How This Book Will Make You a More Successful Writer

By applying rhetorical reading techniques to your writing, you will learn

- To shape your own texts to accomplish your specific purposes in relation to varying situations and audiences

- To use the composing processes of skilled academic writers

- To communicate your understanding of a text through effective summaries and paraphrases

- To write successful analyses and critiques of a text's argument and rhetorical strategies

- To write successful college-level research papers that address significant questions and make important points within a larger conversation

- To follow appropriate conventions for incorporating excerpts from source materials into your own writing without letting them take over your paper

Reading Rhetorically

Second Brief Edition

Reading Rhetorically

Second Brief Edition

JOHN C. BEAN
Seattle University

VIRGINIA A. CHAPPELL
Marquette University

ALICE M. GILLAM
University of Wisconsin–Milwaukee

PEARSON
Longman

New York   San Francisco   Boston
London   Toronto   Sydney   Tokyo   Singapore   Madrid
Mexico City   Munich   Paris   Cape Town   Hong Kong   Montreal

Acquisitions Editor: Lauren A. Finn
Executive Marketing Manager: Sandra McGuire
Project Coordination, Text Design, and Electronic Page Makeup:
    Pre-Press Company, Inc.
Cover Designer/Manager: Wendy Ann Fredericks
Cover Art: Leo Kundas/Spots on the Spot/Images.com
Senior Manufacturing Buyer: Alfred C. Dorsey
Printer and Binder: R. R. Donnelley and Sons
Cover Printer: Lehigh Press, Inc.

For permission to use copyrighted material, grateful acknowledgment is made to the copyright holders on p. 195, which are hereby made part of this copyright page.

Library of Congress Cataloging-in-Publication Data
Bean, John C.
    Reading rhetorically / John C. Bean, Virginia A. Chappell, Alice M. Gillam.—
        2nd brief ed. p. cm.
    Includes index.
    ISBN 0-321-42427-1
    1. College readers. 2. English—Rhetoric—Problems, exercises, etc. 3. Report writing—Problems, exercises, etc. I. Chappell, Virginia A. II. Gilliam, Alice M. III. Title.

    PE1417.B393 2006
    808'.0427—dc22

                                                            2006041660
Copyright © 2007 by Pearson Education, Inc.

Please visit us at www.ablongman.com

ISBN 0-321-42427-1

6 7 8 9 10—DOC—09 08

To our students,
from whom we have learned so much,

and to Eben Ludlow,
our long-time editor and friend,
who inspired this project and has been its guiding light.

Contents

PART **2**   *The Rhetorical Reader as Writer*

Preface

This edition of *Reading Rhetorically* is, like the previous editions, shaped by the belief that students need explicit instruction in analytical reading, not because they have problems with reading, but because college writing assignments demand sophisticated ways of reading. Gratified by the enthusiastic response to the first edition, we have created a second brief edition that preserves the strengths of the first while offering significant improvements based on the suggestions of those who have used the book. This aims-based textbook (1) emphasizes reading as an interactive process of composing meaning and (2) treats academic writing as a process in which writers engage with other texts.

Reading Rhetorically approaches reading as an advanced intellectual process that forms the basis for successful academic writing across the disciplines. Adoption of the regular or brief editions by faculty at a range of two- and four-year institutions for use in a variety of classrooms—including entry-level courses, upper-level writing courses, and even high school college prep courses—suggests that many writing instructors share our belief that academic reading, writing, and inquiry need to be taught as inextricably linked rhetorical acts. This edition adds visual texts—graphs, cartoons, and photographs—to the collection of materials that students are invited to analyze, and the text itself makes greater use of visual displays in tables and lists to help students understand rhetorical concepts.

Reading Rhetorically teaches students to read with an analytical eye and to write about what they have read with rhetorical insight. It defines "reading rhetorically" as attending to an author's purposes for writing and the methods the author uses to accomplish those purposes—the *how* and *what* of a text's message. That is, the book teaches students how to see texts as positioned in a conversation with other texts, how to recognize the bias or perspective of a given text, and how to analyze texts for both content and rhetorical method. This second brief edition maintains emphasis on academic writing as a process in which writers engage with other texts. By sharpening their analytical skills, students learn to write with more rhetorical sophistication. They learn how to analyze other texts by reading them with and against the grain, how to imitate other texts by learning their rhetorical strategies and genre conventions, and how to use other texts for their own purposes in conducting research. Our goal is to offer techniques for rhetorical analysis so that students can learn about, and then apply in their own writing, a variety of rhetorical strategies.

What's New in the Second Brief Edition

Building on the book's strengths, we have revised the text substantially by adding the following features:

- Visual elements throughout the book as well as a two-color design that enhances the book's visual appeal
- A substantially revised first chapter that combines Chapters 1 and 2 from the first edition and concludes with a chart of the distinctive features of various rhetorical aims
- An expanded Chapter 3, which includes strategies for using a text's visual elements to predict content and for connecting the visual to the verbal while "listening" to a text
- A similarly expanded Chapter 4, which adds strategies for analyzing a text's use of visual elements
- Strategies for examining what a text's visual and verbal elements *do* and *say*
- An expanded treatment of the rhetorical analysis paper (Chapter 4), which is presented as the written counterpart of rhetorical reading
- Coverage of American Psychological Association citation conventions and formats as well as those of the Modern Language Association, in Chapter 7 and in the appendix

Distinctive Features

The second brief edition of *Reading Rhetorically* is distinguished by the following features:

- Explanations of rhetorical concepts that provide an analytical framework for reading and writing
- Discussion of reading processes to show students how skilled academic readers construct a text's meaning
- Presentation of writing processes to emphasize strategies for writing about reading
- Treatment of research as a process of rhetorical reading in which students learn to develop research questions and evaluate sources within a rhetorical context
- A discussion of how to evaluate sources that covers Web sources and licensed databases accessed through the Internet
- Presentation of citation methods as integral to rhetorical effectiveness
- An extended example that follows the evolution of one student's writing project from summary to rhetorical analysis to researched critique of a reading
- In the appendix, citation formats for print and electronic materials (including periodicals databases) with an extensive list of model MLA and APA style citations

Structure

The text is organized into two parts that explain the demands of college reading and writing, and offer a conceptual framework and practical strategies for meeting these demands. Part One (Chapters 1 through 4) begins by asking students to reflect on *how* they read and *why*. Chapters 1 and 2 describe the special demands of academic reading and introduce students to the rhetorical reading strategies used by experts: building a context for reading and matching reading strategies to a text's genre and purpose. Chapters 3 and 4 teach *how* to read rhetorically, first by "listening" to what a text is doing and saying, and second by questioning what a text is doing and saying. Chapter 3 offers practice in listening through annotating, mapping idea structure, taking into account a text's visual features, summarizing, descriptive outlining, and writing a rhetorical précis, while Chapter 4 provides practice in questioning through analysis of a text's rhetorical appeals, language, visual elements, and ideology.

Part Two (Chapters 5 through 7) focuses on writing about reading. This section begins with an overview of typical reading-based writing assignments across the curriculum. It then advises students about how to maintain writerly authority and manage their writing process as they write about what they have read. Chapters 6 and 7 teach students how to meet the conceptual and practical demands of research writing. Chapter 6 focuses on how to use rhetorical reading as a research strategy as students formulate research questions and then choose and evaluate readings. Chapter 7 instructs students in the conventions of source-based writing—summary, paraphrase, direct quotation, citation practices—and places these practices in a rhetorical framework.

Strategies for Using *Reading Rhetorically*

The text's organizational structure facilitates easy syllabus design by providing a conceptual framework and practical strategies for reading and writing about a broad range of texts. Students can work their way through these chapters before proceeding to course readings, or they can move back and forth between this text and course readings, trying out the reading and writing strategies on assigned texts.

Acknowledgments

We begin by thanking the teachers who have used the first edition of *Reading Rhetorically* and offered excellent advice for the second edition: Kamala Balasubramanian, Grossmont College; Jami Carlacio, Ithaca College; Jacqueline E. Cason, University of Alaska–Anchorage; Avon Crismore, Indiana University–Purdue University Fort Wayne (and her students); Joan R. Griffin, Metropolitan State College of Denver; Patricia Jenkins, University of Alaska–Anchorage; Martha Marinara, University of Central Florida; Kerri Morris, University of

Alaska–Anchorage; Carol Roberts, Indiana University–Purdue University Fort Wayne; and Martha Van Cise, Berry College.

We would also like to thank the instructors who reviewed the manuscript of the second edition and offered valuable suggestions for improvement: Dominic Delli Carpini, York College of Pennsylvania; Kathleen Baca, Dona Ana Branch Community College; and Kelley Hayden, University of Nevada-Reno.

In Milwaukee, colleagues and students (past and present) whose thinking was invaluable to this revision include Amy Branam, Lynn Bryant, Sarah Caryl, Michelle Dougherty, Derek Hanaman, Jennifer Heinert, Catherine Kalish, Virginia Kuhn, Lesley Kuras, Barrett McCormick, Olivia Taylor, Douglas VanBenthuysen, and Ann Wizenburg. For painstaking assistance with the index, we thank Jessica Demovsky, and for generosity and sharp focus as proofreaders, we thank Patricia Chappell, Cord Klein, and Jane Chappell Singleton.

Deep appreciation goes to two editors, Eben Ludlow and Lauren A. Finn of Allyn & Bacon/Longman, and Marion Castellucci, our development editor, an expert at finding elegant solutions to thorny editorial problems. Their enthusiastic support and wise counsel provided central inspiration for our work. In addition, our sincere thanks go to the able staff at Longman who assisted us at various stages of this book's production.

Finally, we would like to thank our students. Truly, the insights that inform this book largely come from what we have learned from them. For these learning opportunities we are profoundly grateful.

PART 1

Reading Rhetorically

CHAPTER 1

Reading for Academic Writing

The process of reading is not just the interpretation of a text but the interpretation of another person's worldview as presented by a text.

—Doug Brent

Imagine the following scenario: It's early evening, almost the end of the first week of classes. You've conquered the lines at the bookstore, lugged home shopping bags full of books, and lined up your newly purchased textbooks neatly on the shelf next to your desk. You're ready. With the weekend approaching, it's time to figure out just how many of those pages you will need to read by next Monday or Tuesday. Consider this hypothetical list of a weekend's worth of reading assignments early in a college term:

* For Chemistry, the textbook's introductory chapter
* For Political Science, a newspaper editorial of your choice, to be analyzed according to concepts laid out in a textbook chapter on "Interest Groups and the Media," which you are also assigned to read
* For Humanities 101, the Platonic dialog *The Crito*
* For Composition class, this chapter and a reflective essay about reading

In addition, an initial problem statement for your first major composition assignment is due in a week. Deciding on your problem statement will necessitate some reading based on library research—it's up to you to decide where to start, and when.

This scenario and list probably don't fit the specifics of your current situation, but it's likely that their general shape is similar to what you are facing. Probably none of these assignments by itself is overly long. However, taken together and combined with the reading and research assigned for the end of the *next* week, the list may be fairly daunting. Furthermore, because professors seek to introduce students to particular academic methods and subject matters, each assignment necessitates reading with a different purpose and type of awareness. Each asks you to do something different with what you read, such as memorize definitions, understand and apply concepts, track the logic of an argument, or interpret ambiguities and patterns of expression.

Many college students are surprised, even overwhelmed, by the heavy reading they are assigned, and bewildered by their teachers' expectations, not only in English and other humanities classes but in natural science, social science, and preprofessional classes such as introductions to accounting or nursing. Beyond textbook chapters and other readings assigned for specific class sessions, your college reading will include specialized Web sites, books, and articles that you will select and research as you prepare papers and reports in a wide variety of classes.

For the most part, students adapt to these new demands, gradually learn what academic reading entails, and—by the time they are juniors and seniors within their major fields—learn how to do the reading and writing demanded in their disciplines and future professions. But the process is often slow and frustrating, marked by trial and error and the panicky feeling that reading this way is like hacking through a jungle when there might be a path nearby that could make the journey easier.

This book is designed to help you find that path and thus accelerate your growth as a strong academic reader and writer. It aims to describe the special demands and pleasures of academic reading, teach you the reading strategies used by experts, and show you the interconnections between reading and writing in almost all college courses. To explain strategies for handling the demands of college reading assignments and of writing assignments based on readings, the text is divided into two sections.

Part One, "Reading Rhetorically," invites you to explore your changing purposes for reading and teaches you how to *read rhetorically*—that is, to pay attention to an author's purposes for writing and the methods that author uses to accomplish those purposes. All authors have designs upon their readers; they want those readers to see things their way, to adopt their point of view. But rhetorical readers know how to maintain a critical distance and determine carefully the extent to which they will go along with the writer.

Part Two, "The Rhetorical Reader as Writer," focuses on the connections between reading and writing processes. Because most of your college writing assignments will probably involve readings that you are asked to imitate, analyze, or use as source material in pursuing your own inquiry, these chapters show you how to apply rhetorical reading strategies to your own writing. Throughout these chapters, we stress the importance of doing more with a text than just understanding what it says. Reporting about what you have read will be only a beginning point. You will often be expected to write about your reading in a way that shows that you are "doing" a discipline, for example chemistry or political science. You will be asked to find meaning, not merely information, in books and articles. You will be asked to respond to that meaning—to explain it, to analyze it, to critique it, to compare it to alternative meanings that you or others create. To fulfill such assignments, you will need to analyze not just *what* texts say but *how* they say it. This double awareness is what we mean by "reading rhetorically." By analyzing both the content and technique of a given text, a rhetorical reader critically considers the extent to which he or she will accept or question that text.

The Challenges of Academic Reading

Once you get immersed in the academic life—caught up in the challenge of doing your own questioning, critical thinking, analysis, and research—you'll discover that academic reading has unique pleasures and demands. If you ask an experienced academic reader engaged in a research project why she reads, her answer may be something like this: "I'm investigating a problem, and much of my research requires extensive reading. As part of my investigation, I am doing a close analysis of several primary sources. Also I read to see what other researchers are saying about my problem and to position myself in that conversation."

This may seem a curious answer—one that you won't fully understand until you have had more experience writing papers requiring analysis or research. To help you appreciate this answer—and to see how it applies to you—consider that most college courses have two underlying goals:

1. **Conveying conceptual knowledge.** This first goal is for you to learn the body of information presented in the course—to master the course's key concepts and ideas, to understand its theories, to understand how the theories try to explain certain data and observations, to learn key definitions or formulas, and to memorize important facts. Cognitive psychologists sometimes call this kind of learning *conceptual knowledge*—that is, knowledge of the course's subject matter. Transmitting conceptual knowledge is the primary aim of most college textbooks. Certainly that would be the aim of the reading assignment for Chemistry on our hypothetical list at the beginning of this chapter. The assigned pages are undoubtedly packed with specialized terminology that chemistry students need to know if they are to follow lectures, pass exams, and, more generally, understand how chemists think about, label, and measure the physical world.

2. **Conveying procedural knowledge.** A second goal of most college courses is for you to learn the discipline's characteristic ways of thinking about the world by applying your conceptual knowledge to new problems. What questions does the discipline ask? What are its methods of analysis or

research? What counts as evidence? What are the discipline's shared or disputed assumptions? How do you write arguments in this discipline, and what makes them convincing (say in literature, sociology, engineering, or accounting)? Thus in addition to learning the basic concepts of a course, you need to learn how experts in the discipline pose problems and conduct inquiry. Cognitive psychologists call this kind of learning *procedural knowledge*—the ability to apply conceptual knowledge to new problems by using the discipline's characteristic methods of thinking.

Teachers focus on procedural knowledge when they assign readings beyond the typical textbook—newspaper or magazine articles, scholarly articles, or primary sources such as historical documents or literary texts—and ask you to analyze these readings or use them in other discipline-specific ways. Consider the next three assignments in our opening scenario. The political science professor who assigned analysis of the editorial undoubtedly wants students to learn what the textbook says about interest group politics (conceptual knowledge), and then to apply those concepts to analyze current events (procedural knowledge). As you read a variety of editorials looking for one to analyze, you would need to read them through the lens of your political science textbook. A different kind of challenge is presented by the Platonic dialog. Not only does it contain complex ideas, but it also demonstrates a form of discourse and a philosophical way of thinking that has had a lasting impact on European traditions. Still a different kind of challenge is presented by the library research project leading to a problem statement for your first composition. It requires understanding what is meant by "reading rhetorically" and what the instructor means by a "problem statement." Then you would need to read the library sources with the goal of finding a problem to write about. As you read the various kinds of texts assigned in your courses and write different kinds of papers, you will discover that academic disciplines are not inert bodies of knowledge but contested fields full of uncertainties, disagreements, and debate. You will see why college professors want you to *do* their discipline rather than simply study it. They want you not just to study chemistry or political science or history, but to *think like a chemist or a political scientist or an historian.*

The challenges of college reading will vary in different classes and for different people because we all have different backgrounds, learning styles, and interests. It is important to realize that even students with sufficient background knowledge and high interest in a subject will sometimes find course textbooks daunting because each paragraph is dense with new concepts, vocabulary, and information. With so much unfamiliar material, each new sentence can seem just as important as the one before. When it is difficult to separate key concepts from supporting details, you may feel overwhelmed, thinking "I've got to know all of this—how will I ever write anything about it?" This book is designed to help you meet that challenge.

As you learn to read rhetorically you will learn to recognize different authors' purposes and methods, the ways that claims are typically asserted and supported in different disciplines, and the types of evidence that are valued by those disciplines. For example, historians value primary sources such as letters and diaries, government records, and legal documents. Psychologists gather quite different kinds of research data, such as empirical observations of an animal's learning behaviors under different diet conditions, statistical data about the reduction of anxiety symptoms following different kinds of therapy, or "think aloud" transcripts of a person's problem-solving processes after varying amounts of sleep. Your accumulating knowledge about disciplinary discourses will teach you new ways of thinking, and you will learn to use those methods in your own writing.

Reading and Writing as Conversation

Consider again how our experienced researcher at the beginning of the last section answered the question "Why do you read?" It is obvious that she is immersed in *doing* her discipline and that she sees reading as central to her work. But she also says that she is reading "to position herself in a conversation." What does she mean by that? How is reading part of a "conversation"?

To understand reading as joining a conversation, think of writers as talking to readers—and of readers as talking back. For example, suppose our researcher's investigation leads her to new insights that she would like to share with others. If she is a professional scholar, she will write an academic article. If she is an undergraduate, she will write a research paper. In both cases, her audience would be academic readers interested in the same research problem. Her aim is to explain the results of her research, trying to persuade readers to accept her argument and claims. Her motivation for writing is her belief that she has produced something new or challenging or otherwise useful to add to the conversation—something that is different from, or that extends or improves upon, the work of others who have investigated the same problem.

Whenever you write, it is helpful to think of yourself as asserting your voice in a conversation. To prepare yourself for joining this conversation, you must read. As you read, you need to understand not only the text you are reading but also the conversation that it joins. One of the reasons that a particular reading might seem difficult to you—say a journal article on school violence that you find as part of your research for preparing a problem statement—is that you are not yet familiar with the conversation it is part of. That conversation is a multi-voiced conversation. The first voice is that of the article's author; a second voice (actually a set of voices) is the network of texts the writer refers to—previous participants in the conversation. The third voice is yours as you respond to the article while you read, then later if you write something in response to it.

This broad view extends the metaphor of "conversation" to say that texts themselves are in a conversation with previously published texts. Each text acts in relationship to other texts. It asserts a claim on a reader's attention by invoking certain interests and understandings, reminding readers of what has been written about the subject before. For example, articles in scientific journals typically include a summary of important research already conducted on the problem, called a *literature review*. Similarly, political commentators will summarize the views of others so that they can affirm, extend, or take issue with those views. Music, film, and book reviewers are likely to refer not just to the item under review but to the given artist's reputation, which, of course, was established not just by word of mouth but by other texts, texts with which the current reader may or may not be familiar.

The reasons any of us engage in conversation, oral or written, will vary widely according to the occasion and our individual needs. In general, we read because we want—perhaps need—to find out what others are saying about a given matter. Sometimes we may have purely personal reasons for reading, with no intention of extending the conversation further through writing of our own. Ultimately though, in school and workplace writing, we read so that we can make informed contributions to a conversation that is already in progress. Indeed, we are expected to join in.

Entering an oral conversation can sometimes be a simple process of responding to a question. ("Have you seen the new film at the Ridgemont?") But if a conversation is already well underway, finding an opening can sometimes be a complex process of getting people's attention and staking claim to authority on a subject. ("Um, you know, I've seen all of John Woo's films, and I think. . . .") The challenge is even greater if the goal is to redirect the conversation or contradict the prevailing opinion. ("Yes, but, listen! The reading I've done for my cinematography class tells me that his action films are not as innovative as the ads claim.") When we take up writing as a way of entering the conversation, we don't have to worry about interrupting, but we do have to review the conversation for the reader by laying out introductory background.

To explore the similarities between your motives for joining a conversation and your motives for reading, consider how the influential rhetorician and philosopher Kenneth Burke uses conversation as a metaphor for reading and writing.

> Imagine you enter a parlor. You come late. When you arrive, others have long preceded you, and they are engaged in a heated discussion, a discussion too heated for them to pause and tell you exactly what it is about. In fact, the discussion had already begun long before any of them got there, so that no one present is qualified to retrace for you all the steps that had gone before. You listen for a while, until you decide that you have caught the tenor of the argument; then you put in your oar. Someone answers; you answer him; another comes to your defense; another aligns himself against you, to either the embarrassment or gratification of your opponent, depending upon the quality of your ally's assistance. However, the discussion is interminable. The hour grows late, you must depart. And you do depart, with the discussion still vigorously in progress.*

---

*Kenneth Burke, *The Philosophy of Literary Form: Studies in Symbolic Action*, 3rd ed. (Berkeley: U of California P, 1973), 110–11.

● ## FOR WRITING AND DISCUSSION

The following exercise will help you explore the implications of Burke's parlor metaphor for your own reading processes. Write your answers to the questions in a notebook, or as your teacher directs, so that you can compare your responses with those of your classmates.

ON YOUR OWN

1. In what ways does Burke's parlor metaphor fit your experience? Freewrite for a few minutes about an oral conversation in which you managed to assert your voice—or "put in your oar," as Burke says— after listening for a while.

2. Then consider how the metaphor applies to your experience as a reader. Freewrite for another few minutes about a time when reading helped you gather a sense of the general flow of ideas so that you could have something to say about a topic.

3. Not all the "parlors" we enter are filled with unfamiliar conversations. Sometimes we engage in heated discussions on subjects that are very familiar to us. Make a list of one or more communities that you belong to where you feel that you can quickly catch the drift of an in-progress oral conversation. What are some "hot topics" of conversation in these communities? For example, when we were writing this chapter, a hot cultural topic was the legal battle between the entertainment industry and software developers over file-swapping on the Internet to obtain free music. Most of our students were familiar with the software and had strong opinions about file-swapping, particularly the advantages and disadvantages of it for musicians. They could join this conversation immediately. However, many faculty members, especially the older generation, were confused by the lawsuits because they weren't familiar with how the younger generation listens to music and didn't know anything about the software. If you wanted to address a general audience about this issue, how much background information about the music industry, the electronic transfer of digital information, and the varying fortunes of entertainers in post-rock culture would you have to provide to bring these oldsters up to speed?

4. Now let's reverse the situation. Have you ever listened to a conversation in which you were a baffled outsider rather than an insider? (Think of the plight of those oldsters suffering through a conversation about the downloading of MP3 files and the ways that pending lawsuits threaten the survival of indie musicians.) Describe an experience where you had to work hard to get inside an ongoing conversation. Then consider how that experience might be an appropriate analogy for a time when you were frustrated by trying to read a book or article addressed to an insider audience rather than to someone with your background.

WITH YOUR CLASSMATES

Share your responses with other members of your class. See if others have had experiences similar to yours. What have been the topics of conversations where they were in "insider" and "outsider" roles? Help each other appreciate the concepts of insider and outsider audiences and of reading as joining a conversation. ●

Reading Rhetorically as an Academic Strategy

The metaphor of conversation brings out the essential rhetorical nature of reading and writing. The term *rhetorical* always draws attention to a writer's relationship to and intentions toward an audience. However, Aristotle's definition of rhetoric as the art of discovering the available means of persuasion in a given situation highlights *discovery* along with *persuasion*. Writers must thoroughly understand their subject in order to discover the best—the most ethically responsible as well as the most persuasive—methods for presenting their material to others. Rhetoric's partnership of discovery and persuasion makes it clear why reading rhetorically is a powerful academic strategy in all disciplines.

WRITERS' PURPOSES

When we introduced the term *reading rhetorically* early in this chapter, we described authors as having designs on their readers. That phrasing underscores the fact that writers want to change readers' perceptions and thinking, and use both direct and indirect means to do so. Typically, a writer's goal is to change a reader's understanding of subject matter in some way. Sometimes the change might simply confirm what the reader thought beforehand (readers enjoy music and film reviews that affirm their own opinions and political columns that echo their views). At other times the change might involve an increase in knowledge or in clarity of understanding (an article explains how bluenose dolphins use whistling sounds to converse with each other, increasing your awe of sea mammals). Sometimes the change might radically reconstruct a reader's whole view of a subject (an article convinces you to reverse your position on legalization of hard drugs). How much change occurs? The reader decides.

A set of categories for conceptualizing the ways that writers aim to change readers' minds is summarized in Table 1.1 (see pp. 12–13). Based on a scheme developed by rhetoricians to categorize types of writing in terms of a writer's aim or purpose, the table identifies eight rhetorical aims or purposes that writers typically set for themselves—the same eight aims that we used to organize the anthology section of this book. For rhetorical readers, this scheme is particularly powerful because it helps them understand the writer's relation to subject matter and audience. In the table, we describe how texts in each category work, what they offer readers, and the response they typically aim to bring about. We illustrate the differences among the aims with examples of essays and articles that a hypothetical nature writer might compose in response to a proposal to designate one of her favorite hiking and camping areas as a wilderness. (Wilderness designations, intended to preserve threatened land formations as well as animal and plant species, prohibit vehicles and limit human access.)

By labeling the table's fourth column "Desired Response," we emphasize that readers decide not only the extent to which they will accept the ideas and information put forth in a text, but how they will act in response. Readers determine—sometimes unconsciously, sometimes deliberately—whether the information they are reading is reliable, the ideas significant, the presentation convincing. Because writers try to persuade their intended audiences to adopt their perspective, they select and arrange evidence, choose examples, include or omit material, and select words and images to best support their perspective. Your awareness of how a text is constructed to persuade its intended audience (which may not include you) will enable you to decide how well the text meets your purposes for reading.

● FOR WRITING AND DISCUSSION

To explore the spectrum of aims presented in Table 1.1, choose an issue or situation that interests you and create sample writing scenarios and purposes for each of the eight categories on the table. You could base your examples on a single imagined writer as we do (perhaps an entertainment columnist or a sports writer), or you could expand the possibilities by imagining how different people would write with different aims about the same topic (perhaps a family matter such as pets or divorce, or a public matter such as Internet file-swapping or human rights). Choose whatever intrigues you.   ●

WRITERS' PURPOSES VERSUS READERS' PURPOSES

This textbook encourages you to consider the fit between your purposes and the writer's purposes whenever you read. This is an important consideration, one that is particularly pertinent when you are assigned research projects that require you to select sources from among what may be hundreds of possibilities. These potential sources will pose reading challenges different from those of your course textbooks because they will be written for many different audiences and purposes. On any given topic—let's take global warming as a broad example—it's likely your research will turn up books, scholarly articles, popular magazine articles, news reports, and a range of politically charged editorials and op-ed columns, all published in different contexts for readers with a range of different concerns: for experts and nonexperts, theorists and practitioners, politicians, policymakers, and ordinary citizens. As a reader who is planning to write, you will need to determine what among all this material suits *your* needs and purposes.

What do we mean when we refer to *your purposes* as a reader? To understand the answer to this question, consider our earlier statement that you, the reader, decide whether to assent to a writer's views or resist them. As you prepare to

TABLE 1.1 ● A SPECTRUM OF PURPOSES

Rhetorical Aim	Focus and Features	Offers Readers	Desired Response	Examples
Express and Reflect	**Focus:** Writer's own life and experience **Features:** Literary techniques such as plot, character, setting, evocative language	Shared emotional, intellectual experience	**Readers** can imagine and identify with writer's experience. **Success** depends on writer's ability to create scenes, dialog, and commentary that engage readers.	Nature writer's essay narrates her discoveries and reactions when backpacking in area that may be designated "wilderness."
Inquire and Explore	**Focus:** Puzzling problem seen through narration of writer's thinking processes **Features:** Delayed thesis or no thesis; examination of subject from multiple angles; writer's thinking is foregrounded	Shared intellectual experience, new information, new perspectives	**Readers** will agree question or problem is significant, identify with writer's thinking, and find new insights. **Success** depends on writer's ability to engage readers with question or problem and the exploration process.	Nature writer's essay puzzles over the impact of human use on natural areas, loss of recreation opportunities if area is declared wilderness, and the value of wilderness to humans, animals, and landscape.
Inform and Explain (also called *expository writing*)	**Focus:** Subject matter **Features:** Confident, authoritative stance; typically states point and purpose early; strives for clarity; provides definitions and examples; uses convincing evidence without argument	Significant, perhaps surprising, new information; presentation tailored to readers' interest and presumed knowledge level	**Readers** will grant writer credibility as expert, be satisfied with the information's scope and accuracy. **Success** depends on writer's ability to anticipate reader's information needs and ability to understand.	Nature writer's article provides details about rules and process of wilderness designation; reports history of the wilderness process in distant part of the state ten years earlier.
Analyze and Interpret	**Focus:** Phenomena that are difficult to understand or explain **Features:** Relatively tentative stance; thesis supported by evidence and reasoning; new or unsettling analyses and interpretations must be convincing; doesn't assume that evidence speaks for itself	New way of looking at the subject matter	**Readers** will grant writer credibility as analyst and accept insights offered, or at least acknowledge value of approach. **Success** depends on writer's ability to explain reasoning and connect it with phenomena analyzed.	Nature writer pursues ideas about wilderness further in an article analyzing the work of several well-known environmental thinkers, comparing those ideas to provisions of the law.

TABLE 1.1 ● (CONTINUED)

Rhetorical Aim	Focus and Features	Offers Readers	Desired Response	Examples
Persuasion: **Take a Stand**	**Focus:** Question that divides a community **Features:** States firm position, provides clear reasons and evidence, connects with readers' values and beliefs; engages with opposing views	Reasons to make up or change their minds about the question at issue	**Readers** will agree with writer's position and reasoning. **Success** depends on writer's ability to provide convincing support and to counter opposition without alienating readers.	Nature writer prepares opinion piece arguing in favor of the proposed wilderness designation.
Persuasion: **Evaluate and Judge**	**Focus:** Question about worth or value of a phenomenon **Features:** Organized around criteria for judgment and how phenomenon matches them	Reasons to make up or change their minds about the focal question regarding worth or value	**Readers** will accept writer's view of the worth or value of the phenomenon. **Success** depends on writer's ability to connect subject to criteria that readers accept.	Nature writer evaluates the consequences of designating wilderness areas in other states and argues that benefits of preservation outweigh negatives of limited access.
Persuasion: **Propose a Solution**	**Focus:** Question about what action should be taken **Features:** Describes problem and solution, then justifies solution in terms of values and consequences; level of detail depends on assumptions about readers' knowledge	A recommended course of action	**Readers** will assent to proposed action and do as writer suggests. **Success** depends on readers' agreement that a problem exists and/or that recommended action will have good results.	Nature writer urges state residents to support wilderness project, visit area to see where boundaries will be drawn, attend hearing, and write to legislators.
Persuasion: **Seek Common Ground**	**Focus:** Multiple perspectives on a vexing problem **Features:** Lays out the values and goals of the various stakeholders so that others can find commonalities to build on; does not advocate	New perspectives and reduced intensity regarding difficult issues	**Readers** will discover mutuality with opponents; conflict perhaps not resolved; could lead to cooperative action. **Success** depends on readers' discovery of mutual interests.	Nature writer undertakes a common-ground project, interviewing advocates and stakeholders about where wilderness boundaries should be drawn; her goal is to find and highlight points of agreement.

write an academic paper, you need to acquaint yourself with a number of view-points on your subject matter, understand the reasoning and evidence presented by different writers, and determine how to use these ideas in a new context—your own work. Suppose, for example, that in the process of your research on current thinking about global warming you read an article calling for several more years of extensive study before the United States endorses international agreements to reduce emissions from carbon-based fuels. (We'll call this hypo-thetical article "Not Yet.") You must weigh the views in "Not Yet" against the scientific evidence and political reasoning in other articles you read. If this read-ing makes you skeptical of global warming or concerned that the United States will suffer economic loss from stricter regulation of emissions, you might use material from "Not Yet" for evidence that supports your points. In contrast, if your reading provides compelling evidence that global warming is real and is already causing extensive damage, you might summarize "Not Yet" as an op-posing view you wish to rebut. Finally, if your reading leaves you undecided, or if you question the evidence presented by "Not Yet," you would do well to continue your research. Ultimately, your paper might analyze the science and politics of arguments made from a variety of viewpoints on the matter.

To fulfill your own purposes as a reader and writer, you often have to over-come the difficulty of not being part of a text's intended audience. For example, in the situation just described, if you were to explore the current status of re-search on global warming you might encounter highly technical articles that sail over your head because they are written primarily for scientific audiences. Ar-ticles written for policy wonks who know all the details of international treaties might omit background information that you need. When you encounter such materials, you may wish to skim quickly to decide whether to move on to some-thing easier or to keep reading to see what you can learn. Eventually you will read enough materials on the subject to be able to fill in the background and be-gin to read with an expert's understanding.

Until you are thoroughly familiar with the conversation a text is joining, you will also have the challenge of determining how complete a picture of its sub-ject matter a text provides. It is inevitable that no text tells the whole story. To forward an argument, some will deliberately distort opposing perspectives. The genre and purpose of others will make certain perspectives invisible.

As an illustration, suppose you are researching the problem of the melting Arctic ice cap. You become interested in this problem when you read an online article explaining that scientists are divided on how to interpret recent data about the melting of polar ice, whether it is part of a natural cycle that will re-verse itself or part of long-term, irreversible, global warming caused by humans. As you research this issue, you will need to realize how different writers, in try-ing to persuade their intended audiences toward their position on the issue, use rhetorical strategies that best support their own cases. You need to be wary. Some research may be biased by economic or political entanglements—for example, many people charge that global warming research funded by petroleum com-panies should be discounted. Some research may provide what seems like fright-ening data and yet draw only a few cautious conclusions.

FIGURE 1.1 This 2000 photo of Jökulsárlón, a lagoon in southern Iceland, accompanied the *Chronicle of Higher Education* article about ice melt described here. Formed by glacial runoff, the iceberg-filled lake did not exist 100 years ago and doubled in size during the 1990s.

For example, an article in the July 2000 issue of the highly specialized journal *Science* reported that eleven cubic miles of ice are disappearing from the Greenland ice sheet annually, but left it up to the article's intended audience of experts to ponder what kinds of conclusions to draw. However, when the findings of the *Science* article were reported in the popular press, many articles downplayed the scientists' caution and highlighted imagined details of a world fifty years from now with no ice caps—an approach swaying readers to accept uncritically the assumption that the melting ice is an irreversible trend, presumably resulting from human-caused global warming. Once political commentators got hold of the *Science* article, they put a spin on it that reflected their own values and beliefs. Environmentalists used the melting ice cap data to support their case for international regulations to slow or eventually to reverse global warming. Pro-business writers in turn emphasized the original study's cautious call for more research. A more balanced and neutral approach was demonstrated by a *Chronicle of Higher Education* article, also in July 2000, that was headlined, "The Great Melt: Is It Normal, or the Result of Global Warming? Scientists Are Having Difficulty Pinpointing the Causes of Glacial and Sea-Ice Decline." This article provided a background overview for curious academic readers who accept the tentativeness of scientific findings and want to learn about the conflicting interpretations in this controversy. For student writer-researchers, such articles can be gold mines because they provide balanced explanations without attempting to draw the reader to a specific set of conclusions.

Our point here is that the ability to recognize the persuasive strategies built into a text is a powerful academic skill. How can you tell whether a text is trying to give you the whole picture in a fair and reliable way or is simply making another one-sided argument in a hotly contested debate? By learning to read rhetorically.

Questions That Rhetorical Readers Ask

In the language of the epigraph to this chapter, rhetorical readers have learned to recognize and interpret the worldview that a text sets forth. We will discuss *worldview* in more detail later, but for now consider "worldview" to mean a writer's underlying beliefs, values, and assumptions. You probably already recognize these without much effort when you are reading material on familiar subjects. What you already know about a close friend's values makes it relatively easy to recognize whether that friend's e-mail is serious or teasing. Similarly, you can quickly tell whether a review of your favorite musician's latest CD reflects your own musical values and assumptions. In academic settings, though, unfamiliar subject matter and contexts can make analyzing a writer's underlying values and assumptions more problematic. With difficult new material, readers' natural tendency is to concentrate on getting what information and meaning they can from a text without paying attention to its rhetorical strategies. Rhetorical readers, however, analyze rhetorical strategies as a way of understanding a writer's purpose and worldview. This analysis involves eight important questions about how the text works and how you respond to it. Chapter 4 will show in detail how using these questions for critical analysis can reveal a writer's basic values and assumptions and thus help you understand a text more fully.

QUESTIONS FOR READING RHETORICALLY

1. What questions does the text address? (Why are these significant questions? What community cares about them?)
2. Who is the intended audience? (Am I part of this audience or an outsider?)
3. How does the author support his or her thesis with reasons and evidence? (Do I find this argument convincing? What views and counterarguments are omitted from the text? What counterevidence is ignored?)
4. How does the author hook the intended reader's interest and keep the reader reading? (Do these appeals work for me?)
5. How does the author make himself or herself seem credible to the intended audience? (Is the author credible for me? Are the author's sources reliable?)
6. Are this writer's basic values, beliefs, and assumptions similar to or different from my own? (How does this writer's worldview accord with mine?)
7. How do I respond to this text? (Will I go along with or challenge what this text is presenting? How has it changed my thinking?)
8. How do this author's evident purposes for writing fit with my purposes for reading? (How will I be able to use what I have learned from the text?)

TAKING STOCK OF WHY YOU READ

Given this chapter's discussion of writers' and readers' varying purposes, we invite you to pause before moving on to the chapters about specific strategies and reflect upon your own purposes for reading in different situations. In Chapter 2 we will invite you to extend this exploration of *why* you read into an exploration of *how* you read.

● **FOR WRITING AND DISCUSSION**

This exercise asks you to list your recent reading experiences and then to reflect on your motives and strategies, which probably varied with the occasion. The first part asks you to jot down answers on paper; the second part asks you to use these notes in class to compare your responses with those of your classmates.

ON YOUR OWN

1. What have you read so far today? Divide a sheet of paper into two columns.
   a. In the left column, jot down as many items as you can remember reading in the past 24 hours. Try to make this list as long as you can by including texts that you just happened across in the course of the day.
   b. In the right column, note what prompted you to read each item—was it an assignment for school or work? A discussion with a friend? A need to find out something specific, such as tomorrow's weather or the score in yesterday's game, or the latest news from home? Relaxation—thumbing through a magazine or surfing the Web? Or was it chance—the item was "just there," such as a cafeteria menu or a hallway poster?
2. Were the last 24 hours of reading typical for you? If not, draw a line across the bottom of the two columns and list any other items that you would typically read on a given day when school is in session but that you didn't happen to read in the last 24 hours. Perhaps you ordinarily would have read the textbook for a particular course. Perhaps you usually turn on the TV to check the news crawl for sports scores, but you didn't in the past 24 hours. Since this exercise is meant to help you explore your own reading activities, add whatever you think gives a full picture of them.
3. Draw another horizontal line across the page. Extending your view to the past month, note something that you have read in each of the following categories:
   a. Something you found particularly enjoyable
   b. Something you thought particularly important
   c. Something you struggled to understand
   d. Something you were eager to talk about with your family or friends

4. Now, as you look back over your notes, consider what they say about you as a reader, as a college student, and as a person. Freewrite for several minutes about the proportion of time you spend reading "on assignment" as opposed to just following your own inclinations. (By "freewrite" we mean writing rapidly nonstop in order to brainstorm on paper—without worrying about spelling, punctuation, or structure. Your goal is to discover new insights by using nonstop writing to stimulate thinking.)

5. To sum up this taking stock exercise, draw one last horizontal line across the page and address this question: *Why* do you read? Freewrite for several minutes, trying to sum up all that you have discovered through this exercise.

WITH YOUR CLASSMATES

In small groups or as a whole class, compare responses to the reading inventory. As the discussion unfolds, listen carefully so that you can jot down notes about these questions:

1. What patterns of common experience emerged during the discussion?
2. In what ways are your typical reasons for reading different from those of your classmates?

ONCE MORE ON YOUR OWN

Take a few minutes after the discussion to reflect in writing about what you've become aware of through your writing and class discussion. Consider these questions:

1. How was your description of your reading habits similar to and different from what your classmates described?
2. If others seem to enjoy reading more or less than you, how do you explain that difference?
3. What would you like to change about your typical approach to reading? How can you gain greater strength as a reader? ●

Summary

In this chapter we have provided a brief overview of the book and explained how it will help you build a repertoire of reading strategies to meet the challenges of academic reading and writing assignments. In the preceding pages, we

- Defined rhetorical reading as paying attention to both the content of a text ("what") and the author's method of presenting that content ("how")

- Described the special challenges of academic reading, which often requires recognizing how different academic disciplines value evidence and report research
- Used the metaphor of conversation to describe how academic reading and writing involve responding to other texts and adding your own ideas
- Showed the value of rhetorical reading as an academic strategy through which a reader analyzes a text's content and strategies in order to decide how to respond—whether to assent to the writer's ideas, modify them, or resist them
- Provided a table showing how writers' purposes can be arranged on a "spectrum of purposes" that identifies eight different aims
- Pointed out that writers' purposes and readers' purposes for the same text may be quite different
- Provided a list of eight questions rhetorical readers use to judge how a text works and how to respond to it

Finally, as a foundation for your work in this book, we invited you to take stock of your typical reasons for reading.

CHAPTER 2

Strategies for Reading Rhetorically

*It is like the rubbing of two sticks together to make a fire,
the act of reading, an improbable pedestrian task that leads
to heat and light.*

—Anna Quindlen

In the preceding chapter we saw that academic readers read because they are captivated by questions and are challenged to find new or better answers. They also read to pursue their research projects, to see what other researchers are saying, and to position themselves in a scholarly conversation. To read effectively, they have to read rhetorically by attending to both the content and the persuasive strategies in a text. In this chapter, we focus specifically on introducing the rhetorical reading strategies used by experts. We begin by explaining two pieces of background knowledge you will need to read rhetorically: (1) that reading is an active rather than passive process (we say that both reading and writing are acts of composing) and (2) that the choices skilled writers make about content, structure, and style depend on their rhetorical context. Understanding these concepts will help you employ the rhetorical strategies we describe in the last half of the chapter.

Reading and Writing as Acts of Composing

As part of their background knowledge, rhetorical readers know that reading, like writing, is an active process of composing. The idea that writing is an act of composing is probably familiar to you. Indeed, the terms *writing* and *composing* are often used interchangeably. Originally associated with fine arts such as painting, music, or literary writing, the term *composing* still carries with it the idea of originality or creativity even though it has come to mean the production of any kind of written text, from a memo to a Pulitzer-prize-winning novel. Unlike the term *writing, composing* suggests more than just the transcription of a preexisting meaning or idea; it suggests a creative putting together of words and ideas to make a new whole. Except for literally recopying what someone else has written, all writing, even memo writing, is a matter of selecting and arranging language to accomplish a purpose that is unique to a particular situation and audience.

The idea that reading is an act of composing, however, may be less familiar. The ancients thought of reading as a passive activity in which the author via the text deposited meaning in a reader; the text was metaphorically (or even literally) "consumed." The Old Testament prophet Ezekiel, for example, has a vision in which he is instructed by the Lord to open his mouth and literally consume a book that gives him the knowledge he needs to speak to the rebellious Israelites. Commenting on the consumption metaphors associated with reading, Alberto Manguel in *A History of Reading* notes the parallels between the cooking metaphors associated with writing—the author "cooks up" a plot or "spices" up her introduction—and the eating metaphors associated with reading—the reader "devours" a book, finds "nourishment" in it, then "regurgitates" what he has read.*

While the image of Ezekiel's eating a text seems fantastic, the mistaken idea persists that reading is a one-way transaction: author → text → reader. To illustrate the flaws in this model of the reading process, let's try a simple experiment described by reading researcher Kathleen McCormick. Read the following passage and jot down your interpretation of its meaning:

> Tony slowly got up from the mat, planning his escape. He hesitated a moment and thought. Things were not going well. What bothered him most was being held, especially since the charge against him had been weak. He considered his present situation. The lock that held him was strong but he thought he could break it. . . . He was being ridden unmercifully. . . . He felt that he was ready to make his move.†

There are two common interpretations: readers assume that Tony is either in jail or in a wrestling match. Unless you are familiar with wrestling, you probably thought Tony was a prisoner planning a jailbreak. However, if this paragraph appeared in a short story about a wrestler, you would immediately assume that "mat," "escape," "charge," "being held," and "lock" referred to wrestling even if you knew very little about the sport. This experiment demonstrates two important aspects of the reading process: (1) readers use their previous experiences and knowledge to create meaning from what they read; and (2) context influences meaning.

Research such as McCormick's shows that readers make sense of a text not by passively receiving meaning from it but by actively composing a reading of

---

*Alberto Manguel, *A History of Reading* (New York: Penguin, 1997), 170–71.
†Kathleen McCormick, *The Culture of Reading and the Teaching of English* (Manchester, England: Manchester UP, 1994), 20–21.

it. This composing process links the reader's existing knowledge and ideas with the new information encountered in the text. What the reader brings to the text is as important as the text itself. In other words, reading is not a process in which an author simply transfers information to the reader. Rather it is a dynamic process in which the reader's worldview interacts with the writer's worldview; the reader constructs meaning from the text, in effect creating a new "text" in the reader's mind—that reader's active reading or interpretation of the text.

This view of reading as a transaction between text and reader is captured evocatively in the poem "The Voice You Hear When You Read Silently" by Thomas Lux. Take a moment at this time to read Lux's poem and then to do the exercises that follow it.

The Voice You Hear When You Read Silently

is not silent, it is a speaking-out-loud voice in your head: it is *spoken*,
a voice is saying it as you read.
It's the writer's words, of course, in a literary sense his or her "voice"
but the sound of that voice is the sound of *your* voice.
Not the sound your friends know or the sound of a tape played back
but your voice
caught in the dark cathedral of your skull, your voice heard by an internal
ear informed by internal abstracts
and what you know by feeling, having felt.
It is your voice saying, for example, the word "barn" that the writer wrote
but the "barn" you say is a barn you know or knew.
The voice in your head, speaking as you read, never says anything
neutrally — some people hated the barn they knew,
some people love the barn they know
so you hear the word loaded and a sensory constellation is lit:
horse-gnawed stalls, hayloft, black heat tape wrapping a water pipe,
a slippery spilled *chirrr* of oats from a split sack,
the bony, filthy haunches of cows . . .
And "barn" is only a noun — no verb or subject has entered into the
sentence yet! The voice you hear when you read to yourself
is the clearest voice: you speak it
speaking to you.

—Thomas Lux

●   **FOR WRITING AND DISCUSSION**
ON YOUR OWN

1. When you hear the word *barn,* what barn or barns from your own life do you first see? What feelings and associations do you have with this

word? How do you think the barn in your head is different from the barns in your classmates' heads?

2. When you hear the word *cathedral,* what images and associations from your own life come into your head? Once again, how might your class-mates' internal images and associations with the word *cathedral* differ from yours?

3. Now reread the poem and consider the lines "Not the sound your friends know or the sound of a tape played back/but your voice/caught in the dark cathedral of your skull." What do you think Lux means by the metaphor "dark cathedral of your skull"? What seems important about his choice of the word *cathedral* (rather than, say, *house* or *cave* or *gymnasium* or *mansion*)? How does *skull* work (rather than *mind* or *brain* or *head*)? Freewriting for several minutes, create your interpretation of "dark cathedral of the skull."

4. Finally, reflect for a moment about your thinking processes in trying to interpret "cathedral of the skull." Did you go back and reread the poem, looking for how this line fits other lines of the poem? Did you explore further your own ideas about cathedrals and skulls? Our goal is to see if you can catch yourself in the act of interacting with the text—of actively constructing meaning.

WITH YOUR CLASSMATES

5. Compare your responses to questions 1 and 2 with those of your class-mates. How do images of and associations with barns and cathedrals vary?

6. Compare your interpretations of "dark cathedral of the skull." Are there any interpretations that become purely private—that is, that range so far from the text that they can't be supported by evidence in the rest of the poem? (For example, it would be difficult to argue that this metaphor means that the poem is secretly about religion because it uses the term *cathedral.*) Which interpretations make the most sense of the text?   ●

What we have tried to show in the preceding exercise is that a reader's reading or interpretation of the text results from a dynamic *two-way interaction.* On the one hand, the text shapes and limits the range of possible meanings: "The Voice You Hear When You Read Silently" cannot be plausibly interpreted as be-ing about racing in the Indianapolis 500, or about the schizophrenic experience of hearing strange voices in your head. On the other hand, each reader will have a slightly different interpretation or private set of associations with the text based on her or his experiences, knowledge, and attitudes.

When college writing assignments ask you to explain and support your reading of a text, it is important to distinguish between *private* associations that are only loosely related to a text and interpretations that are *publicly* defensible in terms of textual evidence. Private associations are one-way responses in which a certain word, image, or idea in a text sends you off into your own world, causing you to lose track of the network of cues in the text as a whole.

While such private responses are natural, and indeed one of the pleasures of reading, if you are to offer a public interpretation, you must engage in a two-way interaction with a text, attending both to the text's network of cues and to your personal responses and associations with the text. Thus a good interpretation of "dark cathedral of the skull" must connect to the whole of the poem and illuminate its meaning in a way that makes sense to other readers. In short, "good" or sound interpretations are those that are supported by textual evidence and thus are understandable and persuasive to other readers, whose experiences and beliefs may differ from yours.

Texts and Their Rhetorical Contexts

A second piece of background knowledge used by rhetorical readers is their awareness that authors base their choices about content, structure, and style on their *rhetorical context*—what we define as the combined factors of audience, genre, and purpose. Recognizing the influence of context helps rhetorical readers understand a writer's intentions regarding the subject matter and the intended audience, and thus to reconstruct the strategy behind the author's choices.

For example, suppose a writer wants to persuade legislators to raise gasoline taxes in order to reduce fossil fuel consumption. His strategy is to persuade different groups of voters to pressure their congressional representatives. If he writes for a scientific audience, his article can include technical data and detailed statistical analyses. If he addresses the general public, however, the style will have to be less technical and more lively, with storylike anecdotes rather than tabular data. If he writes for an environmental publication, he can assume an audience already supportive of his pro-environment values. However, if he writes for a business publication such as the *Wall Street Journal,* he will have to be sensitive to his audience's pro-business values—perhaps by arguing that what's good for the environment is in the long run good for business.

Besides adapting content and style to different audiences, writers also adapt their work to the genre in which they publish. The term *genre* refers to the conventions of structure, style, format, approach to subject matter, and document design that distinguish different categories of writing from each other. Literature, for example, includes such genres as plays, novels, and poems, and within each of these broad literary genres are subgenres such as the sonnet, epic poem, and haiku. Similarly, nonfiction includes a range of genres from technical reports to newspaper feature articles. Thus, a *Popular Science* article on genetic research will differ in structure, style, and presentation from an article on the same subject in a scholarly journal. The wording and layout of a magazine article about trends in athletic shoe design will be quite different from the wording and layout of a Web presentation of the same trends, where hyperlinks and animation can be used. What's important about these different genres is that readers' expectations vary for different genres.

When you recognize how a text is shaped according to the writer's purpose, audience, and genre, you can decide how to use the text for your own purposes. Say, for instance, that you are reading a newspaper op-ed piece about drilling for oil in the Alaskan Natural Wildlife Reserve (ANWR) to learn more about what is at issue in this controversy. Because it is an op-ed piece for a general audience, you know that it is written in terms that should be understandable to you, but you also know that since it is an op-ed piece, it is the writer's opinion and not an informational article that attempts to be neutral. Thus, your challenge is to read somewhat skeptically, not taking the author's representation of the issue as necessarily the only way the issue might be considered. Let's now turn to a more detailed example.

AN EXTENDED EXAMPLE: ARTICLES ABOUT TEENAGERS' SLEEP HABITS

In this section we provide specific examples of how purpose, audience, and genre affect the way texts are presented. Consider how differently scientific findings are presented in specialized journals versus the popular press. An original scientific study usually appears first as a technical report in a scientific journal. Such articles are written for highly specialized experts and are accepted for publication only after being extensively scrutinized for methodology and integrity by expert peer reviewers (also called referees). When a published scientific article contains newsworthy findings, science writers for general circulation newspapers and magazines or for specialized professional organizations "translate" the original technical material into a form and style appropriate for their targeted audiences. The actual content varies also since the "translators" focus on some parts of the original article and omit other parts. In the original scientific article, the authors carefully review previous literature, describe their methodology in great detail, and usually express their findings cautiously. In the popular press articles, in contrast, the writer usually lavishes attention upon the findings, speculates on their potential usefulness to the public, downplays the original scientists' caution, and says little about methods. Writers for specialized professional publications focus only on aspects of the article relevant to a particular professional field. For example, a scientific study about the effectiveness of a new chicken pox vaccine might be discussed in the *Journal of Community Health Nursing* in terms of patient care and in the *Journal of Health Politics, Policy and Law* in terms of government regulations.

To illustrate the different forms that the information from a scientific study can take, we traced the work of sleep researchers Amy Wolfson and Mary Carskadon through several types of publications whose readers differ in their interests and purposes for reading.* Because these articles represent the variety

---

*Our approach builds on Arthur Walzer's study, "Articles from the 'California Divorce Project': A Case Study of the Concept of Audience," *College Composition and Communication* 36 (1985): 150–159.

of texts you are likely to encounter when you do research for college papers, the following exercise will be good preparation for your work as a rhetorical reader.

● **FOR WRITING AND DISCUSSION**

In this exercise we provide the opening paragraph(s) of five articles concerning a "Sleep Habits Survey" that Wolfson and Carskadon administered to high school students in 1994. They reported their findings at a scholarly meeting in June 1996, and the study itself was published in 1998. The excerpts are from articles printed in five different periodicals that target five different audiences. Each introduction signals the kinds of interests the writers expect their readers will bring to the articles. Read the excerpts *rhetorically* to see what you can discern about the intended readers for each (their interests, their values, their purposes for reading) and then try to match each introduction to its place of original publication on the list that follows the excerpts. To guide your analysis, consider the following questions:

1. What implicit question or problem does each introduction address?
2. Who, in particular, does each article seem to be targeting as readers?
3. What does each introduction suggest about its author's credibility on the subject?
4. How does the introduction draw the reader in? What shared understanding or values does the writer use as a starting point?
5. What beneficial knowledge does each introduction seem to be offering to readers?
6. What clues can you discern in each introduction about the article's genre—for example, scholarly article, newspaper story, magazine feature?

Article 1
An epidemic of sleeplessness is taking a heavy toll on the nation's children and their ability to learn. A majority of kids say they are sleepy during the day and 15 percent admit to falling asleep in school, a survey reveals.

The problem, which hits teenagers especially hard, is of such looming concern that parents and school districts across the country are considering starting high school hours later, so students will not only rise but shine.

"School is starting at a time when their brains are still on their pillows," said Mary Carskadon, an expert on adolescent sleep and a professor at Brown University. "They're just not there."

Article 2
Our understanding of the development of sleep patterns in adolescents has advanced considerably in the last 20 years. Along the way, theoretical models of the processes underlying the biological regulation of sleep have

improved, and certain assumptions and dogmas have been examined and found wanting. Although the full characterization of teen sleep regulation remains to be accomplished, our current understanding poses a number of challenges for the education system.

Article 3
Adolescence is a time of important physical, cognitive, emotional, and social change when the behaviors in one developmental stage are constantly challenged by new abilities, insights, and expectations of the next stage. Sleep is a primary aspect of adolescent development. The way adolescents sleep critically influences their ability to think, behave, and feel during daytime hours. Likewise, daytime activities, changes in the environment, and individual factors can have significant effects on adolescents' sleeping patterns. Over the last two decades, researchers, teachers, parents, and adolescents themselves, have consistently reported that they are not getting enough sleep (Carskadon, 1990a; Carskadon, Harvey, Duke, Anders, & Dement, 1980; Price, Coates, Thoresen, & Grinstead, 1978; Strauch & Meier, 1988).

Article 4
High school will open at 8:30 AM this fall, 65 minutes later than last year, in Edina, Minn, a Minneapolis suburb. School officials hope the 1300 students in grades 9 through 12 will get more sleep and, as a result, be sharper in class.

Area physicians lobbied for the new hours. The Minnesota Medical Association (MMA) wrote the state's 450 school district superintendents in 1994, noting that puberty resets the internal biological clock, prompting teenagers to go to bed later and to need to sleep later than younger children. The MMA cited studies linking inadequate sleep with lower grades and more frequent car crashes. It urged high schools to open at 8 AM or later.

"When the medical community speaks out on an issue of health," said Kenneth Dragseth, Edina superintendent of schools, "it carries a lot of clout."

Article 5
Tired all the time? It's not your fault! Three reasons why:

1. Teens naturally fall asleep later than adults or young children. "People assumed this was because teens wanted independence or had more going on socially," says Mary Carskadon, Ph.D., professor of psychiatry and human behavior at Brown University School of Medicine. Recent studies show that teens secrete melatonin, the hormone that induces sleep, about an hour later than children and adults.

The five introductions you have just read appeared in the publications listed below. Which article introduction goes with which periodical? Briefly freewrite your reasons for linking each piece to its appropriate source. What evidence supports your choice?

- *JAMA: The Journal of the American Medical Association*
- *YM: Young and Modern*
- *Child Development* (published by the Society for Research in Child Development)
- *The Arizona Republic* (daily newspaper in Phoenix)
- *Phi Delta Kappan* (published by the educators' honor society, Phi Delta Kappa)

Additional hint: The *JAMA* article was published under the "Medical News and Perspectives" section.

For the correct answers, see the full article citations at the end of this chapter (but don't look until after you have made your own arguments!).   ●

Learning from the Practices of Experienced Readers

When we ask students to describe the behaviors of good readers, many initially say "speed" or "the ability to understand a text in a single reading." Surprisingly, most experienced readers don't aim for speed reading, nor do they report that reading is an easy, one-step process. On the contrary, experienced readers put considerable effort into reading and rereading a text, adapting their strategies and speed to the demands of the text at hand and to their purpose for reading. Studies of experienced readers show that they consistently do the following:

- Build a context for reading by attending to cues in the text as well to their own purpose and knowledge
- Match their reading strategies with the text's genre
- Vary their reading strategies according to their purpose for reading

Let's look at each in turn.

BUILDING A CONTEXT FOR READING

Experienced readers understand that a text is more than just content or information; it is the work of a real person writing on a specific occasion in order to have real effects on real readers. They understand that the text is part of a larger conversation about a particular topic, and they use textual cues—such as style, format, and terminology—as well as their own background knowledge to speculate about the original context, to make predictions about the text, and to formulate questions.

These strategies for actively building a context for reading are illustrated in Ann Feldman's report of interviews with expert readers reading texts in their own fields.* For example, Professor Lynn Weiner, a social historian, had this to say about a chapter from Philippe Aries' *Centuries of Childhood: A Social History of Family Life* entitled "From the Medieval Family to the Modern Family," written in 1962:

> This work isn't precisely in my field and it is a difficult text. I also know it by its reputation. But, like any student, I need to create a context in which to understand this work. When the book was written, the idea of studying the family was relatively new. Before this time historians often studied kings, presidents, and military leaders. That's why this new type of social history encouraged us to ask, "How did ordinary people live?" Not the kings, but the families in the middle ages. Then we have to ask: "Which families is [Aries] talking about? What causes the change that he sees? . . . For whom is the change significant?" . . . I'll want to be careful not . . . to assume the old family is bad and the new family is good. The title suggests a transition so I'll be looking for signs of it.

As Professor Weiner reads, she continues to elaborate this context, confirming and revising predictions, asking new questions, evaluating what Aries has to say in light of the evidence he can provide, and assessing the value of his ideas to her work as a social historian. She concludes by saying, "A path-breaking book, it was credited with advancing the idea that childhood as a stage of life is historically constructed and not the same in every culture and every time. In my own work I might refer to Aries as I think and write about families as they exist today."

Professor Weiner's description of creating a context for understanding Aries suggests that the ability to recognize what you do not know and to raise questions about a text is as important as identifying what you do know and understand. Even experts encounter texts that they find "difficult." As a college student, you will often be asked to read texts in disciplines that are new to you. Although it may seem challenging to build a context for reading in these situations, it is on these very occasions that it is particularly important to do so. By using textual cues to speculate about the situation that produced the text, you will be in a much better position (1) to identify *what you do understand* about the text and (2) to identify *what you do not yet understand* about the text (terms, concepts, references to other texts). Equipped with this kind of information, you can make better predictions about the text's meaning and decide what you need to know and ask in order to accomplish your purposes for reading.

● FOR WRITING AND DISCUSSION

Even when a text is about an unfamiliar or difficult subject, you can use textual cues to uncover a surprising amount of information that will help you

---

*Ann Feldman, *Writing and Learning in the Disciplines* (New York: Harper, 1996), 16–17, 25–29.

build a context for reading. Imagine that you are enrolled in an introductory philosophy course and have been asked to read philosopher Anthony Weston's *Toward Better Problems: New Perspectives on Abortion, Animal Rights, the Environment, and Justice*. The passage below excerpts key sentences from the opening of Chapter 1, "Practical Ethics in a New Key." In it, find textual cues that might help you build a context for reading. After you have read the passage, answer the questions below.

> Many other "practical ethics" books take up the same topics as this one: abortion, other animals, the environment, justice. Peter Singer covers much the same ground in a book called simply *Practical Ethics.*
>
> The actual practicality of the usual brand of practical ethics, however, is somewhat partial. What we are usually offered is the systematic application of some ethical theory to practice. Singer's book represents an admirably lucid application of utilitarianism. Others apply theories of rights to the same set of issues. . . .
>
> In these well-known kinds of practical ethics, moreover, there is a natural tendency toward a certain kind of closure. The project is to sort out the practical questions at stake in a way that finally allows one or a few facts—one or a few kinds of issues, one or a few aspects of value—to determine the answer. . . .
>
> It is possible, however, to take up practical problems in a radically different spirit, a spirit associated in particular with the work of the American pragmatist John Dewey. This book is an attempt to do so.*

ON YOUR OWN

Jot down brief answers to the following questions:

1. What, if any, background knowledge do you bring to this text?
2. Given your level of background knowledge, how would you go about reading the chapter?
3. What questions can you pose for getting as much as possible from your first reading?
4. What terms or references are unfamiliar to you? Where might you find out more about these terms and references?
5. What do you understand so far about the text's meaning? What don't you understand? What do you predict that Weston will say next?
6. What seems to be Weston's purpose for writing? How will his text be different from other texts?

---

*Excerpted and reprinted from Anthony Weston, *Toward Better Problems: New Perspectives on Abortion, Animal Rights, the Environment, and Justice,* by permission of Temple University Press. © 1992 by Temple University. All rights reserved.

WITH YOUR CLASSMATES

Compare your answers with those of your classmates.

1. What strategies for reading did people offer? Can you agree on a recommended strategy?
2. List the various questions that people formulated for getting as much as possible from the reading. How are they similar and different?
3. List the various predictions your group has made about what will follow in this text. What are various points of agreement and disagreement based upon? Can you clarify any confusion by sharing perspectives? ●

MATCHING STRATEGIES WITH A TEXT'S GENRE

Besides creating a context for reading, experienced readers use their knowledge of a text's genre conventions to guide their reading process. They know that different genres invite different ways of reading. As we explained earlier, genres are distinguished by recurring patterns in form, style, and use of evidence. Familiarity with a particular genre, such as news stories, can guide your reading of that genre, sometimes unconsciously. Knowing from experience that news reports begin with the key facts of the story and then broaden out to offer background information and additional details (what journalists call the *inverted pyramid structure*), you may just read the first paragraph of the report and skip the details if you're in a hurry or not particularly interested in them.

The same predictability permits expert readers to use genre conventions quite consciously to make their reading more strategic and efficient. Illustration comes from the work of researchers who studied the way that physicists read articles in physics journals.* They found that the physicists seldom read the article from beginning to end but instead used their knowledge of the typical structure of scientific articles to find the information most relevant to their interests. Scientific articles typically begin with an abstract or summary of their contents. The main body of the article includes a five-part structure: (1) an introduction that describes the research problem, (2) a review of other studies related to this problem, (3) a description of the methodology used in the research, (4) a report of the results, and (5) the conclusions drawn from the results. The physicists in the study began by reading the abstracts first to see if an article was relevant to their own research. If it was, the experimental physicists went to the methodology section to see if the article reported any new methods while the theoretical physicists went to the results section to see if the article reported any significant new results. These experts, in other words, were guided both by their purpose for reading (based on their own research interests) and by their familiarity with the genre conventions of the scientific

---

*Research reported by Cheryl Geisler, *Academic Literacy and the Nature of Expertise* (Hillsdale, NJ: Earlbaum, 1994) 20–21.

research report (which they used to select the portions of the text most relevant to their purpose).

In your college education, you will encounter a wide range of genres, many of which will be initially unfamiliar. Learning the conventions of new genres is one of the ways you gain expertise in the subjects you are studying. When you major in a subject, you need to learn to read and write in the genres valued by that discipline—for example, business majors learn to read and write business proposals and reports; philosophy majors learn to read and write philosophical arguments; anthropology majors learn to read and write ethnographic narratives, and so forth.

MATCHING STRATEGIES WITH PURPOSE FOR READING

Although all readers change their approach to reading according to their purpose, the situation, and the text at hand, most do so unconsciously, relying on a limited set of strategies. By contrast, experienced readers vary their reading process self-consciously and strategically. Here's how one accomplished undergraduate, Sheri, contrasts her "school" reading process with her "reading-for-fun" process:

When I am reading for class, for starters I make sure that I have all of my reading supplies. These include my glasses, a highlighter, pencil, blue pen, notebook paper, dictionary, and a quiet place to read, which has a desk or table. (It also has to be cold!) Before I read for class or for research purposes I always look over chapter headings or bold print words and then formulate questions based on these. When I do this it helps me to become more interested in the text I am reading because I am now looking for answers.

Also, if there are study guide questions, I will look them over so that I have a basic idea of what to look for. I will then read the text all the way through, find the answers to my questions, and underline all of the study guide answers in pencil.

When I read for fun, it's a whole other story! I always take off my shoes and sit on the floor/ground or in a very comfortable chair. I always prefer to read in natural light and preferably fresh air. I just read and relax and totally immerse myself in the story or article or whatever!*

You'll notice, no doubt, that Sheri's reading strategies combine idiosyncratic habits (the blue pen and cold room) with sound, widely used academic

---

*Sheri's description of her reading process is quoted in Paula Gillespie and Neal Lerner, *The Allyn and Bacon Guide to Peer Tutoring* (Boston: Allyn & Bacon, 2000), 105.

reading habits (looking over chapter headings, checking for study guide questions, and so on). Your own reading process is probably a similar combination of personal habits or rituals and more general types of reading behaviors.

As we noted in Chapter 1 when we introduced rhetorical reading as an academic strategy, your purposes for reading academic assignments will vary considerably. So must your academic reading strategies. You will read much differently, for example, if your task is to interpret or analyze a text than if you are simply skimming it for its potential usefulness in a research project.

One way in which your reading process will vary according to purpose is the rate at which you read. Contrary to popular myth, expert readers are not necessarily "speed" readers. Experienced readers pace themselves according to their purpose, taking advantage of four basic reading speeds.

- *Very fast:* Readers scan a text very quickly if they are looking only for a specific piece of information.
- *Fast:* Readers skim a text rapidly if they are trying to get just the general gist without worrying about details.
- *Slow to moderate:* Readers read carefully in order to get complete understanding of an article. The more difficult the text, the more slowly they read. Often difficult texts require rereading.
- *Very slow:* Experienced readers read very slowly if their purpose is to analyze a text. They take elaborate marginal notes and often pause to ponder over the construction of a paragraph or the meaning of an image or metaphor. Sometimes they reread the text dozens of times.

As you grow in expertise within the fields you study, you will undoubtedly learn to vary your reading speed and strategies according to your purposes, even to the point of considering "efficient" reading of certain texts to involve rereading.

TAKING STOCK OF HOW YOU READ

The first step in self-consciously managing your reading process is to become aware of what you already do when you read. Inevitably, we adjust our reading strategies to fit our purposes. Consider the intricacies of bus and train schedules, the baffling help screens for new Web design software, or the densely packed explanations in your college textbooks. How you read these texts will be governed by your purpose. If you need to know when the next train to Richmond leaves or how to import a pie chart into your marketing proposal, you can skip over lots of irrelevant material. On the other hand, if you are preparing to give a workshop on the essential features of a new computer program or trying to grasp the basic concepts of macroeconomics, you must look beyond specific details to discern overall patterns and meanings.

The beginning of a college writing course is a good time to examine your individual reading processes. In the following exercise, we invite you to think about how you read and how you read differently according to situation and purpose.

● **FOR WRITING AND DISCUSSION**

ON YOUR OWN

Choose two different reading situations that will occur in the next day or two. When you actually do the reading, record all the details you can about these two activities. Use the following questions to guide your two accounts:

1. List your reasons or purposes for undertaking each reading.
2. Describe the setting as fully as possible—the place where you are reading, the surroundings, the level of noise or other distractions, the presence or absence of other materials besides the text (pens, laptop, coffee, etc.).
3. Notice what you do to get started—what do you say to yourself, what do you actually do first, what "rituals," if any, do you have for this kind of reading?
4. What are your initial expectations regarding each reading? Do you expect the reading to be easy or difficult, enjoyable or a chore? Do you expect to learn something new, to be entertained, to be surprised, or perhaps to be inspired?
5. List all of the strategies you use as you read—glancing ahead; pausing to reread; reading word-for-word, scanning, or skimming; taking notes. How do you "manage" this particular reading experience? That is, what do you do to keep yourself moving along?
6. Note how often you stop, and think about why you stop. What do you do when you stop? How do you get restarted?
7. How long does it take you to complete this reading?
8. What are the results of this reading? Did the text meet your expectations? What criteria are you using to judge whether the reading experience was successful or satisfying in this case?

After you have completed your two accounts, compare the various aspects of the way you read the two texts and note differences and similarities, then answer these two additional questions:

9. To what extent did your purposes for reading and the reading situations account for these differences or similarities?
10. What most surprised you about your reading processes?

WITH YOUR CLASSMATES

In small groups or as a whole class, share passages from your two accounts and the results of your comparison. What range of reading situations emerges? How did these differences in situation affect reading processes? What common reading practices emerge? What idiosyncratic reading practices are reported? ●

Summary

This chapter began by explaining two essential pieces of knowledge that you need in order to read rhetorically.

- Reading and writing are acts of composing. Reading is an active process in which readers construe a text's meaning by bringing their own values and experiences to the text.
- Authors vary their texts according to their rhetorical context—audience, genre, and purpose.

This background knowledge prepared you for the second half of the chapter, which focused on three expert strategies you can use to

- Build a context for reading
- Match your reading strategy with a text's genre
- Match your reading strategy with your purpose for reading

SOURCES OF THE ARTICLE EXCERPTS ABOUT TEENAGERS' SLEEP PATTERNS

This list of sources is presented in the same order as the excerpts used in the For Writing and Discussion exercise on page 26. The citations follow Modern Language Association (MLA) format. (Sample MLA formats for other types of sources are presented in the appendix at the end of this book.)

Article 1
McFarling, Usha Lee. "Kids Clobbered by Sleeplessness; Schools Try Later Starting Times." <u>Arizona Republic</u> 27 Mar. 1999, final chaser ed.: A9.

Article 2
Carskadon, Mary A. "When Worlds Collide: Adolescent Need for Sleep Versus Societal Demands." <u>Phi Delta Kappan</u> Jan. 1999: 348-53.

Article 3
Wolfson, Amy R., and Mary A. Carskadon. "Sleep Schedules and Daytime Functioning in Adolescents." <u>Child Development</u> 69 (1998): 875-87.

Article 4
Lamberg, Lynne. "Some Schools Agree to Let Sleeping Teens Lie." <u>JAMA</u> 276 (1996): 859.

Article 5
Rapoport, Jennifer. "The ZZZ-Files." <u>YM: Young and Modern</u> Sept. 1998: 48-49.

CHAPTER 3

Listening to a Text

Read as though it made sense and perhaps it will.

—I. A. Richards

In Chapters 1 and 2 we explained what it means to read rhetorically, high-lighted the value of rhetorical reading as an academic skill, and provided an overview of the strategies experienced readers use when they encounter academic texts. In Chapters 3 and 4 we focus specifically on the nuts and bolts of reading the kinds of texts you will be assigned in college. You will learn to make the strategies used by experienced readers part of your own reading repertoire. These strategies will make you both a better reader and a shrewder writer. Indeed, rhetorical reading strategies overlap with the process of writing by providing you lots of grist for your writing mill.

Our discussion in these chapters extends the metaphor of reading as conversation by using the terms "listening" and "questioning" to describe specific reading techniques. In this chapter we show how listening to a text involves preparation strategies as well as careful reading. As you apply these various techniques for rhetorical reading, your goal is to understand what an author is trying to say. *Listening strategies* help you attend closely to a text and thus give it the fairest hearing possible. When you listen attentively to a text, you are reading with the grain, trying to understand it in the way the author intended. In Chapter 4, we explain *questioning strategies,* which will take you back to the text with a different purpose and approach: to read against the grain in order to compose a deeper, critical reading of the text. Your goal then is to apply your own critical thinking so that you can "speak back" to texts with authority and insight.

Let's turn now to listening strategies. We begin by explaining how rhetorical readers read with pen in hand in order to interact with the text and record their ideas-in-progress. We then offer specific listening strategies that you can use at different stages of your reading process, including strategies that take into account a text's visual features. These are:

1. *Preparing strategies,* which include identifying your purpose, recalling background knowledge, using visuals to plan and predict, reconstructing the text's rhetorical context, and spot reading
2. *Strategies for initial reading,* which include noting organizational signals, marking unfamiliar terms, identifying difficult parts, connecting the visual to the verbal, and making marginal notes
3. *Strategies for rereading,* which include mapping the idea structure, descriptive outlining, composing a summary, and writing a rhetorical *précis*

Writing As You Read

Skilled rhetorical readers write as they read. Often they write in the margins of the text (unless it is a library book) or they keep a reading log or journal in which they record notes. Sometimes they stop reading in the middle of a passage and freewrite their ideas-in-progress. The text stimulates them to think; writing down their ideas captures their thinking for future reference and stimulates further thought. To put it another way, rhetorical reading strategies focus on both *comprehension* (a reader's understanding of a text) and *invention* (the ideas generated in response to a text). Thus, writing while you read helps you generate ideas as well as interact more deeply with the text.

For these reasons, most of the rhetorical reading strategies that we present require you to write. To foster the reading-writing connection, we recommend that you keep a reading log (a notebook or journal) in which you practice the strategies described in this chapter. Keeping a reading log will help you develop advanced reading skills as well as generate a wealth of ideas for essay topics.

Depending on your goals for reading a given text, some of the strategies described in this chapter will probably seem more appropriate than others. Some are used consciously by experienced readers on a regular basis; others are designed to help you acquire the mental habits that have become second nature to experienced readers. Experienced readers, for example, almost always take notes as they read, and they frequently write summaries of what they have read. However, experienced readers would be less likely to write a descriptive outline with *says* and *does* statements (see pp. 55–58)—not because the exercise isn't valuable but because they have already internalized the mental habit of attending to both the content and function of paragraphs as they read. By practicing descriptive outlines on a couple of readings, you too will internalize this dual focus of rhetorical reading. Furthermore, descriptive outlining is a valuable tool to use in your own writing as you analyze a draft in order to make decisions about revision.

To illustrate the strategies we present in the rest of this chapter and in Chapter 4, we will refer to the two reading selections included at the end of this chapter: Larissa MacFarquhar's article, "Who Cares If Johnny Can't Read?" and an excerpt from philosopher Anthony Weston's chapter on environmental ethics in *Toward Better Problems*. We use MacFarquhar's text as an example of the lively popular pieces you are likely to encounter when doing research on contemporary culture. We use Weston's text to illustrate the kind of reading you are likely to be assigned in courses across the curriculum.

Preparing to Read

In completing the "Taking Stock of How You Read" exercise in Chapter 2, you probably discovered that you already have various rituals for reading—a place where you typically read, a favorite snack or beverage that you like to have on hand, and various tricks to keep yourself reading. But did the exercise reveal any time spent preparing to read, such as previewing the text for its gist, scope, and level of difficulty? Taking some time to plan your reading enables you to work efficiently and get the most out of your reading experience from the start. Furthermore, thinking about your purpose will help you maintain a sense of your own authority as you read. The strategies we present in this section encourage you to prepare to read as though you were about to join the text in a multivoiced conversation. As we explained in Chapter 1, the text you are reading is one voice among a network of other voices. Your response to the text constitutes yet another voice in the ongoing conversation about the topic. Practicing the following strategies will prepare you to read in this powerful way:

1. *Identifying your purpose* helps you articulate what you wish to get out of a reading.
2. *Recalling background information* reminds you of what you bring to a text.
3. *Taking a text's visual elements into account* helps you plan your reading and offers you information about genre and purpose.
4. *Reconstructing a text's rhetorical context* alerts you to the writer's purpose, audience, and occasion for writing, and thus enables you to make predictions about the text's content, methods, scope, and level of difficulty.
5. *Spot reading* allows you to flesh out the context for reading by assessing the fit between your aims for reading and the writer's aims for writing.

IDENTIFYING YOUR PURPOSE

Identifying your purpose at the outset helps you set goals and plan your reading accordingly. Your purpose for reading may seem like a self-evident matter—"I'm reading this sociology chapter because it was assigned by my professor." That may be, but what we have in mind is a more strategic consideration of your purpose. How does the reading assignment tie in with themes established in class? How does it fit with concepts laid out on the course syllabus? Is this your first course in sociology? If so, then your purpose might be "to note the types of topics, questions, and special vocabulary used by sociologists." This basic but strategically stated goal might lead you to allow extra time for the slowed down reading that is usually necessary at the beginning of introductory courses.

Let's assume you are skimming articles to select some to read more closely for possible use in a researched argument on gun control. As we discuss in detail in Chapter 6, if you've identified a clear and compelling research question, you will know what you're looking for, and your reading will be more purposeful and productive. At times, your purpose may be at odds with a particular author's purpose in writing the text. Suppose, for example, that you oppose gun control and are reading pro–gun control articles in order to summarize and rebut their arguments. In such a case, you are intentionally reading against the purposes of those authors. Setting goals ahead of time helps you know what to look for. At the same time, you should leave open the possibility that your ideas and purposes for writing might change as you read. Reading pro–gun control articles might cause you to moderate or reconsider your anti–gun control stance. Sometimes you might even discover a new and unexpected purpose. For example, in doing gun control research, you might encounter discussions about conflicts between the right to privacy and background checks and decide that this subissue could become the focus of your paper. Our point, then, is that articulating your purpose for reading will make your reading more efficient and productive.

RECALLING BACKGROUND KNOWLEDGE

Another preparation strategy is to recall your prior knowledge, experience, and opinions regarding the text's subject. What experiences, for example, led to your opposition to gun control? What do you need to learn from your research to write a persuasive argument? A brief review of your background will give you benchmarks for recognizing gaps in your knowledge that you hope to fill through reading and for assessing a given text's effect on your current views or beliefs. Considering your background knowledge will help you determine whether a text has taught you something new, made you consider something you hadn't thought of before, changed your mind, or confirmed your prior knowledge and beliefs. A journal or reading log is the perfect place to brainstorm what you already know or feel about a subject. If you have little knowledge about the subject, jot down some questions about it that will enable you to engage more interactively with what you read.

USING VISUAL ELEMENTS TO PLAN AND PREDICT

One of the first things we notice about a text are its visual features. The color, design, and images on a book or magazine are typically what intrigue us to open it. On Web sites, color, design, and images—and, increasingly, animation—are combined to grab our attention so that we'll pause to read instead of clicking on.

Textbooks also capitalize on color and page design to hold and guide readers' attention; it is common practice for students to leaf through a textbook chapter to spot any illustrations, charts, or graphs, and to note the headings on subsections. Yet while we often notice such features, we seldom actively use them as clues to guide our reading of a text. Careful attention to a text's visual features can help you plan your reading of it as well as enable you to make predictions about its purpose and genre.

To make the most out of the preliminary information provided by a text's visual elements, we suggest a simple approach. Begin by noting the kinds of visual elements present in a text; then use these observations to plan your reading and make predictions, two activities that go hand-in-hand. Generally, these elements fall into the following categories:

- *Print features:* Typeface, size, and style (bold, italics, underlining)
- *Document design:* Paper quality, page layout, bullets, numbers, use of color or shading, and other organizational features such as boxes, subheadings, and highlighted quotes
- *Images:* Drawings, photographs, cartoons, art reproductions
- *Information graphics:* Charts, tables, graphs, maps, and diagrams

Attending to both the obvious and less obvious visual features of a text will alert you to the ways in which these features affect your initial expectations, attitudes, and level of interest. This information, in turn, can help you plan your reading. What do you notice about the "look" of a text? Is the text long or short? Does its appearance draw you into it, or does it make the reading task look daunting? If the text is dense, with long paragraphs uninterrupted by subheadings, you probably expect reading it to be time-consuming and a bit tedious, and you may well decide that you will need to take frequent breaks or that you will save the reading for the time when you are most alert and able to concentrate. On the other hand, if an article or chapter includes pictures or illustrations that pique your interest, or if the text itself is divided into sections by white space or inviting quotations highlighted between the columns (known as *pull-quotes*), you probably expect reading it to be easier and more enjoyable.

Although it may seem as if the visual features of a text are distinct from the verbal, all written texts include print features that affect our attitudes and expectations about a reading. A text set in `Courier font`, for example, resembles typewritten copy and thus has the serious look of a school paper or business letter; a text set in *Lucida Calligraphy*, by contrast, looks ornate, as if it belonged on a fancy invitation or a program for a concert. Or consider the effect of a text or portion of a text written in all caps. IT SEEMS TO BE SHOUTING AT READERS! Additionally, the type of paper on which a text is printed has a particular look and feel. A magazine printed on heavy paper stock has an expensive, sophisticated feel that leads to expectations of high-class content—high fashion if it is a fashion magazine, fine arts if it is an arts magazine, and so on. All of these features affect our expectations about a text.

Increasingly, texts include elements of document design that enhance read-ability and emphasize key points. These reader-friendly visual signals affect our first impressions of a text and provide directions about what's important. They say "pay attention," "remember," "slow down and make sure you understand this," or "follow these steps." Consider, for example, how differently informa-tion about tooth decay and sugary soft drinks might be presented in an infor-mational brochure for teenagers as opposed to the technical research articles for dentists upon which the brochure is based. The brochure might have cartoons, bright colors, large type, and a bulleted list of advice about good tooth care—all intended to enhance readability and persuasiveness. In contrast, the research ar-ticles would probably have an introductory abstract (perhaps set in a different typeface), tables of data, charts and graphs, and the traditional formal headings about "Method," "Results," and "Discussion," all of which would signal the se-riousness and significance of the research as well as the need for readers to pay close attention so that they can understand the articles' main points.

Images, which technology has made easy to include in printed material, also affect our attitude toward a reading and help us make predictions about its tone, content, and purpose. To illustrate their influence, consider Figure 3.1, which was published in a magazine for grant writers alongside an article by Tony

FIGURE 3.1 Illustration from Proscio's "Jabberwocky Junkies"

Proscio entitled "Jabberwocky Junkies." Placed just beneath the title, to the right of the subtitle, this illustration was immediately eye-catching. The cartoon functions not only to draw attention but, in connection with the title, provides important signals about both the content and attitude of the article. You might readily predict that the article takes a humorous attitude toward overblown terms such as "throughput" and "operationalize." This prediction is confirmed by the article's subtitle: "Why we're hooked on buzzwords—and why we need to kick the habit." Later in the article, another visual element—a box entitled "Avoiding Jargon"—offers specific, practical advice. Taken together, these visual elements, along with the title and subtitle, would enable you to predict that the article's purpose is to criticize, with a touch of humor, the use of jargon among grant writers and to offer recommendations for eliminating it.

A text's visual features also reveal its genre, from which you can begin to predict its purpose. In our everyday lives, we easily differentiate an envelope containing a credit card bill from an offer for a new credit card, and we can usually distinguish "serious" fiction from a romance novel by a glance at a book's cover. Similarly, when reading for academic purposes, we encounter many nonacademic and academic genres that are recognizable just by their look. Newspaper articles have short paragraphs to facilitate reading in narrow columns, a characteristic that often makes these articles look choppy when they are reproduced in wide formatting. Book reviews characteristically begin with a short notation, perhaps in boldface, that provides publication information about the book or books under review, and poems are readily recognizable by their layout on the page. As we explained in Chapter 2, rhetorical theorists have found that our knowledge of genres sets up particular expectations and affects how we go about reading a text. Plainly, we approach the reading of a poem quite differently than we do the reading of a scholarly article, résumé, or comic strip. Consider the visual features of this chapter: frequent subheadings, italicized terms, bulleted lists, annotated examples. What do these features suggest about its genre? About how to go about reading it? Even if you were reading a photocopy of this chapter without the context of the book, you would easily recognize that it came from a textbook because its instructional features emphasize important points and break up information for ease of reading and review. Since you are quite familiar with textbooks, you have undoubtedly developed strategies for reading texts like this one—skimming the headings before reading, noting words in bold, using the bulleted information for review.

Beyond textbooks, the broad genre of academic writing generally includes fewer visual elements than popular texts do because academic texts presume an interested and knowledgeable reader. Therefore, it is especially important to preview these texts for any visual signals that might help you plan and predict your reading of them. For example, in texts with long paragraphs and complex reasoning such as *Toward Better Problems*, the Anthony Weston book we have been discussing, headings and sub-headings signal key ideas and thus help readers anticipate main ideas and read strategically.

● **FOR WRITING AND DISCUSSION**

ON YOUR OWN

This exercise invites you to examine the impact visuals can have on a reader's initial responses to a text and ability to predict its genre and purpose. Find two sample texts, one written for a popular audience, the other a scholarly text in your intended major. List the visual features of each type of text, from page design to actual images. Then freewrite in response to the following questions:

1. How do these features affect your attitude toward each reading?
2. How might they guide your reading of each text?
3. What information do they offer about genre and purpose?
4. What do they tell you about what you can expect to get out of the text?

WITH YOUR CLASSMATES

1. Take turns presenting your examples and freewrites.
2. As a group, make a list of the genres represented in the examples shared. Under each genre, list the visual features typical of that genre. Be prepared to present your group's findings about how visual features signal differences in genre and purpose.   ●

RECONSTRUCTING RHETORICAL CONTEXT

In Chapter 2 we showed how a text's content, organization, and style are influenced by a writer's rhetorical context—that is, by the writer's intended audience, genre, and purpose. Reconstructing that context before or as you read is a powerful reading strategy. Sometimes readers can reconstruct context from external clues: a text's visual appearance (as we explained in the previous section), a text's title, background notes on the author, date and place of publication, table of contents, headings, introduction, and conclusion. But readers often have to rely on internal evidence to get a full picture. A text's context and purpose may become evident through some quick spot reading (described below), especially of the introduction. Sometimes, however, context can be reconstructed only through a great deal of puzzling as you read. It's not unusual that a whole first reading is needed. Once context becomes clear, the text is easier to comprehend upon rereading.

To establish a sense of the text's original rhetorical context, use the available sources of information to formulate at least tentative answers to the following questions:

1. What question(s) is the text addressing?
2. What is the writer's purpose?
3. Who is the intended audience(s)?
4. What situational factors (biographical, historical, political, or cultural) apparently caused the author to write this text?

To explore how external clues reveal context, suppose you are enrolled in a philosophy class and have been assigned to read the Anthony Weston book first mentioned in Chapter 2, *Toward Better Problems: New Perspectives on Abortion, Animal Rights, the Environment, and Justice.* The title and subtitle suggest that the book will address the following question: "How can we find better ways to define difficult social problems such as abortion, animal rights, the environment, and justice?" The words "better" and "new" in the title also imply that this book is a response to other books on the subject and that the author's purpose is to propose a change in outlook. The phrase "better problems" is intriguing—is there such a thing as a "good" or "better" problem? This strange notion, along with the promise of "new" perspectives on thorny social issues, seems designed to pique readers' curiosity.

To place the book in a larger context, however, and to identify the intended audience, we need further information. A quick perusal of the back cover tells us the publisher, Temple University Press, has categorized the text as "Philosophy/Applied Ethics," so we might predict that the book was written for an academic audience, or at least a well-educated one, and that Weston will deal with ethical issues from a philosophical perspective (as opposed to a theological, sociological, or political one). This conclusion is further confirmed by information on the cover that Weston teaches philosophy at the State University of New York–Stony Brook, a note that establishes his academic credentials for writing about this subject. If you don't have a strong background in philosophy, this information may further lead you to conclude that this text may be difficult to read—all the more reason to devote time to investigating its context and purpose, which we explore further in the next section. After all, by virtue of enrolling in the philosophy course, you have become part of Weston's intended audience.

SPOT READING

Spot reading is a process that gives you a quick overview of a text's content and structure, thus accomplishing two purposes: (1) determining the fit between the text's purpose and your own purposes for reading; and (2) giving you an initial framework for predicting content and formulating questions. For example, when your purpose for reading is to acquaint yourself with the vocabulary and concepts of a new field, then spot reading will help you to determine whether a book or article is written at an introductory level. If it is, then you can expect textual cues to point to important new vocabulary and concepts. If it is not, then you may decide to find a more introductory text to read first, or you may decide to allot extra time to reread and look up unfamiliar terms.

If the text that interests you has an abstract or introduction, you might begin spot reading there. Other places for productive spot reading are the opening and concluding paragraphs or sections of a text. The opening usually introduces the subject and announces the purpose, and the conclusion often sums up the text's major ideas. If the text is short, you might try reading the opening sentences of each paragraph. If the text is longer, note chapter titles in the table of contents. Sometimes tables of contents, particularly in textbooks, provide chapter contents and subdivisions. If you are working with a text that provides summaries and study questions, read through these before beginning to read the section they describe. Spot reading a table of contents can help you determine what content will be covered and whether a text will help you address a research question. The organizational strategy revealed through a table of contents also provides important information about an author's method, perhaps guiding you to choose certain sections as essential reading.

As illustration, let's return to Weston's *Toward Better Problems* to consider what the chapter titles in his table of contents reveal about his purpose and method.

Chapter 1: Practical Ethics in a New Key

Chapter 2: Pragmatic Attitudes

Chapter 3: Rethinking the Abortion Debate

Chapter 4: Other Animals

Chapter 5: The Environment*

Chapter 6: Justice

Chapter 7: Conclusion

These titles suggest that the first two chapters spell out his theory for constructing "better problems" and "new perspectives" while each of the next four chapters is devoted to one of the topics listed in the book's subtitle. If you were reading this book independently for background on just one of these topics, perhaps environmental ethics, you might read only the first two chapters and then the one on the environment.

This particular table of contents lists major subtopics within all but the first chapter (which is only five pages long). The list of subtopics for Chapter 2 gives further indication not only of Weston's purpose and method but of the chapter's crucial value for understanding his approach in the problem-focused chapters that follow it:

CHAPTER 2: PRAGMATIC ATTITUDES

From Puzzles to Problematic Situations

Reconstructive Strategies

Integrative Strategies

Given the book title's forecast of "better problems" and "new perspectives," it seems reasonable to predict that in this chapter Weston contrasts two ways of

---

*An excerpt from this chapter appears on pages 67–70.

viewing ethical problems—as "puzzles" and as "problematic situations"—and that he favors the latter. From these basic clues you can begin to articulate your own purpose for reading and to formulate questions that will help you understand the text: What's the main difference between thinking of ethical problems as puzzles and thinking of them as problematic situations? Why is the latter approach better than the former?

The framework that spot reading provides for making predictions and posing questions about content will help you make sense of ideas and information as you read. It can also help you anticipate and tolerate difficult-to-understand passages, confident that even though you don't understand every bit of the text on the first reading you nevertheless have some sense of its overall meaning. In short, spot reading helps you to stay in control of your reading process by helping you confirm and revise your predictions and look for answers to your questions. It takes little time and offers a worthwhile payoff in increased understanding.

• FOR WRITING AND DISCUSSION

To demonstrate the value of the various preparation strategies we have described, we invite you to try them out on Larissa MacFarquhar's "Who Cares If Johnny Can't Read?" (pp. 64–66). Later in the chapter we will ask you to read this article carefully. For now, set yourself 10 minutes of preparation time (look at your watch) and try to accomplish the following.

ON YOUR OWN
1. Do some initial spot reading of the text and headnote to get a sense of what the article is about.
2. Based on what you discover about its content, write down a possible purpose you might have for reading it other than for an assignment, or what purpose an instructor might have for assigning it.
3. Freewrite briefly about your background on this topic and your feelings about it.
4. Reconstruct the text's rhetorical context: What question(s) does this text address? Who is the intended audience? What seems to be MacFarquhar's main purpose? What historical or cultural factors cause her to write?
5. Continue to spot read to help you answer the above questions.

WITH YOUR CLASSMATES
Share what you each accomplished in 10 minutes.
1. Compare various purposes proposed by group members.
2. What different backgrounds and feelings emerged?
3. What agreement was there about the text's rhetorical context?

ON YOUR OWN AGAIN

Our goal in presenting this exercise is to show you the value of taking a short time to prepare to read, as opposed to simply plunging into a text. What did you learn from the experience? How successful have we been in convincing you to use these strategies?   ●

Listening As You Read Initially

"Listening" to a text means trying to understand the author's ideas, intentions, and worldview—that is, reading *with the grain* of the text, trying to understand it on its own terms. Just as good listeners attend carefully to what their conversational partners say, trying to give them a fair hearing, so too do good readers attend carefully to what a text says, trying to consider the ideas fairly and accurately before rushing to judgment. In particular, college reading requires you to give an impartial hearing to ideas and positions that are new and sometimes radically different from your own. Moreover, in class discussions, examinations, and paper assignments, you will frequently be asked to demonstrate that you have listened well to your assigned texts. Professors want to know that you have comprehended these texts with reasonable accuracy before you proceed to analyze, apply, or critique the ideas in them. In the language of Kenneth Burke's metaphor of the conversational parlor introduced in Chapter 1, you might think of this listening phase of the reading process as the phase where you try to catch the drift of the conversation and give it the fullest and fairest hearing before "putting in your oar."

Listening strategies help you understand what to listen for, how to hear it, and how to track your evolving understanding of what the text is saying. We have divided this section into two sets of strategies because you need to listen differently the first time you are reading a text than when you are rereading. The first time through, you are trying to understand a text's overall gist and compose a "rough-draft interpretation" of its meaning. The second time through, after you have a sense of the gist, you are aiming to confirm, revise if necessary, and deepen your understanding.

We opened this chapter by urging you to read with a pen or pencil in hand, to adopt experienced readers' practice of marking passages, drawing arrows, and making notes. The following five strategies will guide you through your first reading of a text:

1. *Noting organizational signals* enables you to create a mental road map of the text's idea structure.
2. *Marking unfamiliar terms and references* identifies terms and ideas to look up later.
3. *Identifying points of difficulty* reminds you of passages to bring up in class or reread.

4. *Connecting the visual to the verbal* helps you understand the ways in which visual elements function in relation to the verbal content.
5. *Annotating* a text provides a record to use later for rereading, writing about the text, or reviewing for a test.

NOTING ORGANIZATIONAL SIGNALS

Organizational signals help you anticipate and then track the text's overall structure of ideas. Experienced readers use these signals to identify the text's central ideas, to distinguish major ideas from minor ones, to anticipate what is coming next, and to determine the relationship among the text's major ideas. Organizational signals and forecasting statements (which directly tell you what to expect) function like road signs, giving you information about direction, upcoming turns, and the distance yet to go. For example, experienced readers note words such as *however, in contrast,* or *on the other hand* that signal a change in the direction of thought. Likewise, they note words such as *first, second,* and *third* that signal a series of parallel points or ideas; words such as *therefore, consequently,* or *as a result* that signal cause/effect or logical relationships; and words such as *similarly, also,* or *likewise* that signal additional evidence or examples in support of the current point. Experienced readers often circle or otherwise mark these terms so that a quick glance back will remind them of the structure of ideas.

MARKING UNFAMILIAR TERMS AND REFERENCES

As you read, it is important to mark unfamiliar terms and references because they offer contextual clues about the intended audience and the conversation of which this text is a part. Their very unfamiliarity may tell you that the text is written for an insider audience whose members share a particular kind of knowledge and set of concerns. We suggest that you mark such terms with a question mark or write them in the margins and return to them after you finish your initial reading. Stopping to look them up as you read will break your concentration. By looking them up later, after you have a sense of the text's overall purpose, you will gain insight into how key terms function and how they represent major concerns of a particular field or area of study.

IDENTIFYING POINTS OF DIFFICULTY

Perhaps one of the most important traits of experienced readers is their *tolerance for ambiguity and initial confusion.* They have learned to read through points of difficulty, trusting in I. A. Richards's advice in the epigraph to this chapter, "Read as though it made sense and perhaps it will." When you are reading about new and difficult subject matter, you will inevitably encounter passages that you simply do not understand. As we suggested in our advice about building a context for your reading, explicitly identifying what you don't understand is an important reading strategy. We recommend that you bracket puzzling passages and keep reading. Later you can come back to them and try to translate them into your own words or to frame questions about them to ask your classmates and professor.

CONNECTING THE VISUAL TO THE VERBAL

Nowadays visual elements frequently accompany verbal texts as ways to enhance, support, and extend a text's meaning as well as to increase its rhetorical effectiveness (a topic we discuss in Chapter 4). A number of factors work together to make the use of visual elements particularly powerful. For one thing, we live in a highly visual culture where information is often transmitted through images. Consequently, our attention is more readily attracted and engaged by verbal texts that include visual elements. For another, there is a general belief not only that "a picture is worth a thousand words" but also that "pictures don't lie" and "seeing is believing," despite widespread knowledge that images can be doctored or manipulated. For all of these reasons, careful readers must be alert to the subtle and indirect messages conveyed through visuals.

The importance of visual elements, particularly images, in relation to a text can vary considerably. At one end of the continuum are visual elements that are clearly incidental to the verbal message—for example, generic clip art added to a newsletter. At the other end are texts in which the visual message predominates and verbal elements play only a minor role—for example, the photograph of Christina Aguilera in Chapter 4. Somewhere in between is the special case of cartoons, where the visual and verbal are tightly intertwined, with the visual sometimes leading, sometimes carrying the verbal. In academic writing, visual elements are usually subordinate to the verbal content, with their importance depending on their function.

Here we discuss three common ways in which visual elements can function in relation to the verbal message: (1) by *enhancing* its appeal, (2) by *supporting* its claims, and (3) by *extending* its meaning. Often, visual elements serve more than one of these functions in relation to a text; however, we will explain these three functions separately to highlight their subtle but important differences in relation to the verbal text.

1. **Visuals That Enhance Verbal Content.** Photographs, drawings, and other images often function to attract readers' attention, set a tone, and frame responses to a text. In these ways, they *enhance* the text's verbal content by augmenting it with the vividness and immediacy of visual images. Consider the photograph of the Icelandic lagoon in Chapter 1, which appears along with our description of a series of articles that took different approaches to presenting

© Disney Enterprises, Inc.   **Stage 1**   **Stage 2**   **Stage 3**

FIGURE 3.2 Stephen J. Gould used this composite of images of Mickey Mouse to show how the cartoon character's features became more juvenile over fifty years.

scientific research about the melting of polar ice. The photograph was taken by the author of an overview article and published along with it. The photo's role in the original publication was similar to the role it plays in our text: It adds visual interest to a page that would otherwise include only text at the same time that it gives presence to the matter under discussion.

2. **Visuals That Support Verbal Content.** A second common way in which the visual relates to the verbal is to *support* the verbal message. Authors can provide evidence for their claims by referring readers directly to visual elements. Indeed, the time-honored technique of explaining something by providing a picture is becoming more prevalent, thanks to advances in computer software and printing technology as well as widespread use of the World Wide Web. Consider the images of Mickey Mouse in Figure 3.2, which were used by the late paleontologist and evolutionary theorist Stephen Jay Gould to demonstrate that Mickey's appearance became more youthful over the years, particularly because his head and eyes became larger. Writing in 1979 in honor of Mickey's 50th birthday, Gould used this visual evidence, along with scientific measurement and references, to support his argument that the evolution of Mickey's features toward a more juvenile appearance made him more emotionally appealing to audiences—an idea that, as he demonstrated, coincides with the findings of animal behaviorists, which indicate that "baby faces," be they human or animal, tend to trigger affectionate responses in humans.*

Prominent among visual elements that support verbal content are information graphics, which are typically used to promote readers' comprehension of discrete and detailed points of information. Table 3.1—itself an information graphic—provides a quick list of visuals commonly used for specific explanatory and informative purposes. Most of these are fairly easy to create with standard desktop software. Understanding the purpose and function of information graphics will help you develop your rhetorical reading skills and prepare you to incorporate graphic elements into your texts in college and on the job. Notice that the list of graphics in the table's right column includes photographs and

*Stephen Jay Gould, "Mickey Mouse Meets Konrad Lorenz," *Natural History* 88.5 (1979): 30–36.

TABLE 3.1 ● COMMON TYPES AND USES OF INFORMATION GRAPHICS	
Purpose	**Graphic to Use**
Present detailed or complex data	Table
Bring an object or process to life	Drawing, photograph, flowchart
Show change over time	Line graph
Show relation of parts to the whole	Pie chart
Contrast quantities and phenomena	Table, bar graph
Locate and show distribution of phenomena	Map
Highlight key points	Shaded boxes, bulleted lists

drawings, which become information graphics when labels or computer animation are added. Similarly, elements of page design such as checklists, shaded boxes, and bulleted lists merge into this category when they are used to help readers efficiently find, use, and understand information.

3. **Visuals That Extend Verbal Content.** A third function visual elements can serve is to *extend* the meaning of a verbal text by enlarging or highlighting a particular dimension of it. Visual elements that function in this way can suggest new interpretations, provoke particular responses, or create links to other ideas. In many of these cases, a reader might initially puzzle over the connection between an image and the verbal text it accompanies, not knowing quite how to interpret it until after reading the text. Visuals that work this way often accompany advertisements, by implication connecting physical attractiveness, romantic success, improved economic status, or any number of other desirable attributes with the product being sold. In some cases, a reader might initially puzzle over the connection between an image and the text it accompanies, not knowing quite how to interpret that image until after reading the text. Consider, for example, the drawing by Randy Mack Bishop in Figure 3.3. Bishop is an illustrator for the *Dallas Morning News* whose work is available to newspapers nationwide through NewsArt.com. Before we describe the context in which an editor at the *Milwaukee Journal Sentinel* placed it, take a moment to consider what ideas or issues Bishop's image evokes for you. The drawing came to our attention when it appeared on the op-ed page alongside a reprinted opinion piece by *New York Times* columnist Maureen Dowd with the headline "Scarred for Life: Courage Begets Courage."* Puzzled? We were. In the column, Dowd writes admiringly of her niece's courage in donating part of her liver to her uncle (Dowd's

*Maureen Dowd, "Scarred for Life: Courage Begets Courage," *Milwaukee Journal Sentinel* 3 June 2003: 11A. Published originally as "Our Own Warrior Princess," *New York Times* 1 June 2003: 4.13.

FIGURE 3.3 Editorial art drawing by Randy Mack Bishop

brother); by the end of the piece, Dowd has resolved to become an organ donor herself. By implication, she urges others to do the same. Since the drawing does not connect directly to the text, readers might interpret its meaning variously. However, most would probably agree that the drawing is linked to the abstract idea of courage, suggesting, perhaps, that the support of others enables us to be courageous and to rise above selfish concerns.

ANNOTATING

When you annotate a text, you underline, highlight, draw arrows, and make marginal comments. Annotating is a way of making the text your own, of literally putting your mark on it—noting its key passages and ideas. Experienced readers rely on this common but powerful strategy to note reactions and questions, thereby recording their in-process understanding of a text. By using their pen or pencil to mark the page, they are able to monitor their evolving construction of a text's meaning.

Annotations also serve a useful purpose when you return to a text to reread or review it. They not only remind you of your first impressions of the text's meaning but also help you identify main points and come to new levels of understanding—clearer answers to earlier questions, new insights, and new questions. Indeed, we recommend that you annotate each time you read a text, perhaps using a different colored pen so that you have a record of the new layers of meaning you discover each time you read. Of course, annotating can become counterproductive if you underline or highlight too enthusiastically: a completely underlined paragraph tells you nothing about its key point. To be useful, underlining must be selective, based both on your own purposes for reading and on what you think the writer's main points are. In general, when it is time to review the text and recall its main ideas, notes in the margin about main ideas, questions or objections, and connections among ideas will be far more useful to you than underlining or highlighting.

To illustrate this listening strategy, we have annotated the two opening paragraphs of Weston's "The Need for Environmental Ethics," which is printed at the end of this chapter (pp. 67–70). The annotations were made from the perspective of a student enrolled in an introductory philosophy class that includes a unit on ethics. They demonstrate the student's efforts to uncover Weston's central argument and purpose. We invite you to turn to the selection now and read through the passage and annotations carefully. Think about the student's purpose—and whether the annotations help him achieve his purpose—and consider the uses the student might make of these annotations.

● FOR WRITING AND DISCUSSION

Earlier in this chapter you tried out some "preparing to read" strategies on Larissa MacFarquhar's "Who Cares If Johnny Can't Read?" It is now time for you to read that essay carefully, listening to MacFarquhar's argument.

ON YOUR OWN

As you read the essay the first time, try your hand at marking and annotating.

1. Note organizational signals, unfamiliar terms, and difficult passages.
2. Annotate what you believe to be her key ideas and the most important passages.
3. Record your reactions and questions in the margins.

WITH YOUR CLASSMATES

Compare your markings and annotations of this essay.

1. What differences and similarities were there in different people's underlining, marking, and marginal notes? What do you conclude will be an efficient strategy for you?
2. As a group, make a brief list of MacFarquhar's key points and ideas. Compare your group's list with those of other groups and try to arrive at a consensus. ●

Listening As You Reread

Rhetorical reading, as we have been suggesting, is not a one-step process but may often require careful reading and rereading to confirm and deepen your understanding of a text. Of course not every text requires rereading; however, whenever detailed analysis is required or whenever a text is particularly difficult, a careful second and sometimes third reading is needed.

To help you acquire the mental habits of strong readers and to give you practice with the types of writing you will use frequently as part of college-level analysis and research, we offer the following four strategies:

1. *Mapping the idea structure* provides you with a visual representation of a text's major ideas and the relationships among those ideas.
2. *Descriptive outlining* enables you to distinguish what a text (or visual) *says* from what it *does* rhetorically.
3. *Composing a summary* requires you to focus on and articulate the gist of the text, which is good practice for incorporating source material into your own writing.
4. *Writing a rhetorical précis* provides a structured model for describing the rhetorical strategies of a text as well as capturing the gist of its content.

MAPPING THE IDEA STRUCTURE

One of the goals of rereading is to get a sense of how the text works as a whole—how its ideas connect and relate to one another. Idea maps provide a visual representation of the ways that a text's ideas relate to each other, enabling you to distinguish main ideas from subordinate ones and to understand relationships among the writer's points. You might think of idea maps as X-rays of the text's idea structure.

The time to map a text's idea structure is after you have finished reading it and are sitting back to review its main ideas. To create a map, draw a circle in the center of a page and write the text's main idea inside the circle. Then record the text's supporting ideas on branches and subbranches that extend from the center circle. In Figure 3.4 we offer a sample idea map of the excerpt from Weston's "The Need for Environmental Ethics" found on pages 67–70. Creating a map is not an easy task because it forces you to think about the text's main ideas in a new way. You may even find that creating a map reveals inconsistencies in the text's organizational structure or puzzling relationships among ideas. This, too, is important information and may be an issue you should bring up in class discussion or in your written responses to the text. In any case, creating idea maps is a way to understand a text at a deeper level and thus to evaluate its importance in relation to course content or in relation to a writing project of your own.

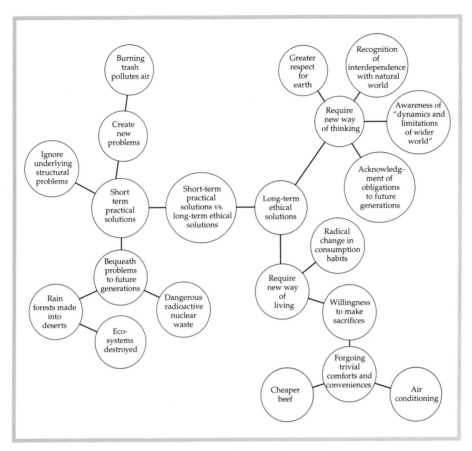

FIGURE 3.4 Idea Map for Weston's "The Need for Environmental Ethics"

DESCRIPTIVE OUTLINING

Making a descriptive outline is a particularly powerful technique for examining how a text is constructed in terms of what discrete parts of it *do* and *say*.* The technique calls for brief statements about the function and content of each paragraph or cluster of related paragraphs in a text. The *does* statement identifies a paragraph's or section's function or purpose, while the *says* statement summarizes the content of the same stretch of text. *Does* statements should not repeat the content but focus instead on the purpose or function of the content in relation to the overall argument. Sample *does* statements might be, "offers an anecdote to illustrate previous point," "introduces a new reason in support of main argument," "provides statistical evidence to support the claim," or "summarizes the previous section."

---

*For our discussion of descriptive outlining, we are indebted to Kenneth Bruffee, *A Short Course in Writing*, 3rd ed. (Boston: Little Brown, 1985), 103.

Does and *says* statements help you see how a text works at the micro level, paragraph by paragraph, section by section. This kind of analysis is particularly useful if you intend to write a summary of the passage, and it is a good way to begin an analysis or critique of an author's rhetorical methods. Because of the analytical distance this technique provides, it also serves as a useful aid to revision of your own writing, helping you to see whether the content of your text matches your intentions.

To illustrate, here are *does* and *says* statements for the two opening paragraphs of the Weston selection:

PARAGRAPH 1

Does: States the problem and illustrates with dramatic examples.

Says: Severe environmental problems are forcing us to realize that there's something profoundly wrong with our relationship to the natural world.

PARAGRAPH 2

Does: Contrasts two approaches to dealing with the problem.

Says: We respond to environmental problems with short-term solutions such as burning trash that then pollutes the air rather than with fundamental changes in our thinking and behavior.

To assist you in writing *does* statements, usually the more difficult statement to write, we offer the following list of verbs that you can use to describe the rhetorical functions performed by a paragraph or section of a text:

VERBS THAT DESCRIBE WHAT TEXTS DO

Each of these verbs might be used to complete a phrase such as "This paragraph [or section] _____."

adds (e.g., adds detail)	dramatizes	opposes
analyzes	elaborates	predicts
argues	evaluates	presents
asks	explains	projects
cites	expresses	proposes
compares	extends	qualifies
connects	generalizes	questions
continues	illustrates	quotes
contradicts	informs	reasons
contrasts	interprets	rebuts
demonstrates	introduces	reflects
describes	lists	repeats
details	narrates	states
	offers	speculates

suggests   supports   traces

summarizes   synthesizes   uses

● FOR WRITING AND DISCUSSION

ON YOUR OWN

Make an idea map of Larissa MacFarquhar's essay. Now make a descriptive outline of the essay, paragraph by paragraph. At first you will find both tasks difficult, and you will probably be forced to reread the article slowly, part by part. (That's one of our points—the need to reread.) Soon, however, your puzzlement will evolve into a much clearer understanding of her argument. Trust us. You may find that it is easier to do the descriptive outline first and then the idea map. To help you get started, here is a descriptive outline of the first three paragraphs of MacFarquhar's essay. This outline was written by a student named Jenny, whose work we will follow closely in this and later chapters.

> Par. 1:
> *Does:* Introduces subject of article and presents three common beliefs about the subject.
> *Says:* Many believe America is in a state of cultural decline because Americans read less than they used to, because they don't read the "classics," and because new media threaten to make the book obsolete.
>
> Par. 2:
> *Does:* Rebuts all three of these common beliefs with facts.
> *Says:* The claims that Americans read less and know nothing about the classics are false, as is the idea that books are becoming obsolete.
>
> Par. 3:
> *Does:* Continues to rebut opposing claims with facts and figures.
> *Says:* Americans are buying and reading more books than they did in the past.

WITH YOUR CLASSMATES

Working in small groups, compare your idea maps and descriptive outlines. Each group can then draw a revised idea map and put it on the board or an overhead for comparison with those of other groups.   ●

The strategies of descriptive outlining can also help you analyze a text's visual features by enabling you to understand more deeply their role and significance in relation to the text's verbal content. To write the *says* statement, you must present the visual element on its own terms, describing it as if it stood alone, without the text. It is important to offer a literal description of the visual image itself.

For example, consider the photograph of Christina Aguilera in Chapter 4 (p. 83), where we reproduce the first page of an article about her to illustrate how images and verbal text can combine to make an argument. Ignoring the overall page layout and text, a *says* statement description of the photograph alone would mention that Aguilera has her feet casually hooked in the rungs of a simple stool, looks directly at the camera, and is wearing torn jeans along with a simple white T-shirt emblazoned with the motto: "A man of quality is not threatened by a woman of equality." In contrast, when you write a *does* statement for a visual element, you need to consider its connection to the verbal text, asking why it is there and how it works in relationship to the text's verbal message. For the Aguilera photograph, a good *does* statement might say that the photo enhances the article's verbal content by piquing interest in the intriguing and probably controversial statement on her T-shirt, and furthermore that the singer's posture and direct gaze invite readers to look closely at the various snippets of text on this page and then the whole article. Since the relationship between image and text is open to interpretation here, as it frequently is, other *does* statements are possible, including ones that might comment on the genuineness or believability of the argument emanating from the T-shirt (e.g., that it "may stretch readers' credulity" or "asserts Aguilera's feminist beliefs").

To write the *does* statement for a visual element, consider its connection to the verbal text, asking why it is there and how it works in relationship to the text's verbal message. A good way to start is to consider the *enhancing, supporting,* and *extending* functions we discussed earlier and compose a *does* statement that specifies one of those functions (for example, "the visual *enhances* by . . ."). If you think that the visual functions in more than one important way, you may wish to write more than one *does* statement.

As further illustration of how descriptive outlining works with visual elements, we offer sample *does-says* outlines of two images presented earlier in the chapter: the straightforward presentation of evidence about Mickey Mouse's appearance in Figure 3.2, and the more abstract image in Figure 3.3, for which a number of interpretations are possible.

Figure 3.2, Composite Disney Images of Mickey Mouse
> **Does:** Supports author's claim by offering visual data
>
> **Says:** Mickey's appearance becomes more juvenile over time as his eyes and head become larger in relation to his body, his nose rounder, and his overall body stockier.

Figure 3.3, Randy Mack Bishop Drawing
> **Does:** Extends the text about organ donation with an inspirational image representing an abstract idea of mutual aid
>
> **Says:** Three figures embracing one another rise together.

In Chapter 4, we discuss ways to analyze more fully the rhetorical work performed by visuals.

COMPOSING A SUMMARY

Probably the best way to demonstrate your understanding of what a writer has said is to compose a *summary*—a condensed version of a text's main points written in your own words, conveying the author's main ideas but eliminating all the supporting details. In academic and professional work, summaries take many forms and fulfill a variety of functions. In research papers, you will often present brief summaries of sources to give readers an overview of another writer's perspective or argument, thus bringing another voice into the conversation. Such summaries are particularly useful to set the context for a quotation. If the source is particularly important, you might write a longer summary—perhaps even a full paragraph. For example, many academic writing assignments call for a *review of the literature,* a section in which you summarize how previous researchers have addressed your research problem. In a persuasive "take a stand" paper, you'll likely use summaries to provide evidence that supports your view as well as to present fully and accurately any arguments that oppose your view (after which you will try to counter these arguments). If you are writing a paper in the social or physical sciences, you will often be expected to write an *abstract* of your paper, since it is conventional in the sciences to begin a published work with a highly condensed overview in case busy readers don't have time to read the whole paper. In business and professional life, the equivalent of an abstract is the *executive summary,* a section that appears at the front of any major business report or proposal. Summary writing, in other words, is not simply a strategy for rhetorical reading; it is one of the most frequent types of writing you will do in your academic and professional life.

Depending on their purpose, summaries can vary in length. At times, you may summarize a text in a single sentence as a way of invoking the authority of another voice (probably an expert) to support your points. For example, suppose you wanted to use Weston's approach to ethical issues in a paper exploring whether the Makah people of the Pacific Northwest should be allowed to hunt whales. In part this is an ethical issue pitting the rights of whales against the rights of native peoples to follow their ancient traditions. You might begin a section by summarizing Weston as follows: "In the introduction to *Toward Better Problems,* Anthony Weston argues that complex ethical problems like environmental issues cannot be viewed as simple puzzles to be solved." After this brief summary, which helps you make your point that environmental issues are many-sided without right answers, you would proceed to explain how the puzzle concept has been wrongly applied in this controversy. Perhaps you would later use ideas Weston develops in his chapters "Other Animals" and "The Environment" as frames for presenting an alternative way of understanding the Makah whaling controversy.

At other times, summaries may be one of your main purposes for writing. A typical college assignment might ask you to summarize the arguments of two writers and then analyze the differences in their views. In the summary part of this assignment, your professor is asking you to demonstrate your understanding of what may be quite complex arguments.

Writing a fair and accurate summary requires that you identify a text's main ideas, state them in your own words, and omit supporting details. The best first step for writing a summary is to create a descriptive outline of the text, where the *says* statements summarize the main point of each paragraph. (A first draft of your summary could be simply your sequencing of all your *says* statements.) Making

---

COMPOSING A SUMMARY

☐ Step 1: Read the text first for its main points.
☐ Step 2: Reread carefully and make a descriptive outline.
☐ Step 3: Write out the text's thesis or main point. (Suppose you had to summarize the whole argument in one sentence.)
☐ Step 4: Identify the text's major divisions or chunks. Each division develops one of the stages needed to make the whole main point. Typically these stages or parts might function as background, review of the conversation, summary of opposing views, or subpoints in support of the thesis.
☐ Step 5: Try summarizing each part in one or two sentences.
☐ Step 6: Now combine your summaries of the parts into a coherent whole, creating a condensed version of the text's main ideas in your own words.

---

a descriptive outline will help you see the text's different sections. Almost all texts—even very short ones—can be divided into a sequence of sections in which groups of paragraphs chunk together to form distinctive parts of the argument or discussion. Identifying these parts or chunks is particularly helpful because you can write a summary of each chunk and then combine the chunks.

To illustrate this process, let's look at the notes Jenny took while following these steps, and then examine her summary of MacFarquhar's essay. (The beginning of Jenny's descriptive outline appears on page 57; these notes begin at Step 3 of the summary procedure.)

JENNY'S PROCESS NOTES FOR WRITING A SUMMARY

Step 3—Text's main idea:

MacFarquhar disagrees with the popular idea that reading is good and TV watching is bad and asks us to think more deeply about what kinds of reading and what kinds of TV watching might be good.

Steps 4 and 5—Text's major chunks and main points of each chunk:

Par. 1-2: Introduces debate about literacy. Main point: Common claim that reading is declining is wrong.

Par. 3-8: Compares old and new reading habits. Main points: Differences between present and past reading habits are exaggerated. Certain genres of reading are very popular today, although not the classics.

Par. 9-14: Discusses two related questions: Does it matter what one reads? Or is reading valuable in and of itself? Main point: It is too simple to say that reading is good and TV watching is bad.

Par. 15: Concludes with new question. Main point: We are asking the wrong question. We should be asking why certain kinds of reading and television matter in terms of cultural health.

CHECKLIST FOR EVALUATING SUMMARIES

Good summaries must be fair, balanced, accurate, and complete. This checklist of questions will help you evaluate drafts of a summary.

- ☐ Is the summary economical and precise?
- ☐ Is the summary neutral in its representation of the original author's ideas, omitting the writer's own opinions?
- ☐ Does the summary reflect the proportionate coverage given various points in the original text?
- ☐ Are the original author's ideas expressed in the summary writer's own words?
- ☐ Does the summary use attributive tags (such as "Weston argues") to remind readers whose ideas are being presented?
- ☐ Does the summary quote sparingly (usually only key ideas or phrases that cannot be said precisely except in the original author's own words)?
- ☐ Will the summary stand alone as a unified and coherent piece of writing?
- ☐ Is the original source cited so that readers can locate it?

JENNY'S SUMMARY

In "Who Cares If Johnny Can't Read?" published in the online journal <u>Slate</u> on April 16, 1997, Larissa MacFarquhar informs readers that those who think that Americans no longer read books are mistaken. According to MacFarquhar, Americans are reading more than ever, although they are reading genre fiction and self-help books instead of the classics. This preference for "popular" books leads MacFarquhar to raise two related questions: Does it matter what people read or only if they read? Many persons today, says MacFarquhar, believe that reading in and of itself matters because reading is considered more intellectually stimulating and culturally valuable than watching television. MacFarquhar opposes this view by suggesting that watching television can sometimes be more stimulating and culturally valuable than reading. What matters, she believes, is the quality of what is being watched or read (par. 15).*

---

*Because MacFarquhar's essay was published online, page references for quotes cannot be provided. Jenny is following her teacher's request for in-text references to the paragraph numbers in the reprint at the end of this chapter.

HOW TO STRUCTURE A RHETORICAL PRÉCIS

☐ **Sentence 1:** Name of author, genre, and title of work, date in parentheses; a rhetorically accurate verb (such as "claims," "argues," "asserts," "suggests"); and a THAT clause containing the major assertion or thesis statement in the work.

☐ **Sentence 2:** An explanation of how the author develops and supports the thesis, usually in chronological order.

☐ **Sentence 3:** A statement of the author's apparent purpose, followed by an "in order to" phrase.

☐ **Sentence 4:** A description of the intended audience and/or the relationship the author establishes with the audience.

WRITING A RHETORICAL PRÉCIS

A *rhetorical précis* differs from a summary in that it is a less neutral, more analytical condensation of both the content and method of the original text. ("Précis" means "concise summary.") If you think of a summary as primarily a brief representation of what a text says, then you might think of the rhetorical précis as a brief representation of what a text both says and does. Although less common than summary, a rhetorical précis is a particularly useful way to sum up your understanding of how a text works rhetorically.

Part summary and part analysis, the rhetorical précis is a powerful skill-building exercise often assigned as a highly structured four-sentence paragraph.[†] These sentences provide a condensed statement of a text's main point (the summary part), followed by brief statements about its essential rhetorical elements: the purpose, methods, and intended audience (the analysis part).

JENNY'S RHETORICAL PRÉCIS

In her online article "Who Cares If Johnny Can't Read" (1997), Larissa MacFarquhar asserts that Americans are reading more than ever despite claims to the contrary and that it is time to reconsider why we value reading so much, especially certain kinds of "high culture" reading. MacFarquhar supports her claims about American reading habits with facts and statistics that compare past and present reading practices, and she challenges common assumptions by raising questions about reading's in-

---

[†]For the rhetorical précis assignment, we are indebted to Margaret K. Woodworth, "The Rhetorical Précis," *Rhetoric Review* 7 (1988): 156–65.

trinsic value. Her purpose is to dispel certain myths about reading in order to raise new and more important questions about the value of reading and other media in our culture. She seems to have a young, hip, somewhat irreverent audience in mind because her tone is sarcastic, and she suggests that the ideas she opposes are old-fashioned positions.

Summary

This chapter focused on the nuts and bolts of preparing to read and listening to a text.

- To read effectively, you need to read with pen in hand, interacting with texts by making annotations as you read.
- Before reading, practice preparatory strategies such as identifying your purpose for reading, recalling background knowledge, reconstructing the text's rhetorical context, using visual features to plan and predict, and spot reading.
- While reading, note organizational signals, mark unfamiliar terms and references, make connections between the visual and the verbal, and annotate the text with marginal comments and queries.
- To deepen your understanding of a text, reread and employ such strategies as the following: idea mapping, writing descriptive outlines, summarizing, and writing a rhetorical précis.

In the next chapter we show how rhetorical readers "speak back" to a text through questioning.

• A BRIEF WRITING PROJECT

Your instructor will identify a text for you to read carefully and annotate using the rhetorical reading strategies suggested in this chapter. Then submit to your instructor the following three pieces of writing:

1. A descriptive outline of the text
2. A 150- to 200-word summary of the text
3. A four-sentence rhetorical précis of the text •

LARISSA MACFARQUHAR

Who Cares If Johnny Can't Read?
The Value of Books Is Overstated.

This essay was published on April 16, 1997, in *Slate,* Microsoft's online magazine about politics and culture. Larissa MacFarquhar, a widely published book reviewer and magazine writer, was then a frequent contributor to that magazine as well as a contributing editor of *Lingua Franca,* a magazine about higher education, and an advisory editor at the *Paris Review,* a prestigious literary journal. The title of the following selection alludes to Rudolf Flesch's 1955 *Why Johnny Can't Read,* one of the first books to declare a national literacy crisis. To find out more about *Slate* and read other articles by MacFarquhar, go to its Web site at http://slate.msn.com.

———— • ————

Among the truisms that make up the eschatology of American cultural decline, one of the most banal is the assumption that Americans don't read. Once, the story goes—in the 1950s, say—we read much more than we do now, and read the good stuff, the classics. Now, we don't care about reading anymore, we're barely literate, and television and computers are rendering books obsolete. 1

None of this is true. We read much more now than we did in the '50s. In 1957, 17 percent of people surveyed in a Gallup poll said they were currently reading a book; in 1990, over twice as many did. In 1953, 40 percent of people polled by Gallup could name the author of *Huckleberry Finn;* in 1990, 51 percent could. In 1950, 8,600 new titles were published; in 1981, almost five times as many. 2

In fact, Americans are buying more books now than ever before—over 2 billion in 1992. Between the early '70s and the early '80s, the number of bookstores in this country nearly doubled—and that was before the Barnes & Noble superstore and Amazon.com. People aren't just buying books as status objects, either. A 1992 survey found that the average adult American reads 11.2 books per year, which means that the country as a whole reads about 2 billion—the number bought. There are more than 250,000 reading groups in the country at the moment, which means that something like 2 million people regularly read books and meet to discuss them. 3

In his book about Jewish immigrants in America at the turn of the century, *World of Our Fathers,* Irving Howe describes a time that sounds impossibly antiquated, when minimally educated laborers extended their workdays to attend lectures and language classes. Howe quotes an immigrant worker remembering his adolescence in Russia: "How can I describe to you . . . the excitement we shared when we would discuss Dostoyevsky? . . . Here in America young people can choose from movies and music and art and dancing and God alone knows what. But we—all we had was books, and not so many of them, either." 4

5   Hearing so much about the philistinism of Americans, we think such sentiments fossils of a bygone age. But they're not. People still write like that about
books. Of course, most aren't reading Dostoyevsky. The authors who attract
thousands and thousands of readers who read everything they write and send
letters to them begging for more seem to be the authors of genre fiction—
romances, science fiction, and mysteries.

6   Romance readers are especially devoted. The average romance reader spends
$1,200 a year on books, and often comes to think of her favorite authors as close
friends. Romance writer Debbie Macomber, for instance, gets thousands of letters
a year, and when her daughter had a baby, readers sent her a baby blanket and a
homemade Christmas stocking with the baby's name embroidered on it. It's writers like Macomber who account for the book boom. In 1994, a full 50 percent of
books purchased fell into the category of "popular fiction." (Business and self-help
books were the next biggest group at 12 percent, followed by "cooking/crafts" at
11 percent, "religion" at 7 percent, and "art/literature/poetry" at 5 percent.)

7   These reading habits are not new. Genre fiction and self-help books have con-
stituted the bulk of the American book market for at least 200 years. A survey
conducted in 1930 found that the No. 1 topic people wanted to read about was
personal hygiene. And you just have to glance through a list of best sellers
through the ages to realize how little we've changed: *Daily Strength for Daily
Needs* (1895); *Think and Grow Rich* (1937); *Games People Play: The Psychology of Human Relationships* (1964); *Harlow: An Intimate Biography* (1964).

8   Romance writers tend to be clear-eyed about what it is they're doing. They
don't think they're creating subversive feminine versions of Proust. They're producing mass-market entertainment that appeals to its consumers for much the
same reason as McDonald's and Burger King appeal to theirs: It's easy, it makes
you feel good, and it's the same every time. The point of a romance novel is not
to dazzle its reader with originality, but to stimulate predictable emotions by
means of familiar cultural symbols. As romance writer Kathleen Gilles Seidel
puts it: "My reader comes to my book when she is tired. . . . Reading may be the
only way she knows how to relax. If I am able to give her a few delicious, relaxing hours, that is a noble enough purpose for me."

9   But then, if romance novels are just another way to relax, what, if anything,
makes them different from movies or beer? Why should the activity "reading romances" be grouped together with "reading philosophy" rather than with "going for a massage"? The Center for the Book in the Library of Congress spends
lots of time and money coming up with slogans like "Books Make a Difference."
But is the mere fact of reading something—*anything*—a cultural achievement
worth celebrating?

10   We haven't always thought so. When the novel first became popular in
America in the latter half of the 18th century, it was denounced as a sapper of
brain cells and a threat to high culture in much the same way that television is
denounced today. In the 1940s, Edmund Wilson declared that "detective stories
[are] simply a kind of vice that, for silliness and minor harmfulness, ranks somewhere between smoking and crossword puzzles." You almost never hear this
kind of talk anymore in discussions of American reading habits: *Not all reading
is worth doing. Some books are just a waste of time.*

As fears of cultural apocalypse have been transferred away from novels 11
onto a series of high-tech successors (radio, movies, television, and now computers), books have acquired a reputation for educational and even moral worthiness. Books are special: You can send them through the mail for lower rates,
and there are no customs duties imposed on books imported into this country.
There have, of course, been endless culture wars fought over what kind of books
should be read in school, but in discussions of adult reading habits these distinctions tend to evaporate.

The sentimentalization of books gets especially ripe when reading is com- 12
pared with its supposed rivals: television and cyberspace. Valorization of reading over television, for instance, is often based on the vague and groundless notion that reading is somehow "active" and television "passive." Why it is that the
imaginative work done by a reader is more strenuous or worthwhile than that
done by a viewer—or why watching television is more passive than, say, watching a play—is never explained. Sven Birkerts' maudlin 1994 paean to books, *The
Gutenberg Elegies: The Fate of Reading in an Electronic Age,* is a classic example of
this genre. *Time* art critic Robert Hughes made a similarly sentimental and mysterious argument recently in the *New York Review of Books:*

> Reading is a collaborative act, in which your imagination goes halfway to meet
> the author's; you visualize the book as you read it, you participate in making
> up the characters and rounding them out. . . . The effort of bringing something
> vivid out of the neutral array of black print is quite different, and in my experi-
> ence far better for the imagination, than passive submission to the bright icons
> of television, which come complete and overwhelming, and tend to burn out
> the tender wiring of a child's imagination because they allow no re-working.

I cannot remember ever visualizing a book's characters, but everyone who 13
writes about reading seems to do this, so perhaps I'm in the minority. Still, you
could equally well say that you participate in making up TV characters because
you have to imagine what they're thinking, where in a novel, you're often provided with this information.

Another reason why books are supposed to be better than television is that 14
books are quirky and individualistic and real, whereas television is mass-pro-
duced corporate schlock. But of course popular books can be, and usually are,
every bit as formulaic and "corporatized" as television. The best books might be
better than the best television, but further down the pile the difference gets
murkier. Most of the time the choice between books and television is not between Virgil and Geraldo but between *The Celestine Prophecy* and *Roseanne.* Who
wouldn't pick *Roseanne?*

If the fertility of our culture is what we're concerned about, then 15
McLuhanesque musing on the intrinsic nature of reading (as if it had any such
thing) is beside the point. Reading *per se* is not the issue. The point is to figure
out why certain kinds of reading and certain kinds of television might matter in
the first place.

ANTHONY WESTON

The Need for Environmental Ethics

Anthony Weston teaches philosophy and Interdisciplinary Studies at Elon College in North Carolina. His publications include *Toward Better Problems* (1992), *Back to Earth: Tomorrow's Environmentalism* (1994), and *A Practical Companion to Ethics* (1996). *Toward Better Problems,* the book from which this excerpt is taken, was first introduced in Chapter 2. As we explained there, *Toward Better Problems* applies pragmatic philosophy to pressing ethical issues of our time: abortion, animal rights, the environment, and justice. However, Weston's aim in this book is not so much to solve these complex ethical problems as it is to transform these problematic situations into more manageable or "better" problems. "The Need for Environmental Ethics" is the opening section of the chapter on the environment. Other sections of this chapter include "Beyond Anthropocentrism," where Weston proposes that we move beyond our purely "human-centered" perspective to consider and respect nature "in its own right," and "Integrative Strategies in Environmental Politics," where Weston proposes seeking common ground in the fight for more enlightened environmental policies.

1 We are beginning to struggle with the intimation that something is seriously wrong with our relation to the natural world. It is a little like suspecting cancer but not wanting to know. But the danger signs are all around us. Garbage dumped a hundred miles off the Atlantic coast is now washing up annually on beaches. The federal government is continuing its increasingly desperate search for a way to dispose of the highly toxic radioactive wastes that American nuclear reactors have been generating since they began operating, so far without any permanent disposal plan at all. A state-sized chunk of South American rain forest is slashed, cut, or burned every year, in large part to clear land to graze beef cattle, though the resultant pasture is of marginal quality and will be reduced to desert within ten years. And our society, affluent beyond the wildest dreams of our ancestors and most of the rest of the human race, increasingly fortifies itself inside artificial environments—we see the countryside through the windshield or the airplane window, we "learn about nature" by watching TV specials about endangered African predators—while outside of our little cocoons the winds laugh for no one and increasingly, under pressure of condominiums and shopping malls, the solace of open space is no more.

2 Short-term solutions of course suggest themselves. If the seas can no longer be treated as infinite garbage pits, we say, let

Effective analogy

Examples of "danger signs"

Check recent news about Yucca Mt. as a nuclear dumping site

Examples of our relation to the natural world— all distance us

Artificial environments = cocoons

"Winds laugh for no one"? What does he mean?

Short-term, practical versus fundamental—key issues for Weston

us incinerate the garbage instead. Rain forest cutting could be curtailed by consumer action if North Americans paid a little more for home-grown meat. Sooner or later, we suppose, "science" will figure out something to do with nuclear wastes. And so on. This kind of thinking too is familiar. The problems may seen purely practical, and practical solutions may be in sight. Environmental ethics, however, begins with suspicion that something far deeper is wrong, and that more fundamental change is

Key issue to track   called for.

Beyond Ecological Myopia

3   For one thing, these "solutions" are short term indeed, and ignore or obscure the structural crises that underlie the immediate problems. Incinerating trash just treats the air as a waste dump instead of the sea, with consequences that even proponents of incineration admit are unpredictable. The only workable short-term solution is recycling, and the only workable long-term solution is to stop producing so much garbage in the first place, especially materials that are not biodegradable. But this calls for an entirely different way of thinking: for greater respect for the earth, more awareness of the dynamics and the limits of the wider world, and more insistent reminders that our children's children will inherit the world we are "trashing." And these new ways of thinking in turn call for a different way of living. Sometimes the practical demands are not so very difficult—using paper cups instead of styrofoam is hardly a major lifestyle change—but even this calls for a kind of mindfulness that today we lack. In the background is the suggestion that we need to recognize systematic ecological constraints on economic activity, a kind of constraint that is still unfamiliar and controversial, at least in America.

4   Nuclear wastes are an even clearer case. Even proponents admit that long after the normal operation of nuclear power plants is past, we will be left with enormously toxic waste products from their operation, including the reactors themselves, which after their forty or so years generating electricity may take hundreds of thousands of years to drop back to safe levels of radioactivity. Operating wastes are presently stored at reactor sites and in temporary federal storage areas and tanks, most of them nearly full and some notoriously already leaking. It is not obvious that there is any adequate permanent disposal method. Burying the wastes, even in the most apparently stable site, puts all future life at the mercy of geological changes, which are virtually certain over hundreds of thousands of years. Meanwhile, no state or community will voluntarily accept the proposed storage facilities, let alone have the wastes shipped, as they must be, by truck or rail, across half the nation.

5   Public opposition to nuclear power focuses, for the most part, on the danger of accidents: on the dangers of injury to *us*. But the waste problem mortgages the entire future of the earth. Any significant leakage would be devastating.

Even very low-level leakage will cause genetic damage, not just to humans, but to all plants and animals, which over generations can have immense consequences. Again, then, our habitual short-term perspective comes into question; again an ecological point of view suggests radical change.

6   Finally, the devastation of the rain forests too is motivated almost exclusively by short-term and commercial considerations. Since the land can be bought very cheaply (or can simply be expropriated), nothing stands in the way of the most shortsighted and complete exploitation. The soil, however, is very poor—rain forests are self-sustaining and self-nurturing systems, biotic efflorescences that virtually run of themselves—and so exploitation is complete indeed. In ten years the land will not even support cattle. Like the bare hills of the Mediterranean stripped of their forests by the ancients and since irreparably eroded, the land will become unable to support any life at all. And so for the sake of a few more years of slightly cheaper hamburgers we are turning the most exquisite jungle in the world into desert, and along with it threatening up to 60 percent of the world's plant and animal species, many of them unknown, with unknown me-dicinal and other benefits, not to mention the completely unpredictable climatic effects of turning enormous areas of the world's wettest ecosystems into the world's driest, the loss of atmospheric recharge, and so on.

7   Like our willingness to saddle our descendants with radioactive wastes into the unimaginably distant future, our willingness to sacrifice the unknown potentials of rain forest ecosystems to the most trivial and short-term advantage shows an astonishing arrogance toward the human future. And to recognize this disproportion is already to take a major ethical step. Merely to take our own descendants seriously might well require a different way of life. That alone may be enough to require of us a far more respectful and conserving attitude toward the earth, and certainly requires us to avoid making massive, little-understood, and irreversible ecological changes, like destroying the rain forests or leaving genetically lethal wastes to the perpetual guardianship of our children's children's children. *Maybe* the most pressing and vital interests of the race could justify such a thing. Maybe we could justify turning some of the rain forests into deserts if in some unimaginable crisis only ravaging the rain forests could save life on earth. But ten years of slightly cheaper meat does not justify it. Maybe our children could understand reactor waste left littering the landscape of the future if the electricity it made possible saved civilization from some unheard-of threat, or accomplished some great task. But the "need" to run air conditioners is the saddest of excuses. Especially when the alternative is not even so serious as having to sweat in the summer, God forbid, but merely requires designing slightly more energy-efficient appliances and building houses that aren't heat sinks in the sun. Traditional cultures know how to build naturally cool houses.

8 Only we seem to have lost the ability.

       "Environmental ethics," then, urges upon us at minimum a much more mindful and longer-term attention to the way we interact with and depend on nature. It urges attention to everything from the medicinal and nutritional uses of rain forest plants to the psychic need for open spaces and various kinds of ecological dependence of which we are not yet even aware. The implications are radical. We need to think of the earth itself in a different way: not as an infinite waste sink, and not as a collection of resources fortuitously provided for our use, but as a complex system with its own integrity and dynamics, far more intricate than we understand or perhaps *can* understand, but still the system within which we live and on which we necessarily and utterly depend. We must learn a new kind of respect.

Questioning a Text

A good question is never answered. It is not a bolt to be tightened into place but a seed to be planted and to bear more seed toward the hope of greening the landscape of idea.

—John Ciardi

Whereas the previous chapter focused on listening to a text *with the grain* in order to understand it as fully as possible, in this chapter we focus on questioning a text, which involves reading it analytically and skeptically, *against the grain.* If you think of listening to a text as the author's turn in a conversation, then you might think of questioning the text as your opportunity to respond to the text by interrogating it, raising points of agreement and disagreement, thinking critically about its argument and methods, and then talking back.

What It Means to Question a Text

Learning to question a text is central to your academic success in college. Your professors will ask you to engage with texts in ways that you may not be used to. They expect you to do more than just "bank" the knowledge you glean from reading; they expect you to use this knowledge to do various kinds of intellectual work—to offer your own interpretations or evaluations, to launch a research project of your own, to synthesize the ideas among readings and draw independent conclusions.

However, questioning does not necessarily mean just fault-finding, and it certainly doesn't mean dismissing an author's ideas wholesale. Rather, it entails carefully interrogating a text's claims and evidence and its subtle forms of persuasion so that you can make sound judgments and offer thoughtful responses.

Your job in critiquing a text is to be "critical." However, the term *critical* means "characterized by careful and exact evaluation and judgment," not simply by "disagreement" or "harsh judgment." In questioning a text, you bring your critical faculties as well as your experience, knowledge, and opinion to bear on it, but you do so in a way that treats the author's ideas fairly and makes judgments that can be supported by textual evidence.

This chapter offers you a repertoire of useful strategies to help you question a text and explore your responses to it. At the end of the chapter, we show you an analytical paper that student writer Jenny (whose work you followed in Chapter 3) wrote in response to an assignment calling for a rhetorical analysis of Larissa MacFarquhar's article, "Who Cares If Johnny Can't Read?" In that paper, Jenny uses the questioning strategies described in this chapter to analyze MacFarquhar's argument and methods. Our purpose is to demonstrate how such strategies can enable you to write critical analyses valued by college professors.

Strategies for Questioning a Text

The six questioning strategies in this section offer powerful ways to question a text's argument, assumptions, and methods by examining a writer's credibility, appeals to reason, strategies for engaging readers, language, and any visual elements, as well as the worldview or ideology that informs the text. The first three strategies examine an author's use of the three classical rhetorical appeals identified by Aristotle:

- *Ethos:* the persuasive power of the author's credibility or character
- *Logos:* the persuasive power of the author's reasons, evidence, and logic
- *Pathos:* the persuasive power of the author's appeal to the interests, emotions, and imagination of the audience

Although these three appeals interconnect and sometimes overlap—for example, a writer may use a touching anecdote both to establish credibility as an empathic person (*ethos*) and to play on the reader's emotions (*pathos*)—we introduce them separately to emphasize their distinct functions as means of persuasion. The last three questioning strategies involve vehicles through which appeals are made, implicitly and explicitly:

- *Language:* the words authors use to create a persona, connect with the audience, and represent their ideas as reasonable and compelling
- *Visual elements:* the drawings, photographs, graphs, and other images that are used to enhance, support, and extend rhetorical appeals
- *Ideology:* the worldview or set of values and beliefs invoked by a text

EXAMINING A WRITER'S CREDIBILITY

To change readers' minds about something, writers must make themselves credible by creating an image of themselves that will gain their readers' confidence. In most cases, writers want to project themselves as knowledgeable, fair-minded, and trustworthy. To examine a writer's credibility, ask yourself, "Do I find this author believable and trustworthy? Why or why not?" Experienced readers always try to find out as much as possible about an author's background, interests, political leanings, and general worldview. Sometimes they have independent knowledge of the writer, either because the writer is well known or because the reading has a headnote or footnote describing the writer's credentials. Often, though, readers must discern the writer's personality and views from the text itself by examining content, tone, word choice, figurative language, organization, and other cues that help create an image of the writer in the reader's mind. Explicit questions to ask might include these: Does this writer seem knowledgeable? What does the writer like and dislike? What are this writer's biases and values? What seems to be the writer's mood? (Is he or she angry? Questioning? Meditative? Upset? Jovial?) What is the writer's approach to the topic? (Formal or informal? Logical or emotional? Scientific or personal?) What would it be like to spend time in this writer's company?

● **FOR WRITING AND DISCUSSION**

ON YOUR OWN

1. To help you consider an author's image and credibility, try these activities the next time you are assigned a reading. Describe in words your image of this author as a person (or draw a sketch of this person). Then try to figure out what cues in the text produced this image for you. Finally, consider how this image of the writer leads you to ask more questions about the text. You might ask, for example, Why is this writer angry? Why does this writer use emotionally laden anecdotes rather than statistics to support his or her case? What is this writer afraid of?

2. Try these activities with Larissa MacFarquhar's article at the end of Chapter 3. What kind of an image does she create for herself in this text? How would you describe her in words or portray her in a drawing? Take a few minutes to find and jot down the cues in the text that create this image for you.

WITH YOUR CLASSMATES

Compare your impressions of MacFarquhar with those of your classmates. Do any contradictory traits come up? That is, do some people in the group interpret the textual cues differently? Some people, for example, might see a comment as "forthright" and "frank" while others might see it as "rude." What aspects of her character (as represented in the text) do you as a group agree on? What aspects do you disagree about? ●

EXAMINING A WRITER'S APPEALS TO REASON

Perhaps the most direct way that writers try to persuade readers is through logic or reason. To convince readers that their perspective is reasonable, skilled writers work to anticipate what their intended readers already believe and then use those beliefs as a bridge to the writer's way of thinking. They support their claims through a combination of reasons and evidence.

For example, imagine a writer arguing for stricter gun control laws. This writer wants to root his argument in a belief or value that he and his readers already share, so he focuses on concerns for the safety of schoolchildren. The line of reasoning might go something like this: Because the ready availability of guns makes children no longer safe at school, we must pass strict gun control laws to limit access to guns. Of course, readers may or may not go along with this argument. Some readers, although they share the writer's concern for the safety of schoolchildren, might disagree at several points with the writer's logic: Is the availability of guns the main cause of gun violence at schools or are there other more compelling causes? Will stricter gun control laws really limit the availability of guns? If this same writer wished to use evidence to strengthen this argument, he might use statistics showing a correlation between the rise in the availability of guns and the rise in gun violence in schools. Here, the writer would be operating on the assumption that readers believe in facts and can be persuaded by these statistics that increased gun violence in schools is linked to the availability of firearms.

Experienced readers are alert to the logical strategies used by authors, and they have learned not to take what may appear as a "reasonable" argument at face value. In other words, they have learned to question or test this reasoning before assenting to the position the author wants them to take. To examine a writer's reasoning, you need to be able to identify and examine carefully the basic elements of an argument—claims, reasons, evidence, and assumptions. The following questions will help you examine a writer's reasoning:

- What perspective or position does the writer want me to take toward the topic?
- Do the writer's claims, reasons, and evidence convince me to take this perspective or position?
- Do I share the assumptions, stated or unstated, that authorize the writer's reasoning and connect the evidence to the claim?

Claims

The key points that a writer wants readers to accept are referred to as *claims*. For example, Anthony Weston's initial claim in the selection at the end of Chapter 3 is this: "We are beginning to struggle with the intimation that something is seriously wrong with our relation to the natural world." Or take another example. Early in her essay on page 64, MacFarquhar claims that "None of this [a series of beliefs about reading] is true." Once you have identified various claims in a text, then you can raise questions about them, especially about their wording and scope. Is the meaning of key words in the claim clear? Can particular words be interpreted in more than one way? Is the claim overstated? For example, one might ask of Weston's claim, "To whom do 'we' and 'our' refer?" "What evidence is there that 'we' are beginning to struggle with this awareness?" "What is wrong with our relation to the natural world? 'Wrong' in what sense or according to what ethical standards?" "How serious is this problem?" Similarly, one could ask of MacFarquhar, "Are none of these beliefs true in any sense?"

Reasons

Reasons are subclaims that writers use to support a main claim. A reason can usually be linked to a claim with the subordinate conjunction "because." Consider the gun control argument mentioned earlier, which we can now restate as a claim with reason: "We must pass gun control laws that limit access to guns [claim] because doing so will make children safer at school [reason]." This argument has initial appeal because it ties into the audience's belief that it is good to make children safe at school, but as we have discussed earlier, the causal links in the argument are open to question. To take another example, Weston offers readers the following reasons for accepting his approach to environmental problems:

> We are beginning to struggle with the intimation that something is seriously wrong with our relation to the natural world [claim]
>
> - because the danger signs of environmental damage are occurring all around us [reason]
> - because short-term solutions have caused other environmental problems that will have dire consequences for future generations [reason]

If readers are to accept the first reason, they must agree that there are danger signs all around us and that these signs are serious enough to call for action. However, some readers may believe that environmentalists exaggerate the dangers posed by environmental problems. If readers are to accept the second reason, they must believe not only Weston's claims that short-term solutions don't work but also his predictions about the serious consequences for future generations.

As these examples illustrate, once you've identified the reasons that the author offers for various claims, then you can proceed to examine the adequacy of these reasons. Do they really support the claim? Do they tie into values, assumptions, and beliefs that the audience shares?

Evidence

The facts, examples, statistics, personal experience, and expert testimony that an author offers to support his or her view of the topic are referred to as *evidence*. To examine the author's use of evidence, consider whether the evidence is reliable, timely, and adequate to make the case. Or ask whether there is more than one way the evidence can be interpreted. When MacFarquhar argues that none of the "truisms" many people believe about reading are true, she relies heavily on evidence. She offers facts, statistics, expert testimony, example, and so forth throughout the essay mainly to refute positions with which she disagrees. Readers skeptical of MacFarquhar's argument might question her interpretations of some facts and statistics: Couldn't people just be saying that they are reading a book because they're embarrassed to admit they're not? Couldn't people have learned the name of the author of *Huckleberry Finn* from television and not from reading? Similarly, in our gun control example, skeptics could question whether the statistical correlation between rising availability of guns and rising gun violence in schools is in fact a causal relationship. The fact that A and B happened at the same time does not mean that A caused B. Or readers might question Weston's use of the destruction of South American rain forests as an example of an environmental "danger sign" and ask for clear scientific evidence for his claim that this land will become desert within ten years.

Assumptions

In an argument, the often unstated values or beliefs that the writer expects readers to accept without question are referred to as *assumptions*. You can interrogate an argument by casting doubt on those assumptions. For example, when Weston argues that fundamental changes in our relationship to the environment are needed to address environmental problems, he assumes that such changes will make a difference and that the value of improving the environment outweighs potential negative effects on the economy. Some readers may question these assumptions by arguing that policies to improve the environment won't actually work or that the negative effects will outweigh the benefits. Similarly, part of the gun control argument is based on an assumption that gun control legislation will in fact limit the availability of guns. You can question this assumption by pointing to the existence of black markets.

● **FOR WRITING AND DISCUSSION**

ON YOUR OWN

Find a newspaper or magazine opinion piece (an editorial or an individual op-ed piece), and identify its claims, reasons, evidence, and assumptions. You may find that some of these elements are missing or only implied. Then analyze the writer's reasoning in the opinion piece by answering the three questions we listed on page 74 as fundamental to examining a writer's reasoning.

WITH YOUR CLASSMATES

1. Briefly summarize your opinion piece and your analysis of it with a small group of classmates.
2. After each group member has presented his or her editorial, try to decide which of the editorials involves the most persuasive reasoning and why. Present the results of your discussion to the rest of the class. If there is disagreement about which piece involves the best reasoning, then present more than one to the class, explaining the differences of opinion. ●

EXAMINING A WRITER'S STRATEGIES
FOR ENGAGING READERS

The third of the classical rhetorical appeals is to an audience's interests and emotions—the process of engaging readers. How does a writer hook and keep your interest? How does a writer make you care about the subject? How does a writer tweak your emotions or connect an argument with ideas or beliefs that you value?

Rhetoricians have identified four basic ways that writers engage readers at an emotional or imaginative level by influencing the reader to identify (1) with the writer, (2) with the topic or issue, (3) with a certain group of fellow readers, or (4) with certain interests, values, beliefs, and emotions. Let's look at each in turn.

In the first approach, writers wanting readers to identify with them might use an informal conversational tone to make a reader feel like the writer's buddy. Writers wanting to inspire respect and admiration might adopt a formal scholarly tone, choose intellectual words, or avoid "I" altogether by using the passive voice—"it was discovered that. . . ." In the second approach, writers wanting readers to identify with the topic or issue might explain the importance of the issue or try to engage readers' emotions. In urging community action against homelessness, for example, an author might present a wrenching anecdote about a homeless child. Other methods might be the use of vivid details, striking facts, emotion-laden terms and examples, or analogies that explain the unfamiliar in terms of the familiar. In the third approach, writers try to get readers to identify with a certain in-group of people—fellow environmentalists or feminists or Republicans or even fellow intellectuals. Some writers seek to engage readers by creating a role for the reader to play in the text. For example, Weston invites readers to think of themselves as serious and intelligent, interested in tough ethical issues. In the fourth approach, writers appeal to readers' interests by getting them to identify with certain values and beliefs. For example, a politician arguing for changes in the way Social Security is funded might appeal to voters' desires to invest in high-yield stocks. If workers could pay lower Social Security taxes, they could invest the difference in the stock market. If you are aware of how all of the above appeals work, you will be able to distance yourself from arguments in order to examine them critically.

● **FOR WRITING AND DISCUSSION**

Consider all of the ways in which Larissa MacFarquhar tries to engage readers of her text. What kind of a relationship does she try to establish with readers? How does she try to make you care about her topic? How does she try to engage and keep your interest? What interests and values does she assume her audience shares? Do you consider yourself part of her intended audience? Why or why not? ●

EXAMINING A WRITER'S LANGUAGE

Besides looking at a text's classical appeals, you can examine a text rhetorically by paying careful attention to its language and style. Diction (which includes tone, word choice, and level of formality), figurative language, sentence structure and length, and even punctuation are all techniques through which a writer tries to influence the reader's view of a subject. Consider, for example, the connotation of words. It makes a difference whether a writer calls a person "decisive" rather than "bossy," or an act "bold" rather than "rash." Words like "decisive" and "rash" are not facts; rather they present the writer's interpretation of a phenomenon. You can question a text by recognizing how the writer makes interpretive words seem like facts.

At times, you might overlook features of the writer's language because they seem natural rather than chosen. You probably seldom stop to think about the significance of, say, the use of italics or a series of short sentences or a particular metaphor. Readers rarely ask what's gained or lost by a writer saying something one way rather than another—for example, calling clear-cut logging in the Northwest a "rape" rather than a "timber extraction process."

Take, for example, Weston's use of analogy in the first paragraph of the passage from *Toward Better Problems* (p. 67). He compares our "intimation that something is seriously wrong with our relation to the natural world" to the situation of "suspect[ing] cancer but not wanting to know." Since no single word probably evokes more fear than the word "cancer," Weston is able to connect a fear with which readers can readily identify with a less common one, the fear that our attitude toward nature is causing catastrophic environmental damage that we or our descendants will pay for. Further, this analogy implies a whole range of associations that Weston need not spell out. In both cases, we "do not want to know" because knowing will force us to face eventual suffering and loss; it will make us feel hopeless and helpless. Consequently, we repress the knowledge, hoping the problem will magically go away. Or consider the last two sentences in the first paragraph of MacFarquhar's essay: "Once, the story goes—in the 1950s, say—we read much more than we do now, and read the good stuff, the classics. Now, we don't care about reading anymore, we're barely literate, and television and computers are rendering books obsolete." Try reading those sentences aloud, paying particular attention to the punctuation. It's hard to say them out loud in anything but a mock serious, singsong, sarcastic tone of voice. Her tone tells us that these are not her own sentiments but rather sentiments she is ascribing to others. To signal her distance from and disdain for these views, she makes the claims sound vague and baseless ("once . . . in the 1950s, say"), exaggerated ("we're barely literate"), and trite (classics are "the good stuff"). By contrast, the voice in the next paragraph is very businesslike—the sentences are short and clipped; the information is presented in listlike fashion. We know it is this voice we are supposed to listen to. Through language that creates particular tones of voice, MacFarquhar tries to get readers to think about the subject—commonplace beliefs about reading—in the same way she does.

Experienced readers have developed antennae for recognizing these subtle uses of language to manipulate responses. One way to develop this sensitivity is to ask why a writer made certain choices rather than others. For example, if you were examining paragraph 9 of MacFarquhar's essay, you might note her striking comparison of reading romance novels to drinking beer and getting a massage. What effect does she achieve through these specific comparisons? What would be different if she'd compared reading romances to going dancing or floating down a river?

● **FOR WRITING AND DISCUSSION**
BACKGROUND
What follows below is the introduction to an article by freelance writer Bruce Barcott entitled "Blow-Up," which appeared in the February 1999 issue of *Outside,* a magazine described by its editors as "driven by the search for innovative ways to connect people to the world outdoors." After you have read the introduction, consider the following questions: What do you think is the author's persuasive intention in the whole article? How does the use of language in this introduction help contribute to the author's persuasive intentions? Pay attention to word choice, tone, sentence patterns, punctuation, figurative language, levels of diction, and other language features.

ON YOUR OWN
Write out your own analysis of the use of language in this passage.

WITH YOUR CLASSMATES
Share your analyses. See if you can reach consensus on the ways that this writer uses language for persuasive intent.

Introduction to "Blow-Up"
1   By God we built some dams!
2   We backed up the Kennebec in Maine and the Neuse in North Carolina and a hundred creeks and streams that once ran free but don't anymore. We stopped the Colorado with the Hoover, high as 35 houses, and because it pleased us we kept damming and diverting the Colorado until the river no longer reached the sea. We dammed our way out of the Great Depression with the Columbia's Grand Coulee, a dam so immense you had to borrow another fellow's mind because yours alone wasn't big enough to wrap around it. The Coulee concrete was not even hardened by the time we finished building a bigger one still, cleaving the Missouri with Fort Peck Dam, a structure second only to the Great Wall of China, a jaw-dropper so outsized they put it on the cover of the first issue of *Life,* and wasn't that a hell of a thing? We turned the Tennessee, the Colorado, the Columbia, and the Snake from continental arteries into still bathtubs.

We dammed the Clearwater, the Boise, the Santiam, the Deschutes, the Skagit, the Willamette, and the McKenzie. We dammed the North Platte and the North Yuba, the South Platte and the South Yuba. We dammed the Blue, the Green, and the White as well. We dammed Basher Kill and Schuylkill; we dammed Salt River and we dammed Sugar Creek. We dammed Crystal River and Muddy Creek, the Little River and the Rio Grande. We dammed the Minnewawa and the Minnesota, and we dammed the Kalamazoo. We dammed the Swift and we dammed the Dead.

3   One day we looked up and saw 75,000 dams impounding more than half a million miles of river. We looked down and saw rivers scrubbed free of salmon and sturgeon and shad. Cold rivers ran warm, warm rivers ran cold, and fertile muddy banks turned barren.

4   And that's when we stopped talking about dams as instruments of holy progress and started talking about blowing them out of the water. ●

EXAMINING A TEXT'S USE OF VISUAL ELEMENTS

Besides language, another vehicle for rhetorical appeals is the use of visual elements, which merit close attention when you analyze any text. The common belief that pictures are more truthful and compelling than words can make visual images powerful persuasive devices. Moreover, images can shape perceptions, emotions, and values without the reader's conscious awareness, thus making their influence particularly seductive. Questioning the ways in which visual elements make a text more persuasive allows you to step back and avoid the automatic consent implied in the "seeing is believing" cliché.

In Chapter 3, we discussed how consideration of a text's visual elements helps you understand a text's message more fully. Here we discuss how analysis of a text's visual elements helps you recognize and question those elements' rhetorical effects. To analyze the ways in which visual elements work, you need to consider a visual's rhetorical appeals (how the visual works) and its persuasive function in relation to the verbal text (why it is there). We suggest that you begin your analysis of visual elements with the following questions:

- How does the visual element relate to the writer's overall point or argument? Is this relationship explicit or implied?
- How important is this visual element to the author's argument?
- What kinds of rhetorical appeals does the visual element employ? How does it work rhetorically to influence the intended audience?

Visual Elements as Ethical Appeals

Visual elements frequently enhance a writer's credibility and authority. Thus, an article by a yoga teacher includes a picture of him in an advanced yoga position;

an article by a scientist reporting a new scientific breakthrough includes a picture of the scientist working in her lab. Similarly, newspapers and magazines include head shots of syndicated columnists whom they regularly publish. These usually flattering photographs may offer an image of the writer as smiling and approachable or, perhaps, as intellectual, sophisticated, or down to earth. Head shots also offer information about the author's age, ethnicity, and gender (if not evident from the writer's name), and this information is likely to affect our reading of the text, sometimes without our being aware of it. When the subject is affirmative action or racial profiling, for example, the race and perhaps gender of the author are likely to affect readers' perceptions of his or her credibility on the issue.

Of course, these photographs can be misleading. Many writers use the same picture for years, thus preserving the image and credibility of a younger person. The late Ann Landers' column still pictured her as a woman in her mid-forties when she was well into her seventies. Consider the difference it would have made if readers pictured the advice she offered as coming from an elderly, white-haired woman. In short, rhetorical readers need to question even these apparently straightforward visual appeals based on a writer's *ethos* as well as their implications. For example, the yoga teacher pictured in an advanced pose may be an expert practitioner of yoga, but does it follow logically, as the picture (and article) implies, that he is a good teacher of yoga?

The key questions to ask in analyzing how visual elements establish a writer's *ethos* are the following:

- How does the visual element contribute to the writer's image, credibility, and/or authority?
- How does the image of the author created by the visual element influence your reading of the text?
- To what extent does the visual image fit the image created by the text?

Visual Elements as Logical Appeals

Drawing on the idea that "seeing is believing," writers often support their claims with visual evidence. Thus, the most common use of visual elements as logical appeals is to supply evidence to verify or support a writer's argument. Whether the visual element is a pie chart, a table of data, or a picture, these elements appear to add concreteness and factuality to an author's claims. Indeed, the genre conventions of scholarly journals dictate that authors provide information graphics to help readers understand and evaluate the strength of the research.

Visual elements play an even more central role in academic and journalistic writing that analyzes and critiques them. As we saw in Chapter 3, for example, when Stephen Jay Gould argued that Mickey Mouse's image has become more childlike over the years, the sample images of Mickey at various stages of his career (Figure 3.2) provided essential supporting evidence.

In response to our increasingly visual culture, however, it is important to question whether images themselves are reliable. Technology makes it easy for almost anyone to doctor a photo, and even ordinary photographs can be misleading because they omit the larger context and are often published without information about who took the picture or why. An illustration of this problem of context is provided by two photographs that became rallying points for opposing sides in the spring 2000 custody battle over Elián Gonzales. As you may recall, Gonzales, a young Cuban boy, was rescued off the coast of Miami, Florida, after his mother and several others died during their flight from Cuba. His father in Cuba wished to claim him and take him back to Cuba, and his mother's relatives in Miami wished to keep him in the United States. A photograph taken when federal agents removed Elián from the home of one of his Miami relatives showed an agent clad in combat gear seeming to point a gun at the terrified Elián, who was being held protectively by an unidentified man. The other photo, released by the father's lawyer a day or so later, showed a smiling Elián in the arms of his father with a woman holding another small child looking happily on. The former photo, as you might imagine, caused public outrage and seemed to support the claims of his Miami relatives that Elián wanted to remain with them. By contrast, the image of the beaming reunited family seemed to support his father's claims that Elián belonged with him. Which picture revealed the truth about this case? Both omitted vital information about the circumstances surrounding the moment when the photographs were taken.*

The following questions will help you analyze how visuals interact with logical appeals:

- Does the writer make explicit the relationship between the visual element and his or her argument?
- How would you define this relationship? Is it the focal point of the argument? Or does it provide additional support or evidence for the author's claims?
- Is the visual evidence reliable, timely, and adequate to make the case?
- Does the visual itself make a kind of argument, and if so, is it convincing?

● FOR WRITING AND DISCUSSION

Some arguments are made through a combination of visual and verbal elements, such as the argument implied by the introductory page of an *Us Weekly* cover story featuring Christina Aguilera (Figure 4.1). Try translating this page into a paragraph-long written argument. To do so, you will need to identify the central claims made by the page's combination of verbal and visual elements, the evidence used in support of those claims, and the

---

Slate commentator William Saletan has written a detailed analysis of the contrasting implications of the photographs: "The Elián Pictures," 24 April 2000, <http://slate.msn.com/id/81142/>. A court decision eventually returned Elián to his father's custody in Cuba.

FIGURE 4.1 First Page of an Article About Christina Aguilera in *Us Weekly*

assumptions that connect the claims and evidence. After you have composed a written version of this visual argument, apply the questioning strategies suggested throughout this chapter to analyze and assess the argument's persuasiveness. ●

Visual Elements as Audience Appeals

Probably the most powerful rhetorical use of visual elements is to appeal to an audience's emotions, values, and interests. Three common and often overlapping ways in which visual elements create audience appeals are by setting a tone, fostering identification, and evoking emotions and values.

To see how graphic elements can set a tone or context that frames a reader's response, consider your expectations of an article that is accompanied by an image of Dr. Martin Luther King Jr., delivering his "I Have a Dream" speech in front of the Washington Monument. It seems likely that you would anticipate that the article deals with a serious issue, perhaps civil rights, racial justice, or the role of social protest movements. Similarly, the drawing of the three embracing figures discussed in Chapter 3 (Fig. 3.3, p. 52) combined with the headline "Scarred for Life: Courage Begets Courage" prepares readers for an inspirational article—although, importantly, neither the drawing nor the headline gives any hint of the specific content of Maureen Dowd's column about organ donation. To discover the meaning of this rather ambiguous image and decidedly dramatic title, readers had to stop their perusal of the newspaper to read the article. Undoubtedly, you can think of many occasions when a striking image caught your attention and triggered an emotional reaction that, in turn, prompted you to read something that you might otherwise have ignored. Since photographs and drawings are frequently the first thing we notice about a text, it is important to pause and consider how they frame our attitude toward the subject both before and after reading.

Visual elements can also create identification with a person, situation, or topic. The photograph of Christina Aguilera in Figure 4.1, for example, invites readers of *Us Weekly* to identify with Aguilera as well as with the message on her T-shirt. This identification, in turn, encourages those casually flipping through this magazine to read the cover story that follows.

Closely tied to identification are the emotions and values often elicited by visual images. A story about widespread starvation in Africa, for example, is made more compelling if accompanied by pictures of skeletal children with distended bellies. We not only identify more readily with the human toll but also feel sadness and compassion, and these responses shape our reading of the story. Or recall the power of the now iconic photograph of the soot-covered New York City firefighters raising the American flag in the aftermath of the 9/11 terrorist attack, evoking as they did admiration and gratitude for their bravery as well as a sense of patriotic pride. The use of this image automatically associates whatever text it accompanies with these emotions and values. No matter how compelling the image, however, we still need to ask for what purpose our emotions and values are being evoked. Is the topic at hand really analogous to the heroism of the firefighters on 9/11? While we cannot avoid "gut" responses to visual images, it is important to stop to consider their intended effect and to question their reliability, recognizing that photographs and images, like words, are selected and constructed to create particular emotional responses.

The key questions to ask in relation to the use of visuals to appeal to your emotions, interests, and values are the following:

- What purpose does the visual element seem to serve in relation to the text?
- To which emotions, interests, and values does the visual element appeal? What assumptions are being made about readers' values, interests, and emotions?
- How do specific parts of the visual element work to elicit a response? How do the parts work together as a whole?
- Are there other ways of reading or interpreting these elements?

EXAMINING A TEXT'S IDEOLOGY

Another approach to questioning a text is to identify its *ideology,* a more technical term for the word *worldview,* which we introduced in the epigraph to Chapter 1. An ideology is a belief system—a coherent set of values and concepts through which we interpret the world. We sometimes think that ideology applies only to other people's worldviews, perhaps those of zealots blinded by a certain rigid set of beliefs. In fact, the term *ideology* applies to all of us. Each of us has our own beliefs, values, and particular ways of looking at the world. Our perspectives are inevitably shaped by family background, religion, personal experience, race, class, gender, sexual orientation, and so on. As you continue with your education, you may even discover that your perspective is influenced by the types of courses you are taking—science majors are sometimes skeptical about the ambiguities of literary texts, for example, and humanities students can similarly resist the details required in laboratory reports. Moreover, each of us is to some extent "blinded" by our worldviews, by our way of seeing. For instance, middle-class persons in the United States, by and large, share a variety of common beliefs: "Hard work leads to success." "Owning your own home is an important good." "Punctuality, cleanliness, and respect for the privacy of others are important values." "All persons are created equal." If we are among the privileged in this country, we literally may not be able to see existing inequities and barriers to success faced by less privileged Americans.

If we are to become astute readers, we must look for signals that reveal the ideology informing a text. One way to begin doing so is to look for patterns of opposites or contrasts in a text (sometimes called *binaries*) and see which of the opposing terms the writer values more. We generally understand things through contrast with their opposites. We would have no concept of the term *masculine,* for example, without the contrasting term *feminine.* To understand light, we have to understand dark (or heavy). Our concept of liberal depends on its contrast with conservative. We could list hundreds of these opposites or binaries: civilized is that which is not primitive; free is that which is not enslaved; abnormal is that which is not normal; people of color are those who are not Caucasian. When these binaries occur as patterns in a text, one term is generally valued above the other. When you examine the pattern of those values, you can begin to uncover the text's ideology. Sometimes the opposite or devalued terms are only implied, not even appearing in the text. Their absence helps mark the text's ideology.

For example, suppose you are reading an article that opposes a proposed five-day waiting period for the purchase of handguns. If you make a list of valued words, concepts, or ideas and then match them against their nonvalued opposites, you might produce the two-column pattern shown in Table 4.1. Lists such as these can help you clarify a text's ideology—in this case, conservative, individualistic, and supportive of the rights of individuals against the state.

Sometimes it is not immediately evident which terms are valued by a text and which ones are devalued. In such cases you can often identify a major contrast or binary in the text—for example, loggers versus tree huggers, school vouchers versus neighborhood schools, old ways versus new ways, scientific medicine versus alternative medicine. You can then determine which of the opposed terms is more valued. Once you can identify the main controlling binary, you can often line up other opposites or contrasts in the appropriate columns.

If you were to use these oppositions to draw conclusions about the ideology informing Weston's text (see Table 4.2), you might say something like the following: "Weston's text seems informed by liberal values generally and 'green' or environmentalist values, particularly. He is critical of many aspects of American life—our wealth, isolation from nature, and habits of consumption—and

TABLE 4.1 ● BINARY PATTERNS IN ANTI–WAITING PERIOD ARTICLE

Words, Concepts, and Ideas Valued by This Text	Words, Concepts, and Ideas Not Valued by This Text
2nd Amendment: the right to keep and bear arms	Bureaucratic bungling that will result in infringements on the right to keep and bear arms
Reliance on individual self to oppose an assailant	Reliance on police to oppose an assailant; administration of waiting periods would drain police resources
Conservatives	Liberals
Limited government	Active government
Examples of well-known shootings where waiting period would have been irrelevant—no statistical evidence of effectiveness of waiting period or other gun control laws	Examples of mentally ill persons with guns harming or killing people
Examples of criminals thwarted by individual citizens with guns	Examples of children killed by accidental shootings (excluded from text)
Hard time for hard crime, victim's rights	Plea bargaining, lax enforcement of existing gun control laws

TABLE 4.2 ● BINARY PATTERNS IN THE WESTON EXCERPT	
Words, Concepts, and Ideas Valued by This Text	Words, Concepts, and Ideas Not Valued by This Text
Facing up to problems	Ignoring problems
Engagement with nature	Distance from nature
Natural environments—e.g., open spaces	Artificial environments—e.g., shopping malls
Fundamental change in our relation to nature and our consumption habits	Short-term solutions that don't change our relation to nature or our consumption habits

implicitly calls into question the value Americans place on 'progress' and 'a better life' over preservation of the natural world."

If the text includes visual elements, these often provide clues about ideology. Think about how the photograph of Aguilera appeals to various beliefs and values, such as the value of the liberated, powerful woman who doesn't care whether her albums sell as long as she can "do it [her] way." The ideology of this page is complex, however, because the words and images invoke competing beliefs and values—for instance, sex appeal versus independence, financial success versus the willingness to forgo it based on principle.

● **FOR WRITING AND DISCUSSION**

ON YOUR OWN

Return to the introduction to "Blow-Up" (p. 79). Make a two-column chart of the binaries you find in that passage. Put the words, concepts, or ideas that the author values in the left column. Place the opposing words, concepts, or ideas that the author doesn't value in the right column. (Remember, the nonvalued terms may only be implied and not actually appear in the text.) Then write a short analysis of the author's ideology, following the models we provided based on the anti-waiting period argument and Weston's text.

WITH YOUR CLASSMATES

Share your list of binaries and your analysis of Barcott's ideology. Try to reach consensus on both. ●

Exploring Your Responses to a Text

The previous section has explained six questioning strategies based on examining the details of a text. In this section we explain a different approach to interrogating a text, one that asks you simply to explore your own reactions to something you've read. This approach encourages you to record on paper your first gut reactions to a text and then, after reflection, your more sustained and considered responses. We describe in this section three informal, easy-to-use strategies for helping you explore and articulate your own reaction to a text: (1) before/after reflections, (2) the believing and doubting game, and (3) interviewing the author.

BEFORE/AFTER REFLECTIONS

To consider how much a text has influenced your thinking, try writing out some before and after reflections by freewriting your responses to the following statements.

1. What effect is this text trying to have on me? What kind of change does the writer hope to make in my view of the subject?

Here is how Jenny answered this question after she first read Larissa MacFarquhar's article.

MacFarquhar wants me to reject certain commonplaces about reading—that Americans don't read much any more, for example—and to question other common assumptions such as the assumption that reading is always a more worthwhile activity than watching TV or that reading the classics is better than reading romance fiction.

2. Before reading this text, I believed this about the topic: _____
_____. But after
reading the text, my view has changed in these ways: _____
_____.
3. Although the text has persuaded me that _____,
I still have the following doubts: _____.
4. The most significant questions this text raises for me are these: _____
_____.
5. The most important insights I have gotten from reading this text are
these: _____.

● **FOR WRITING AND DISCUSSION**

We gave you an example of Jenny's before/after reflection responding to the question "What kind of change does the writer hope to make in my view of the subject?" Based on your reading of the MacFarquhar article, write out your own before/after reflections for statements 2 through 5. Share your responses with classmates. ●

THE BELIEVING AND DOUBTING GAME

Playing the believing and doubting game with a text is a powerful strategy both for recording your reaction to a text and for stimulating further thinking. Developed by writing theorist Peter Elbow, the believing and doubting game will stretch your thinking in surprising ways. You begin the game by freewriting all the reasons why you believe the writer's argument. Then you freewrite all the reasons why you doubt the same argument. In the "believe" portion, you try to look at the world through the text's perspective, adopting its ideology, actively supporting its ideas and values. You search your mind for any life experiences or memories of reading and research that help you sympathize with and support the author's point of view or ideas. If you find the author's ideas upsetting, dangerous, or threatening, the believing game may challenge—even disturb—you. It takes courage to try to believe views that you feel are dead wrong or contrary to your most deeply held beliefs. Nevertheless, to be a strong rhetorical reader, you need to look at the world through perspectives different from your own.

According to Elbow, the believing game helps you grow intellectually by letting you take in new and challenging ideas. In contrast, the doubting game helps you solidify your present identity by protecting you from outside ideas. Like an antiballistic missile, the doubting game lets you shoot down ideas that you don't like. The "doubt" portion of this game thus reverses the believing process. Here you try to think of all of the problems, limitations, or weaknesses in the author's argument. You brainstorm for personal experiences or memories from reading and research that refute or call into question the author's view. (Of course, the doubting game can be threatening if you already agree with the author's views. In such a case, doubting causes you to take a stand against your own beliefs.)

In the following example, student writer Jenny plays the believing and doubting game with MacFarquhar's article. Note how this exercise promotes critical thinking that goes beyond just expressing her subjective opinions. The results of playing the believing and doubting game are nearly always a bit surprising.

JENNY'S BELIEVING-DOUBTING GAME FREEWRITE

Believe

It's easy for me to believe what MacFarquhar has to say about how Americans are not reading less than they used to but actually more, especially books like romance fiction. I used to read every Sweet Valley High book I could get my hands on. As a kid, I also loved the Judy Blume books. It irritates me when people think that the only reading that counts is Shakespeare or something. I've learned a lot about life from reading Judy Blume's books. For example, Hey, God, It's Me Margaret is about a girl whose parents get divorced just like mine did. It really meant a lot to me to read about a character who had some of the same experiences and feelings I had. If reading is not about helping you get through life, then what is it about? Like MacFarquhar says, book clubs are a big thing nowadays and that proves that reading is as popular as ever. I heard that a professor here offered a literature course called "Oprah's Books," and so many students enrolled that they had to open up another section of the course. My next door neighbor and her middle-school-aged daughter even belong to a mother/daughter book club. MacFarquhar also presents a lot of facts about reading that are hard to argue with. Also, it has always irked me that people think you are an idiot if you like to watch a lot of TV. I think many shows today are as good as many books. Even though some people call it just "fluff," I love Will and Grace and try not to miss it. Plus, I know that many educated adults (including some of my profs!) watch HBO shows like the Six Feet Under and The Sopranos even though some people call them nighttime soap operas. I agree with MacFarquhar that TV and video games are not destroying people's love of reading and that Americans are reading more than ever!

Doubt

It's harder for me to doubt what MacFarquhar is saying because I generally agree with everything she has to say. I suppose some people might call into question her statistics. How reliable are the responses people give to Gallup polls? MacFarquhar seems to think facts and statistics absolutely prove that people read a lot—but can't facts and statistics be manipulated? I know a lot of my teachers feel that students' reading abilities and knowledge of the classics are not what they were in the past. I must admit that I did get a lot out of the "classics" that I have had to read in high school and college even though I wouldn't have read them on my own. I particularly remember reading Heart of Darkness in high school, and just recently reading The Great Gatsby. Recently, I was watching a television report on the famine in Africa, and the news report quoted a line from The Heart of Darkness—"The horror of it all"—and it really made me feel good that I knew what the reporter was referring to. I also guess I can see why people are concerned that television and video games are replacing reading. My younger brother is just addicted to video games, and he never reads. I know, even for myself, sometimes I sit down to watch just one favorite program and end up watching the next show even though I'm not that interested in it and it isn't even that good. So I realize that TV can be addictive and a lot of it does feel more passive than reading. The only other thing that makes me doubt or question what she has to say is her attitude. I don't like the way she sometimes seems to insult people who have a different point of view.

INTERVIEWING THE AUTHOR

Another strategy for exploring your reactions to a text is to imagine interviewing the author and brainstorm the questions you might ask. This strategy urges you to identify the text's hot spots for you. These might be places where you want the author to clarify something, expand on something, or respond to your own objections or counterviews. Here are some questions Jenny developed to ask MacFarquhar.

JENNY'S INTERVIEW QUESTIONS

Are Gallup polls really conclusive evidence that more Americans are reading? Couldn't people just be saying that they are reading a book out of embarrassment? You offer convincing evidence that the books that are the most popular in contemporary America are genre fiction and self-help books, but what do you think of this? Do you think it's a loss or problem that not many Americans read the classics? You seem to think that watching TV can be as valuable as reading. Why do you think that? What would you say to the accusation that you spend most of your time attacking others' positions without really offering your own opinions?

Writing a Rhetorical Analysis Paper: Guidelines and an Example

A rhetorical analysis paper is the written counterpart of rhetorical reading. Writing this kind of paper gives you the opportunity to draw together and apply all the listening and questioning strategies discussed in this and the previous chapter for a two-fold purpose: articulating your own insights about how a text works to influence its readers and communicating those critical insights to other readers. Here we offer general guidelines for writing a rhetorical analysis paper, followed by a student example.

GUIDELINES FOR WRITING A RHETORICAL ANALYSIS

Getting Started

We suggest you begin your rhetorical analysis with the following preliminary activities:

1. Write a summary of the text you are going to analyze to make sure that you understand it well enough to represent its meaning accurately and fairly.
2. Make a descriptive outline in order to determine the distinction as well as the relationship between what a text says and what a text does.
3. Write a rhetorical précis of the text. (See p. 62 for instruction on writing a rhetorical précis.)
4. Try one of the three exploratory activities to identify a strong response or significant effect the text had on you as a reader.

Selecting a Focus for Your Analysis

To write an effective rhetorical analysis, you will need to focus on some aspect of the text's rhetorical methods, an aspect that merits close examination or critique. We suggest one of two approaches. You can start deductively with the effect the text had on you as a reader—a strong positive or negative response, a tension or contradiction you found in the text, or some aspect of the text that confused or surprised you. If you begin with your response, you will need to analyze the text to discover the rhetorical features that account for this response. How do they work? Why are these features effective or ineffective? Alternatively, you can start inductively by identifying and then analyzing particularly striking rhetorical features. If you begin inductively, you will need to consider how these features work and to what effect. What new understanding of the text does your analysis reveal?

Whether you begin deductively or inductively, you will need to select specific rhetorical features to write about. Choose features that you consider particularly effective or ineffective, or in which you detect inconsistencies or tensions between two different appeals. To frame your analysis, choose among the questions about texts' rhetorical methods suggested throughout the chapter.

Drafting Your Paper

Once you have determined a focus, reread the text carefully to find specific examples of these features, taking notes on how they contribute to the effect you have identified. Use these notes to draft a working thesis that states the gist of the insights your rhetorical analysis will offer about the text's meaning and methods. You can revise and refine this working thesis after you draft the whole paper. In your final draft, the thesis should clearly introduce the new understanding that results from your analysis and indicate what that analysis says about the text's effectiveness or ineffectiveness.

The full draft of your paper should have the following elements:

1. An introduction that includes (a) a brief summary of the text, (b) contextual information about the text, and (c) your thesis about the text's rhetorical effect
2. A series of body paragraphs that develop the thesis by (a) discussing specific rhetorical features that produce the rhetorical effect and (b) providing specific textual evidence to back up your points
3. A conclusion that makes clear (a) why the new understanding your paper presents is important and (b) why the insights of your analysis are significant to other readers

AN EXAMPLE OF A RHETORICAL ANALYSIS PAPER

In Chapter 3, we looked at the summary and rhetorical précis of Larissa MacFarquhar's "Who Cares If Johnny Can't Reader" written by Jenny, the first-year writing student whose work we have been following. We now present the paper Jenny wrote about MacFarquhar's essay in response to the assignment below. We have annotated Jenny's paper to highlight the questioning strategies that she uses to analyze the article as well as the rhetorical writing strategies she uses to support her analysis.

JENNY'S ASSIGNMENT TO WRITE A RHETORICAL ANALYSIS PAPER

Write an essay of approximately 750 words in which you examine a key rhetorical strategy (or several related ones) used by Larissa MacFarquhar to engage readers with her point of view regarding reading and its value. Your purpose is to offer your readers a new perspective on how the text works rhetorically, a perspective gleaned from your analysis of the text.

Caring If and What Johnny Reads

States topic's relevance to her

Gives publication information

Offers one-sentence summary of LM'sarticle

Identifies the key rhetorical strategy, *logos*, which her paper will examine

States thesis

Elaborates thesis

Offers support for her claim that LM belittles those with opposing views

Points out LM's use of evidence to support her claim that Americans do care about reading

1   As a future elementary school teacher, interested particularly in language arts, I am always drawn to stories about reading and its supposed decline due to television and the Internet. Therefore, I was curious to see what Larissa MacFarquhar had to say about the subject in her essay, "Who Cares If Johnny Can't Read," published in the online magazine Slate in 1997. As the attention-getting title of her essay suggests, MacFarquhar questions some common assumptions regarding reading, specifically that Americans read less than they used to and that reading books is better and more intellectually stimulating than watching television or surfing the Internet. To challenge each of these common beliefs, MacFarquhar relies mainly on logical argument. A close examination of her essay, however, reveals that her argument is not entirely convincing. She is successful in showing that reading has not declined in America. However, she is less successful in challenging the belief that reading has unique value because she focuses more on disproving (and belittling) the ideas of others than she does on presenting a convincing argument of her own.

2   MacFarquhar begins by challenging the view that Americans "don't care about reading anymore." Her mocking description of this belief suggests that it is the opinion of old fogies who glorify the past and blame new technology for this "cultural decline": "Once, the story goes—in the 1950s, say—we read much more than we do now, and read the good stuff, the classics. Now . . . we're barely literate, and television and computers are rendering books obsolete" (par. 1).* To show just how mistaken these ideas are, she goes on to offer evidence that Americans are actually reading more than ever: "In 1957, 17 percent of

---

*As in her summary in the previous chapter, Jenny's in-text citations refer to the paragraph numbers on the reprint of "Who Cares If Johnny Can't Read?" at the end of Chapter 3.

people . . . said they were currently reading a book; in 1990 over twice as many did" (par. 2). In 1992, she reports, Americans bought over 2 billion books, and a survey conducted that year "found that the average adult American reads 11.2 books a year" (par. 3). Although some readers may doubt the reliability of this statistical data, most are likely to be convinced that reading is alive and well in America.

MacFarquhar has more difficulty challenging the assumption that reading is intrinsically more valuable than watching television or surfing the Internet. Again, she attempts to influence her readers by representing the assumptions she wishes to challenge as old-fashioned. For example, she describes Sven Birkerts's book The Gutenberg Elegies: The Fate of Reading in an Electronic Age as a "maudlin 1994 paean to books." She also says that Time art critic Robert Hughes's argument that books stimulate the imagination in a way that television cannot is "sentimental" and "mysterious" (par. 12).

She uses logical argument to question the idea that books have a unique intellectual value. She disputes the idea that reading in and of itself is a valuable activity no matter what the content by asking rather sarcastically, "Why should the activity 'reading romances' be grouped together with 'reading philosophy' rather than with 'going for a massage'?" (par 9). Even the writers of romance fiction, she argues, admit that their novels are not great literature and are written mainly as "mass market entertainment" (par. 8). MacFarquhar supports her implicit claim that the value of reading depends on its content by quoting 1940s critic Edmund Wilson, who wrote that detective fiction was "a kind of vice, that, for silliness and minor harmfulness, ranks somewhere between smoking and crossword puzzles" (par. 10). Initially, MacFarquhar's argument seems surprising and even convincing. However, it is inconsistent with her earlier dismissal of concerns about the failure of

---

Marginal annotations:

Cites examples of this evidence

Evaluates logical persuasiveness of LM's evidence

3 Provides a transition to her next point of analysis—LM's second main claim that reading is "overvalued"

Offers further examples of LM's tendency to belittle those with opposing views

4 Analyzes LM's first reason for challenging the value placed on reading

Develops analytical point by citing textual evidence

Points out inconsistency in LM's reasoning

contemporary readers to read the classics, which she refers to sarcastically as "the good stuff."

Moves to LM's second reason for challenging the value placed on reading

5   Although we may acknowledge that the value of reading increases if the content is better, many of us believe that reading is a uniquely valuable intellectual activity in and of itself. MacFarquhar, however, disagrees. She disputes the idea that reading is active and television watching passive, calling this notion "vague" and

Critiques evidence LM uses to refute the argument that reading is more active than TV watching

"groundless" (par. 12). In particular, she cites her own experience to challenge Hughes's contention that books stimulate the imagination: "I cannot remember ever visualizing a book's characters, but . . . perhaps I'm in the minority" (par. 13). Since this is the only evidence she offers, she also could be accused of making a claim that is weak and groundless. Moreover, because she is

Points out a serious weakness in LM's argumentative approach

concentrating so much on discrediting the views of book advocates, she gets trapped into offering a negative argument against book reading based on her own experience rather than a positive argument that book reading and television may both be intellectually valuable but in different ways. This different-but-equal view seems to be the point of her last sentence: "The point is to figure out why certain kinds of reading and certain kinds of television might matter in the first place" (par. 15).

Concludes essay by offering a mixed evalua-tion of the effectiveness of MacFarquhar's argument

6   In conclusion, MacFarquhar's argument is only partially convincing. While I am persuaded that Americans are still reading books and that the value of reading is somewhat dependent on the quality of what is read, I am not persuaded that the activity of reading lacks intrinsic value. Not only does MacFarquhar put off some readers by her dismissive attitude toward those who advocate reading, she also fails to offer convincing evidence that reading is not a uniquely valuable activity. As a future teacher, I continue to care deeply about if and what Johnny reads.

Works Cited

MacFarquhar, Larissa. "Who Cares If Johnny Can't Read?"
     Slate 16 Apr. 1997. Rpt. in Reading Rhetorically. 2nd
     Brief ed. Ed. John C. Bean, Virginia A. Chappell, and
     Alice M. Gillam. New York: Longman, 2005. 64–66.

● FOR WRITING AND DISCUSSION

ON YOUR OWN

In your reading log, write a response to Jenny's paper. How does her reading of MacFarquhar compare with yours? What issues or ideas does she leave out? Is hers a fair criticism of the essay? Does she back up her analysis with adequate and convincing evidence? If you had been given the same assignment, what rhetorical aspects of the text would you have written about?

WITH YOUR CLASSMATES

Share your responses with classmates. Working as a whole class or in small groups, list some additional ideas or insights that Jenny might have incorporated into her paper.   ●

Summary

This chapter has explained strategies for questioning a text, which involves carefully interrogating a text's argument and methods in order to critique it and join its conversation. We presented questioning strategies for examining

- The writer's credibility
- The argument's reasoning and logic
- The writer's appeals to the audience's interests and emotions
- The text's language
- The text's use of visual elements
- The text's ideology

We then explained three easy-to-use methods for exploring your own reactions to a text: writing out before/after responses, playing the believing and doubting game, and imagining an interview with the author. Finally, we offered guidelines for writing a rhetorical analysis paper and an example, Jenny's rhetorical analysis of MacFarquhar's article. This example shows how the questioning strategies described in this chapter can help you write a college-level analysis of a text.

P A R T 2

The Rhetorical Reader as Writer

Writing About Reading: The Special Demands of Academic Writing

Academic writing, reading, and inquiry are inseparably linked; and all three are learned by not doing any one alone, but by doing them all at the same time.

—James Reither

As our epigraph suggests, academic tasks often require you to read, write, and inquire simultaneously. Reading, as we have been suggesting all along, is an act of inquiry—a process in which you both listen to and question a text. Similarly, writing is an inquiry process that usually involves reading. The next three chapters focus on helping you do the kind of writing most frequently required by college professors: writing that grows out of reading. However, it is not just college or the academic life that requires writing based on reading. To dramatize the practical value of rhetorical reading as an integral part of effective writing well beyond academic study, we invite you to consider the following scenarios:

- A public relations intern at a regional theater company is asked to report on how comparable theaters around the country are presenting themselves on the World Wide Web. Her supervisor expects detailed information about the visual and verbal content of the other Web pages along with an overview of their various advertising strategies. The intern also wants to communicate her own marketing and design expertise because she hopes to do such a good job that she'll be hired to revamp this theater's Web page.
- A management trainee at an electric utility is assigned to research the cost and competitive features of microform readers and printers that the company might purchase as part of its overhaul of document-handling procedures. As he works, he discovers that he not only has to boil down

extensive technical data in the stacks of sales material he's collected but must also decipher marketing lingo that makes it difficult to compare the equipment directly. He knows that his own boss wants a report that will enable a speedy purchasing decision by a management committee. He also knows that a good report will speed up his own promotion out of "trainee" status.

- A law clerk assisting a judge with an important legal opinion must summarize reams of government documents and position papers about a controversial new environmental policy. He knows that the judge expects his report to provide legal, not political, criteria for analyzing and evaluating the opposing arguments in the case.

- The judge, who chairs the board of a nonprofit women and children's shelter, sits down to write an annual report for volunteers and donors. She must distill a year's worth of dry monthly reports into a short, readable text that will thank the shelter's supporters for past effort and inspire them to further generosity.

All these writers must read and synthesize multiple texts so that they can create a new document with an audience and purpose quite different from those of the original materials. The workplace and community contexts we have described may be unfamiliar to you, but the rhetorical problems facing these reader/writers are parallel to those that you will need to solve when you are asked to incorporate material from outside sources into your own academic writing. These writers may have never heard the term "rhetorical reading," but the effectiveness of the texts they write will depend on how well they analyze both content and technique in their sources and then, on the basis of this analysis, select material that will serve their purposes for influencing the thinking of the next set of readers.

Overview of Part Two

In Part One of this book, we introduced you to the whys and hows of rhetorical reading, arguing for its value in deepening your understanding of what you read and in generating ideas for writing. Now, in Part Two, we turn our attention to the special demands of using the ideas gleaned from reading to create new texts. In Chapter 5, we begin by describing typical reading-based writing assignments that you are apt to receive in classes across the curriculum. Then we turn to the problem of how to assert your authority when you use readings—that is, how you make an argument in your own voice rather than patch together quotes and paraphrases from your sources. Finally, we offer tips on how to manage your writing process—how to produce effective texts that assert your authority as a writer and meet the expectations of college professors.

Chapter 6 guides you through the task of searching for and selecting readings to use in your research-based writing. It explains how to formulate and then use strategic questions to find and evaluate readings that fit your purposes for writing. Chapter 7 covers the nuts and bolts of incorporating the ideas and words of others into your own text. It discusses the rhetorical choices involved when you decide to summarize, paraphrase, or quote a source, and it explains the conventions for doing so ethically and effectively.

Typical Reading-Based Writing Assignments Across the Curriculum

In college, a reading assignment is often only the first step in a complex series of activities that lead toward writing something that will be graded. What you write will naturally vary from situation to situation and can range from a quick answer on an essay exam to an extensive source-based paper. In this section, we discuss five common college writing assignments in which reading plays a major role:

1. Writing to understand course content more fully
2. Writing to report your understanding of what a text says
3. Writing to practice the conventions of a particular type of text
4. Writing to make claims about a text
5. Writing to extend the conversation

These roles can be placed along a continuum, starting with writing tasks in which the ideas in the readings predominate and moving to assignments in which the readings are subordinated to your own ideas and aims. The first two assignment types focus primarily on using writing to learn course subject matter and to practice careful listening to texts. The last three focus primarily on writing your own analyses and arguments for academic audiences. Writing teachers sometimes distinguish these two categories of assignment goals by the terms "writing to learn" versus "learning to write."

WRITING TO UNDERSTAND COURSE CONTENT MORE FULLY

"Writing-to-learn" assignments aim to deepen your understanding of the reading material by asking you to put the author's ideas into your own words or to identify points of confusion for yourself. The primary audience for these types of writing is often yourself even though teachers sometimes ask you to turn these writings in so that they can check on your understanding and progress. The style is informal and conversational. Organization and grammatical correctness are less important than the quality of your engagement with the content of the reading. These assignments typically take one of the following forms.

In-Class Freewriting

The point of freewriting is to think rapidly without censoring your thoughts. Freewriting is often done in class as a way to stimulate thinking about the day's subject. A typical in-class freewrite assignment might be this:

> Choose what for you personally is the single most important word in the text we read for today. You need not speculate about which word the author or your instructor or any other classmate would choose. Just choose the word that seems most important to you. This word may occur only once, a few times, or perhaps it appears frequently. Then explore in writing why you chose the word as the most important word in the essay.*

Reading or Learning Logs

Reading or learning logs are informal assignments that ask you to record your understanding, questions, and responses to a reading. Some teachers give specific prompts to guide your entries while others just ask that you write entries with a certain regularity and/or of a certain length. A typical question about the Larissa MacFarquhar essay might be "How would you describe the author's voice in this essay?" If a teacher asks you simply to write your own reflections in a log, you might use some of the questions rhetorical readers ask presented in Chapter 1 about the text's method and your response to it.

Double-Entry Notebooks

Double-entry notebooks are a special kind of reading log in which you conduct an ongoing dialogue with your interpretations and reactions to the text. Here's how they work: Divide a notebook page with a line down the middle. On the right side of the page record reading notes—direct quotations, observations, comments, questions, objections. On the left side, record your later reflections about those notes—second thoughts, responses to quotations, reactions to earlier comments, answers to questions or new questions. Rhetorician Ann Berthoff, who popularized this approach, says that the double-entry notebook provides readers with a means of conducting a "continuing audit of meaning."† In keeping a double-entry journal, you carry on a conversation with yourself about a text.

One-Page Response Papers or Thought Pieces

Written for an instructor, one-page response papers or "thought" pieces are somewhat more formal than the previous writing-to-learn assignments but still a great deal more informal than essay assignments. They call for a fuller response than the previous types of writing-to-learn assignments, but the purpose

---

*We thank Joan Ruffino, an instructor at the University of Wisconsin–Milwaukee, for this freewriting assignment.
†Ann Berthoff, *The Making of Meaning* (Montclair, NJ: Boynton Cook, 1981), 45.

will be similar—to articulate an understanding of a text and to respond to it, often within the context of major themes or concepts being addressed in a particular course. Usually, a teacher will give students a specific question as a prompt for these papers. Here is a sample thought piece written in response to a prompt from a freshman seminar in psychology. The teacher asked the students to write about the insights they gleaned about obsessive-compulsive disorder (OCD) from reading Lauren Slater's "Black Swans," in which the author narrates the onset of her ongoing battle with OCD.

Reading Lauren Slater's "Black Swans" taught me some basic information about OCD, but more importantly, it taught me how terrifying this disease can be. It begins with a single obsessive thought that leads to a cycle of anxiety, repetitive behaviors such as repeatedly washing one's hands, and avoidance of situations that produce the obsessive thoughts. In severe cases, like Slater's, the person completely avoids life because the obsessive thought invades every aspect of one's life. The essay also makes it clear that experts understand very little about the causes for this disease or about how to treat it.

What impressed me most about this essay, however, was Slater's ability to put me in her shoes and make me feel some of the terror she felt. She vividly describes her experience at being stricken with this condition without warning. A single thought—"I can't concentrate"—suddenly blocked out all other thoughts. Ordinary surroundings like the blue floor of her room appeared strange and frightening. Even her own body seemed foreign to her and grotesque: "the phrase 'I can't concentrate on my hand' blocked out my hand, so all I saw was a blur of flesh giving way to the bones beneath, and inside the bones the grimy marrow, and in the grimy marrow the individual cells, all disconnected. Shattered skin." To me, this was the most frightening description in the essay. I can't imagine being disconnected from my own body. I think the most terrifying aspect of this disease is the sense of being completely out of control of your mind. Slater describes it as, "My mind was devouring my mind." While one can never really know what the disease feels like without actually experiencing it, this essay gives us a disturbing glimpse of what it might be like.

Effective response papers or thought pieces, like the one above, identify significant points in the reading and offer a personal response or interpretation of those significant points. In this book, there are numerous places where we give short writing-to-learn tasks designed to help you learn and apply key concepts of rhetorical reading.

WRITING TO REPORT YOUR UNDERSTANDING OF WHAT A TEXT SAYS

Another common reading-based assignment asks you to report your understanding of what a text says. For example, you will frequently need to summarize readings in a paper and to explain an author's ideas as part of an essay exam. You may also be asked to write an annotated bibliography that provides brief summaries of sources related to a particular topic or question. In Chapter 3, we discussed how to write summaries and the various purposes they serve in college reading and writing assignments. In your own writing, a summary of an article might be short; for example, you might write a one-sentence summary in order to put into context a quotation you are going to use in your research paper. Or it might be fairly detailed; for example, you might want to summarize the complete argument of an important article on a controversial issue. Sometimes an entire paper can be a sequence of summaries, as when you write a review of literature about a particular topic—for example, about new treatments for obsessive-compulsive disorder in a psychology course or about scientific studies of the relationship between pesticides and cancer in a biochemistry course. Although summaries or reports of your understanding of a text will vary in length and purpose, they are all expected to be accurate, fair, and balanced. In short, they require you to listen carefully to the text.

WRITING TO PRACTICE THE CONVENTIONS OF A PARTICULAR TYPE OF TEXT

Assignments that ask you to analyze and practice the conventions of a particular type of writing—its organizational format, style, ways of presenting evidence, and so on—use readings as models. Such assignments are common in college courses. In a journalism class, for example, you would learn to write a news report using the inverted pyramid structure; in a science course you might be asked to write up results of experiments in the form of a laboratory report. Similarly, in courses using this textbook, you might be asked to write aims-based essays modeled after some of the readings in the anthology—that is, to write your own reflective essay, informative essay, exploratory essay, or proposal argument.
   Generally, using readings as models involves the following activities:

- Identifying the features that characterize a particular type of text
- Noting the ways in which rhetorical situation affects the features identified in model texts
- Coming up with your own topic and reason for writing this particular type of text
- Using the features of the model text (or texts) and your own rhetorical situation to guide your writing

Let's say, for example, that you've been asked to write a proposal argument. Proposals typically include three main features: description of the problem, proposal of a solution, and justification of that solution. As you read sample proposals, you will find that various authors deal with these features differently depending on their audience and purpose. In some cases, for example, there is a great deal of description of the problem because the intended audience is unfamiliar with it; in other cases, there is very little description because it is presumed that the intended reading audience already knows a lot about the problem. The key is to adapt the model's characteristic structure and style to your own rhetorical purpose, not to follow the model slavishly.

In courses across the curriculum, your ability to analyze and adopt the conventions particular to a given discipline's ways of writing will help you write successful papers. For example, when you are asked in a philosophy class to write an argument in response to Immanuel Kant's *Critique of Pure Reason,* you are primarily being asked to engage with the ideas in the text. But secondarily you are also being asked to practice the conventions of writing a philosophical argument in which counterexamples and counterarguments are expected. It pays, then, to be alert to the structure and style of material you are assigned to read in any field of study as well as to the ideas.

WRITING TO MAKE CLAIMS ABOUT A TEXT

Assignments in this category ask you to analyze or critique readings. Many academic writers take as their field of study the texts produced by others. Literary critics study novels, poems, and plays; cultural critics analyze song lyrics, advertisements, cereal boxes, and television scripts; historians analyze primary source documents from the past; theologians scrutinize the sacred texts of different religions; lawyers analyze the documents entered into court proceedings, the exact wording of laws and statutes produced by legislators, or the decisions of appellate court judges.

Many college composition courses ask students to write rhetorical analyses of texts. These assignments ask you to analyze one or more readings by identifying specific rhetorical methods and strategies used by the author, showing how these rhetorical choices contribute to the text's impact, and evaluating the choices in light of the author's evident purpose. Your claims must go beyond what a text says to make judgments and draw conclusions. In these types of assignments, the text and your ideas about the text are of equal importance. Assignments asking for analysis or critique are not invitations for you to refer briefly to the text and then take off on your own opinions about the topic, nor are they invitations merely to summarize or rehearse what the text has said. Rather, these assignments expect you to engage critically with a specific text. On the one hand, you will be expected to represent what the text said accurately and fairly. On the other hand, you will be expected to offer your own analysis, interpretation, or critique, one that enables readers to see the text differently. Chapter 4 includes guidelines for writing a rhetorical analysis as well as a sample assignment and a student paper, Jenny's rhetorical analysis of MacFarquhar's article.

WRITING TO EXTEND THE CONVERSATION

These assignments treat texts as voices in a conversation about ideas. They typically call for you to read and synthesize material from several sources. Here, your own ideas and aims take center stage; your source texts play important but less prominent backup roles. The most familiar form this assignment takes is the research or seminar paper. What distinguishes such college work from high school research paper assignments is the expectation that the paper will present your own argument, not the arguments provided by the sources. In other words, you are expected to articulate a significant question or problem, investigate relevant data, research what published authors have said about it in print or on the Web, and then formulate your own argument. To write these multisource papers successfully, you should use other texts primarily to position yourself in the conversation and to supply supporting data, information, or testimony. The argument—your main points—must come from you.

A helpful way to approach these assignments is to treat the texts you have read as springboards for further research and discovery. Think of the readings you encounter in your research as voices in a conversation that your essay will join. By giving you the opportunity to define your own purposes for writing in dialogue with other texts, such assignments prepare you for the research assignments typical of many college courses, where your goal is to synthesize material from a number of sources and then produce your own paper, inserting another voice—your own—into the ongoing conversation. To illustrate this kind of research writing, we include at the end of Chapter 7 Jenny's researched argument on romance novels, a paper that grew out of her work with Larissa Mac-Farquhar's essay.

Asserting Your Authority as a Reader and Writer

"I have nothing to say! It's all been said!" This complaint is a familiar one. In the midst of a complicated reading and writing project, it's not unusual for any of us—students, teachers, or professional writers—to lose sight of our original goals and thus lose our confidence that we have ideas worth writing about.

Throughout this book, we have argued that reading is an active, constructive process. We don't need to convince you that writing, too, is an active process; after all, to write, one must actually make words appear on a page or screen. Nevertheless, as we turn to the subject of connecting reading and writing, we do want to warn you against *passive writing,* writing that just translates what's on someone else's page onto your page. Passive writing is packed full of summaries, paraphrases, and quotes (sometimes very lengthy quotes) but contains very little content from the writer. Some teachers refer to such writing as "patchwriting"—patches from source materials stitched together by a few sentences of the student's own. Such papers don't make their own arguments. They just cut and paste their sources' writing in order to fill the page. Passive writing of this sort doesn't assert its author's reason for writing and so it doesn't give its audience a reason for reading.

Passive writing occurs because many people (not just students!), when confronted with already published materials, find it difficult to maintain their own sense of purpose as authors: they lose track of their *author-ity*. Perhaps uncertain about the source text's content or purposes, they begin to insert quotations or paraphrases into their own texts without clear purpose. Perhaps awed by the rush of facts and abstractions in materials they are reading, they yield their authority as readers/writers to previously published texts. They begin to copy rather than compose, to cut and paste rather than argue. In effect, they let themselves be silenced by the experts. When they simply must put words on a page (because the assignment is due), the resulting product resembles a pasted-together collage of quotes and paraphrases. By letting their source materials take over the paper, writers not only fail to gain their readers' confidence but lose the opportunity to make their own contribution to the discussion.

As you work with the advice in this chapter, you will begin to discover a powerful truth: rhetorical reading leads to rhetorically powerful writing. Just as rhetorical reading involves analyzing and critiquing an author's method as well as content, rhetorically effective writing asserts its purpose and method along with its content. Strong writers use the knowledge and understanding gained from their reading to build their own authority so that they can, in turn, *author* their own texts. These strong texts will engage readers because they not only "say" clearly what they mean but "do" what they intend: extend the conversation by providing new information and asserting new ideas that will alter their readers' view of the subject.

Managing Your Writing Process

To assert your authority as a writer, you need to think of writing as an active process of making new meaning, of adding your voice to an ongoing conversation about a subject. It is not a matter of just retrieving something that is fully formed in your head or of finding other voices to cobble together; rather, it is a matter of finding a compelling reason to write and then actively constructing a text that accomplishes that purpose. Perhaps Kenneth Burke, whom we mentioned in Chapter 1, puts it best when he describes the unique contribution each speaker or writer makes to a conversation as "putting in your oar."

Recognizing that the process of creating a text will vary from writer to writer and from situation to situation, we offer in this section a variety of strategies that will help you claim your own authority as a writer. You should think of the strategies and processes we describe as *recursive*; in other words, you don't go lockstep through the strategies in a strictly linear fashion but frequently circle back to repeat earlier strategies because you have discovered a new angle or refined your main idea or purpose for writing.

STRATEGIES FOR GETTING STARTED

As a college writer, you are more likely to succeed when you can make an assignment your own. Rather than writing just to fulfill an assignment, you need to construct your own "take" on the subject by imagining yourself writing to a real audience for a real purpose. You assert your own authority by creating your own *exigence*—a useful term from rhetorical theory that means a circumstance that is other than it should be, a situation in need of attention. To resolve the situation, you write to bring about some kind of change in your audience—to correct a misunderstanding, to talk back to something someone else has said, to propose a solution to a problem, to explore and shed new light on an issue, to change your audience's thinking or attitudes, to make your audience appreciate something or value it differently, to call for action.

In writing projects that involve reading, the exigence or reason for writing grows either out of your analysis and response to a single text (you have something new to say about the text that is surprising or challenging to your audience) or out of your own research question, which then leads to a search for texts that will expand and complicate your understanding of your subject. Your increased understanding, in turn, provides you with insights and information you need to develop an argument that brings about a desired change in your audience's view of a subject. When your writing project involves reading, here are some strategies for getting started.

- For assignments that ask you to analyze and respond to a text, the questioning strategies explained in Chapter 4 should generate responses that can serve as points of departure. As you consider various starting points for writing about a text, consider what kind of change you want to make in *your* readers' thinking about this text and why this change is important. For example, do you want readers to see an inconsistency or contradiction they might otherwise miss? Do you want them not to be taken in by a particular persuasive ploy or faulty reasoning? Do you want to impress upon them the broad significance of what the text has to say?
- For assignments that ask you to begin with your own question, issue, or stance and to conduct research, you might begin by brainstorming a list of questions or problems that intrigue you. What are the points of disagreement? Why does this question or problem matter? To whom is this question or issue important and why? These questions can help you refine your starting point or stance and thus help guide your research. In Chapter 6 we discuss question analysis, a technique for formulating strategic questions to guide you through the process of finding, evaluating, and selecting sources.

Whatever kind of writing assignment you are given, the starting point of the writing process should be a problematic question or a risky claim. Although it might be tempting to start with ideas that are familiar or safe, that you are already firmly committed to or that are already settled in your mind, this approach usually leads to flat, perfunctory writing that fails to engage readers. The better approach is instead to start with a question that is genuinely puzzling to you or with a tentative claim that provokes multiple perspectives and invites audience resistance or skepticism.

STRATEGIES FOR GENERATING IDEAS

Once you have identified a starting point, you'll need to develop your ideas by analyzing more fully the single text you are writing about or by finding additional texts that can expand, deepen, and challenge your understanding of your research question. In either case, the rhetorical reading strategies in Chapters 3 and 4 should help you generate ideas for your writing project. Here are a few additional suggestions.

- A useful place to begin is to consider your rhetorical situation: Whose minds are you trying to change about what, and why? What kind of information do you need to establish your credibility? How can you make your readers concerned about your topic? What kind of supporting evidence will be persuasive to them? What values or interests do you share with your readers? What differences in opinions or values might you need to try to overcome?

- If you are writing to make a claim about a particular text, reread the text with your starting point in mind and note all the textual details you might use to support your claim. Likewise, look for counterevidence that you will have to account for in some way. Perhaps this counterevidence will cause you to modify your claim.

- If you are assigned to do library or Internet research, consider how a given source will advance your purpose for writing. (Chapter 6 offers extensive advice on both finding and evaluating sources.) As you take notes from the texts you plan to use as sources, consider how you might use each source in your paper. Does this source provide background information? Support for your claims? An alternative perspective? A compelling example or illustration of a point? With answers to these questions in mind, try out various organizational plans by making an informal outline or drawing an idea map of how the materials you've read connect with each other. This kind of preliminary planning can help you see the "big picture" of your evolving ideas.

- Conferencing with your teacher, peer group, or a writing center tutor is another good way to generate ideas for writing. When you try to explain your rough or tentative ideas to someone else, it's likely you will discover new ideas and connections that you didn't see before. Moreover, your conferencing partners will also ask you questions that will trigger new lines of thinking or enable you to see gaps in your current thinking that may require further analysis or research.

STRATEGIES FOR WRITING A FIRST DRAFT

Good first drafts are usually messy, confusing, and imperfect. Fear of this messiness, or fear of the blank screen or page, often prevents writers from producing idea-generating early drafts and thus reduces the time available for multiple revisions. To get past such fears, it can be helpful to think of first drafts as *discovery drafts*. Their purpose, in other words, is to extend the process of figuring out what you have to say and how to say it. A writer's most original ideas often appear in the final paragraph of these drafts, at the point where the writer discovered them. This is not a problem at the rough draft stage because your goal is simply to start working out ideas. During revision you can reshape these ideas to meet your readers' needs. What follows are some strategies for getting your ideas onto screen or paper so that you can work with them, learn from them, and use them to guide your next steps in writing:

- Try to produce a complete first draft without worrying about perfection or even clarity for readers. When you get stuck, make notes to yourself in caps about ideas that might go in a particular section—a transition, an example, another point in support of your claim, or even just your doubts. If you have a vague idea but can't figure out how to say it, freewrite, again in caps, "WHAT I REALLY WANT TO SAY IS. . . ."
- Another strategy for overcoming the fear of getting started is to "blind write": Turn off the monitor on your computer so that you can't see what you're writing, and write for a while. The idea of blind writing is to silence your internal critic that finds fault with every sentence. What you want to do is get the words flowing so that you can determine how the ideas you have generated so far work, where the gaps are, what is still not clear to you.
- If you have trouble with introductions, try starting in the middle or with a particularly strong or well-formulated point. When you have most of the paper drafted and know what it will say, you can come back and write a focused opening.
- If your paper assignment calls for a particular organizational format— such as a classical argument, a technical report, an evaluative review of literature—use that format as an idea-generating template for producing various parts of your text. For example, a classical argument includes an introduction that explains the significance of the issue, provides background information, and gives the writer's thesis or claim; a section that supports the claim through a sequence of reasons and evidence; a section that summarizes and responds to opposing views; and a concluding section that calls for action or relates the argument to larger issues. Structures like this can help you build your first draft section by section. The specific requirements for each section will provide you with implicit questions to address in it. When you write out the answers, you'll have a discovery draft.

- Try talking out your draft by having a conversational partner (classmate, writing center tutor, teacher, or friend) listen to your ideas and take notes, or try talking directly into a tape recorder and then transcribing what you said. Since we're more accustomed to talking than we are to writing, we can often discover what we have to say orally better than we can in writing.

STRATEGIES FOR EVALUATING YOUR DRAFT FOR REVISION

Producing an initial draft is only the first step in producing a final polished product. For most college assignments, success requires substantial revision through multiple drafts. Effective revision is not just minor repair or sentence correction but literally reseeing a draft's ideas. As you gain experience as a writer, you will find that the urge to revise begins when, in reading a draft, you discover confusing passages, points that need support and development, contradictions or flaws in thinking, gaps in your argument, places where the text fails to anticipate audience questions or objections, and so forth. Sometimes you will even decide to change your thesis and reorganize. To see these sorts of things requires a critical distance that is not easy to achieve. Therefore, you will benefit from specific techniques that enable you to adopt a reader's perspective toward your own text. Here are some suggestions.

- Try to "listen" to your own text in some of the ways outlined in Chapter 3. Write a descriptive outline of your draft, draw an idea map, or write a rhetorical précis. Because these strategies ask you to take your draft apart in various ways, they will inevitably provide you with a new, more "objective" view of your text and in the process reveal various problems—missing connections among ideas, digressions, gaps, vagueness, and so on.
- Most of us compose on screen these days, but reviewing your draft screen by screen can make you lose sight of the big picture. Instead, we recommend that you print your draft periodically and read from hard copy, annotating it for problems and ideas for revision.

STRATEGIES FOR PEER RESPONSE AND REVISION

One of the best ways to see your text differently is through another reader's eyes. Because you know what you meant to write, it is often difficult to see any gaps or confusing points in what you actually wrote. Other readers, not privy to your inner thoughts, can spot these problems much more readily. A common technique for getting this kind of perspective on your draft is through peer response. Peer response groups allow you to receive feedback from a "live" audience, whether this feedback comes in the form of written comments by a peer or face-to-face response to your draft. The benefits of working in a peer response group go beyond the insights you gain about your own draft; you also benefit from the experience of offering feedback to others. For one thing, you learn to recognize and understand various kinds of writing problems better by seeing them in someone else's writing. This understanding, with practice, helps you detect them in your own writing. In addition, offering constructive feedback helps you develop a language for talking about what's working and what's not working in writing. This language, in turn, helps you analyze your own writing. Put simply, receiving and giving peer response enables you to achieve the kind of critical distance on your own writing that is so crucial to revision.

Tips for Offering Feedback to Others

- Get a sense of the whole before formulating your responses. If the peer is reading a draft aloud, listen to the whole draft before jotting down a few notes. Ideally, you should make your notes while listening to the paper being read aloud a second time so that you can confirm or rethink your first impressions. For convenience, you might record your responses in three columns: positive comments, negative comments, and questions. If you are reading the draft and will write out your response, read the paper through completely, using wavy lines or marginal notes to mark passages that you want to look at again or comment on. A second reading will then help you fill out a peer response form or decide on the most constructive feedback you might offer the writer. If you are not given explicit guidelines for responding, be sure to be selective in your comments. Although you may mark various passages with a question mark or underline a number of confusing sentences, select only two or three major concerns to comment on in detail. When there are too many comments, writers are not sure where to start with their revision. They feel overwhelmed and discouraged rather than motivated to revise.
- Respond honestly and productively. Perhaps the most frequent complaint we hear from student writers about peer response groups is that the responders didn't offer any real feedback but instead offered vague, polite comments.
- Offer your comments from a reader's perspective, not an evaluator's. Instead of saying—"This is illogical"—say "I don't follow your reasoning here. After you offered example X, I was expecting you to come to conclusion Y." Or if the paper seems disorganized, explain where as a reader you get lost.
- Make sure that your comments are text-specific, not general. Rather than praising a paper by saying, "I liked your introduction," say "The personal anecdote you started with really captured my attention and made me want to read on." Or rather than saying that "Some points are unclear,"

identify specific points that were unclear to you as a reader and try to explain what was unclear about them, the questions they raised.
- Ask questions to help the writer generate ideas for clarification and support and to help the writer extend and complicate his or her thinking about the topic. Depending on the paper's aim, you may want to play the devil's advocate and introduce objections or other points of view to help the writer make a more convincing argument.

Tips for Using Feedback to Revise
- When possible, ask for feedback in terms of your rhetorical aim and your own assessment of your draft's rhetorical effectiveness. That is, think about the change you hope to make in your reader's attitude, understanding, or opinion about your subject matter and ask your peer responders whether your text accomplished this purpose. Ask specific questions about passages that you have already identified as potentially problematic. For example, you might ask readers if you need further evidence to support a particular point or if you need to explain an unfamiliar term more fully. Or you might ask if you come on too strong in a given passage or if your tone is appropriate in light of your purpose.
- Try to keep an open mind as you listen to or read through peer responses. That is, try to resee your paper from the reader's perspective. Let go of the urge to defend what you've written. Remember that the feedback from response groups is meant to help you improve your writing and should not be viewed as a personal attack. Experienced writers regularly seek feedback on their writing and understand that it enables them to see their writing in a way they can't on their own.
- Expect to get some mixed or contradictory feedback from peers. Try on these varied and conflicting perspectives to determine what in the text is causing these mixed responses or confusion. If several readers identify the same problem, you should probably try to fix it even if you don't fully agree with the feedback. Ultimately, however, it is up to you to weigh the feedback you receive and decide which responses you will attend to in your revising process.
- Use peer feedback to develop a revision plan. Two considerations should guide your revision plan: (1) what the feedback tells you about this draft's successes and failures, and (2) your sense of which responses are the most important to address first. Generally, you should attend to higher-order concerns (focus, organization, development of ideas, logic) before lower-order concerns (sentence-level and grammatical and mechanical problems). You might find that problem sentences disappear once you focus on higher-order concerns. By revising for clearer ideas, you may create clearer sentences without grammatical tangles.

STRATEGIES FOR EDITING AND POLISHING
YOUR FINAL DRAFT

College professors expect final drafts that are carefully edited and proofread. Editing can be difficult, however, because most of us have trouble seeing the surface errors in our own writing—omitted words, spelling and punctuation errors, wrong or repeated words. We literally fail to see what's on the page, instead substituting what we intended to write for what's there. Consequently, you must train yourself to detect and correct errors in sentence structure, word choice, spelling, punctuation, citation conventions, and grammar or usage. We suggest the following strategies for producing a polished final draft:

- As simple as it may sound, reading your text aloud to yourself or someone else (classmate, friend, tutor) is one of the most effective ways to catch missing words, wrong words, and other kinds of errors. Conversely, sometimes it's helpful to have someone else read your paper back to you. Although there are many errors that you cannot detect through just hearing your paper, you can often recognize snarled or unclear sentences and awkward wording when you hear someone else's voice reading it.
- Another effective strategy is to read through your paper line by line, using another sheet of paper to cover the part of the text you have not yet read. Such a practice slows down your reading and forces you to look at each word and sentence, making it more likely you'll see what's really on the page, not what you hope is there.
- Computer programs now provide a number of editing aids—spelling and grammar checkers. You may want to turn these checkers off while you are drafting because they can intrude on your composing process. Once you are ready to proofread, however, take advantage of them, particularly the spelling checker. But do not rely on them solely to detect the errors in your paper. Spelling checkers, for example, do not detect homonym errors—*its* when you need *it's*—and they don't flag misspellings that turn out to be correctly spelled words that are not what you meant—*cant* for *want*. Similarly, grammar checkers mechanically mark things like passive voice or repeated words that may actually be appropriate in a particular writing context. For example, the computer highlighted the second *that* in the following sentence: "I believe that that is wrong." But this sentence might be perfectly appropriate in a context where what the second *that* refers to is perfectly clear. As a rule of thumb, use such computerized aids as only *one* of several steps in your editing process. Many experienced writers have an intense dislike for grammar checkers, which can only perform countable calculations and do not actually understand language.
- You may find that having a friend or classmate read over your final paper is a necessary step in your editing process because no matter how careful you are, there are errors that you miss.

- To improve your editing skills, try to keep track of the kinds of errors you habitually make, and try to be on the lookout for these errors as you proofread.
- To check on word choices, punctuation, grammar, and usage rules as well as citation conventions, keep nearby a recently published handbook and dictionary or a CD-ROM reference guide.

Summary

We began this chapter with an overview of five typical types of reading-based writing assignments: writing (1) to understand course content more fully, (2) to report your understanding of what a text says, (3) to practice the conventions of a particular type of text, (4) to make claims about a text, and (5) to extend the conversation. We then discussed the importance of the following:

- Asserting your own authority when you use readings; that is, making your points in your own voice rather than patching together quotes and paraphrases from sources
- Claiming and maintaining your authority as you generate ideas and draft your paper
- Reading and analyzing your own drafts rhetorically so that you attend both to your content ("what") and your methods ("how") as you revise through multiple drafts

Using Rhetorical Reading to Conduct Research

*The only way in which a human being can make some approach
to knowing the whole of a subject is by hearing what can be
said about it by persons of every variety of opinion and studying
all modes in which it can be looked at by every character of
mind. No wise [person] ever acquired wisdom in any mode but
this; nor is it in the nature of human intellect to become wise
in any other manner.*

—John Stuart Mill

As the opening epigraph suggests, wisdom emerges only through careful examination of many differing perspectives. John Stuart Mill's admonition to hear "every variety of opinion" on a subject, although probably not literally possible to follow, serves as an important reminder that new knowledge is made only through our interaction with the thinking and writing of others, including—perhaps, especially—those with whom we do not expect to agree. In this chapter we address the difficult challenge of finding and selecting materials that will provide you with reliable and diverse perspectives on the questions and issues you investigate for college writing assignments. As our chapter title suggests, our intent is to demonstrate the value of rhetorical reading as a research strategy.

This chapter will show you how to use rhetorical reading strategies to handle the challenges you face when you need to write a paper that synthesizes material from outside readings, challenges such as (1) finding sources that speak directly to the questions your paper seeks to address, and (2) evaluating the reliability of potential sources. The next chapter will then demonstrate practical techniques for incorporating material from your sources into your own writing so that your papers make new knowledge out of your diverse sources. Together, the two chapters will show you how to find sources for and write rhetorically effective papers that contribute your voice and ideas to extend the conversation about a topic.

First, we show how to formulate initial research questions and predict where you will find the best materials—before you even begin looking for sources— through a systematic process called *question analysis.* The middle section of the chapter provides background information contrasting search tools (library databases and Web search engines) and publication contexts for various types of print sources. Finally, we show how you can evaluate potential sources by asking questions about relevance, currency and scope, authors and experts, and publishers (of print sources) and sponsors (of Web sources). We will illustrate our discussion by following the work of Jenny, the composition student working on Larissa MacFarquhar's "Who Cares If Johnny Can't Read?", as she responds to the writing assignment below. Her final essay—a researched argument entitled "Romance Fiction: Brain Candy or Culturally Nutritious?"—appears at the end of Chapter 7.

JENNY'S ASSIGNMENT TO EXTEND THE CONVERSATION

Here is the writing assignment Jenny received to evaluate a particular genre of reading or television. The assignment invites students to "extend the conversation" by contributing their own ideas to an ongoing conversation initiated by other writers.

> In the last paragraph of "Who Cares If Johnny Can't Read?" Larissa MacFarquhar poses the following challenge to readers: "Reading *per se* is not the issue. The point is to figure out why certain kinds of reading and certain kinds of television might matter in the first place." Write a paper in which you extend the conversation introduced by MacFarquhar's challenge. Choose a particular kind of reading with which you are familiar—romance fiction, science fiction, detective fiction, inspirational books—or a kind of television program—the Nature channel, police dramas, reality TV—and ask these questions: Is this kind of reading or television culturally valuable? If so, how? If not, why not?
>
> Your paper should include the following: a working definition of "cultural value" and criteria for judging it; your own experience with this kind of print or media text; and the published opinion of others regarding its cultural value. It should be four to six pages long and include MLA in-text citations and a works cited list.

Formulating Questions

Knowing what you are looking for is essential to successful research-based writing. Whether you are fulfilling an assignment for a first-year writing class or for a capstone seminar in your major, the first step in your research process—the step before you begin searching for sources—is articulating your purpose: What is it that you want to investigate and write about?

CLARIFYING YOUR PURPOSE

When you are doing research for a writing assignment, your goal is to find source readings that will support your writing project in two basic ways: (1) by helping you uncover and understand the ongoing conversation about the subject, and (2) by providing information and concepts you can use to develop your paper. The question analysis process that we describe in the next section will help you determine in advance what you will be "listening" for once you begin looking at sources. In Chapter 2 we described how experienced readers approach their reading purposefully and predict content by recognizing genre conventions and reconstructing rhetorical context. Similarly, experienced researchers go to the library (perhaps via their Internet browser) with more than a generalized "topic" in mind. They begin with a carefully worked out question and a set of expectations about how they will recognize relevant answers. You need to do the same. As your research progresses, you will probably revise your original question, narrowing or broadening it as you catch the drift of the ongoing conversation about it. (Most researchers—not only students—find that they must narrow their initial questions significantly just to make their project feasible for the amount of time available and the number of pages allotted for the assignment.) Your question will undoubtedly change somewhat as your project unfolds until it eventually becomes part of your paper's introduction. Combined with the answers you find, it will lead into your thesis statement to signal your paper's purpose to your readers.

But first you need the question. How else will you recognize answers?

In the past, you may have encountered research assignments that asked you to do little more than report on a topic by gathering information and funneling it into paragraphs. The expectations and standards of your college teachers who assign papers with research components will be quite different. In the language of our service economy, these professors expect you to provide "value-added" content that demonstrates your own thinking about the subject of your paper. The information you need for your paper is "out there" in publications and on Web sites; indeed, we are awash in information. But what it means is not always apparent. Your task, like that of the writers in the workplace scenarios in Chapter 5, is to survey the raw data of the information you collect, discover patterns of meaning within it, select relevant material from it, and then explain that material's significance to your readers. The value you add comes from the analysis and organization you provide to help your readers make sense out of the disconnected array of available information.

This multilayered researching/reading/writing process involves rhetorical reading at its most challenging. In our electronic information age, where thousands, even millions, of research sources are available within seconds of a mouse click, locating information is only a small step in the research process. Some new college students make the mistake of thinking that, with so much information available, researching a paper is a quick, easy matter. It's true that computers make it easy to obtain potential source materials. With the full text of many magazine and journal articles available through library databases such as EBSCO-host, Lexis-Nexis, or ProQuest, it's possible to collect many sources without even looking up a call number and going to the stacks. But making sense of the information in all those potential sources presents a wholly different challenge.

Think of research-based writing assignments this way: Your job is to conduct an inquiry, not to shop around for sources. We offer a cautionary tale. Consider what went wrong when a student we'll call Stacey treated a research assignment as a hunt for bargains instead of an inquiry. Her assignment was an explanatory paper that would examine the potentially negative consequences of something that interested her. She had heard that Barbie dolls were being redesigned to have more natural proportions, so she thought Barbies would be an interesting "topic." She skipped the assigned step of writing out an initial question because, as she wrote in a later reflection, she thought that since Barbie was in the news, it would be faster just to do some computer searches and see "what there was to say." She felt overwhelmed at first by all the sources she found in just one periodicals database, so she just chose the first three articles for which full text was available online.

The result was a paper that amounted to the "patch-writing" we caution against in Chapter 5. It interspersed engaging descriptions of her own favorite Barbies between three long paragraphs that summarized a feminist's reflections about her childhood dolls, a psychological study about gender stereotypes and eating disorders, and a commentary about the negative impact of Teen Talk Barbie's dislike for math class. There was nothing about Barbie's new figure, her original topic. The descriptions of Stacey's dolls were fun to read and showed that she was a fluent writer with a good vocabulary. But other than that, the paper was three long, loosely connected summaries. It lacked purpose. Stacey had not defined a purpose for her reading and research, and so she did not have one for her paper.

QUESTION ANALYSIS

What could Stacey have done instead? The question analysis (QA) technique we recommend is a systematic examination of your initial research question in terms of what you already know about your subject matter and what you hope to find out by doing research.* The QA prompts that follow will enable you to make a preliminary map of the terrain you need to cover so that you can plan your research and consider in advance what kind of sources are going to be most useful for you to retrieve, read, and eventually integrate into your paper. Because QA is preliminary to your active search for sources, just as note-taking and

---

*The term *question analysis* comes from the work of academic librarian Cerise Oberman, who first broached it in "Question Analysis and the Learning Cycle," *Research Strategies* 1 (Winter 1983): 22–30.

freewriting during planning stages of the writing process are preliminary to active drafting, it will help you begin your actual searching with a focused sense of purpose. Then you can use your rhetorical reading skills to select the sources most relevant to your purposes. Students who use QA for the first time are often surprised to discover how much they already know about where they are likely to find relevant sources and what issues those sources will raise. The QA process takes you out of a passive role like Stacey's, waiting to see what you can find, and puts you in charge of your research.

Prompts for Question Analysis

Jot down answers to these questions *before* you begin searching for sources.

1. What question do you plan to investigate in this paper?
2. What makes this question worth pursuing?
3. What kind of expert would be able to provide good answers or the current best thinking about finding answers? (Perhaps a physician? Wildlife biologist? Water resource engineer? CPA? Social worker?)
4. Where do you expect to find particularly good information about the matter? General interest publications? Specialized publications? Are you aware of a specific source with material relevant to your needs?
5. How recent must materials be to be relevant? What factors might make information outdated (such as a congressional election or the announcement of important medical findings)? Do you need information recorded *before* a particular event? For situations that change rapidly, such as AIDS research or foreign policy, even a few months could make a difference in the relevance of some material to your project. Defining a particular calendar period will help you search more efficiently.
6. What individuals or interest groups have a major stake in answering your question in a particular way? For example, players' unions and sports team owners look at salary caps from different perspectives; lumber companies and environmental activists evaluate the effectiveness of the Endangered Species Act differently.
7. What kinds of bias do you need to be especially alert for on this particular question? Neutral sources are valuable, but bias of some kind is unavoidable, so it's important to recognize how it is operating in your sources.
8. Finally, jot down some words or phrases that you might use to begin searching.

The first two QA prompts ask you to jot down not only the question that you will address in your paper, but also your reasons for pursuing that question. Thinking carefully about the importance of your question will help you negotiate complexities you may find in your sources. For academic writing projects, a question with an obvious or simple answer is probably not worth investigating. You'll want to choose a question without clear-cut answers. Perhaps experts have been unable to discover an answer or are at odds with each other because of different values, political perspectives, or research approaches. Ask yourself also why pursuing the question is important. What benefits will come from answering the question? What readers are interested in the question? Why are you yourself interested in the question? Whatever your purpose, if you clarify it for yourself in advance, you will greatly reduce the risk of losing sight of your purpose once you dive into the search process. To illustrate the QA process, we invite you to examine the following excerpts from Jenny's answers to the QA prompts.

EXCERPTS FROM JENNY'S RESEARCH LOG

Question Analysis

1. My question: How do people defend romance novels? (I'm assuming some people do!) What do they say is the value of them? What criteria do they use? Maybe I have to set up criteria, but I'd like some experts to base my ideas on and use for support!

2. Why it's worth pursuing: Because (1) MacFarquhar uses romance novels as an example, so they'll fit the "extending the conversation" idea, (2) lots of people read them—including me, sometimes, (3) I need to understand what my future students might be reading. . . .

3. Experts I need: teachers, librarians, maybe that Center for the Book that LM mentions

4. Sources I think will work: I hope there will be good material in regular newsstand magazines, possibly women's magazines, maybe magazines/journals for teachers & librarians.

5. Dates? They have to be pretty current, from 1997 (LM's article) to now.

6. People with a stake in this: teachers, except I don't know which way they'd lean. Some of my teachers thought they were OK!

7. Bias to watch for: Publishers and bookstores—they want to sell books, no matter what kind. I have to watch out for material that's just hyping romance writing. Would data about bestsellers prove cultural value? Probably not. Need to find serious discussion, not just somebody arguing back at MacFarquhar.

8. Words for searching: "romance novels" (obviously), "reading" ?? (possibly too broad) "readers" ?? Maybe look for reviews of books by specific authors—Nora Roberts, Amanda Quick—and see how reviewers talk about them for evidence of cultural value. Look for author names on bestseller list? Ask at bookstore?

● **FOR WRITING AND DISCUSSION**

Working individually or in small groups, use the question analysis method to develop a more productive approach than Stacey's for researching a paper about the potential negative effects of Barbie dolls.

1. Start by brainstorming a few possible research questions. Then choose one that you consider significant to use for practicing all eight steps of the QA method.
2. Compare notes with other classmates or groups to see how many different approaches to the subject your class can come up with. ●

Planning Your Search:
Background Information

The QA prompts asking about experts, publication type, controversy, and bias all draw attention to matters that are important for rhetorical reading: the credibility, intended audience, and evident purpose of the sources you might examine. Initial clues about these matters will often be evident in the basic bibliographic information for a source. In other words, the same information that helps you locate materials may also help you quickly assess the reliability and relevance of a potential source. That assessment will in turn help you make good decisions about how far you want to pursue retrieval of that source.

The background information we provide here about the kinds of sources you might retrieve will help you use the QA questions and the questions for evaluating sources in the next section. At the end of the chapter we include more excerpts from Jenny's research log to illustrate how one student applied these guidelines to her own work. As you look over Jenny's log entries, note that as she sifts through potential sources and refines her purpose she continues to ask questions.

PUBLICATION CONTEXTS

QA questions 3 and 4 ask you to consider—before you start searching—what types of materials to look for and where you might find them. In general, your preferred sources should be those that have undergone solid editorial and fact-checking processes. Whether you access your materials in the library stacks, through an electronic library database, or through a Web search engine, you must scrutinize their contexts and purposes for relevance and reliability. We recommend searching your library's catalogue and periodicals databases before jumping on the Web, which contains garbage as well as gold. It can be difficult to assess the credibility of Web authors or the motives of a site sponsor; furthermore, the Web's global reach and the vastness of its contents make finding relevant and reliable overviews difficult. For example, when Jenny did a Web search for "romance novels," she turned up 147,000 hits, which a quick sampling suggested were mostly book lists and fan mail.

The abundance and immediacy of information now available through the Internet make careful scrutiny crucial to your research work, especially during the early stages of your research, when your main goal is to catch the drift of the published conversation relevant to your research question. Once you have read some good overview materials from sources you know are reputable, you will be more adept at judging whether the opinions expressed on an impressive Web page or in a Web log (or "blog") are grounded in genuine expertise. As knowledgeable as some of those opinions might seem, as enjoyably irreverent as critiques of media icons on "watchdog" Web sites such as Cursor.org or the Media Research Center (mrc.org) might be, these assertions usually come directly from just one person, with no intermediaries to check facts or calm him or her down. Whether you are reading in print or on line, the more you feel like someone is shouting, or the more ads that come along with the source, the more cautious you need to be. For academic papers, you need sources with a calm, evenhanded approach.

For currency and reliability (but not always evenhandedness), periodicals with large circulations and good reputations are your best bet. The editorial process at national newspapers, magazines, and journals is typically rigorous, more rigorous than for most materials that appear only on the Web. This editing work represents major investments of time and money. It involves multiple readers, fact-checking, quote-checking, and even background-checking of sources who are quoted. With so many people not only checking content but staking their professional reputations on quality and credibility, such materials clearly deserve preference. This is not to say that there are no reliable materials on Web sites. Many Web materials have undergone rigorous editorial processes, and print periodicals often publish archives and major articles on the Web. But for the sake of efficiency in both searching and evaluating, we recommend print periodicals for their consistent reliability.

LIBRARY DATABASES AND WEB SEARCH ENGINES

Library databases (such as ProQuest or Lexis-Nexis) and Web search engines (such as Yahoo! or Google)—all at your command from a desktop computer—will lead you to significantly different types of material because they search entirely different parts of the Internet.* Libraries pay substantial subscription fees for the database services that give you access to electronic archives of material that has appeared in print periodicals—magazines, scholarly journals, and major newspapers. "We pay for quality," librarians at both public and university libraries commonly stress at student orientations. In contrast, Web search engines search the free access part of the Internet. You can use these engines without charge because their revenue comes from advertisers. When you enter keywords in the search box of one of these engines and click "search," the software scours

---

*We follow the practice of using "Internet" to refer to the entire network of linked computers around the world and "Web" to refer to material available through the graphical interface used by browsers such as Netscape and Internet Explorer.

computers around the globe—all the computers linked to the free access portion of the Web—to find postings that include your word or phrase. Every item or "hit" on your results list represents a place on one of those computers where the words are found. Within seconds you can accumulate an overwhelming number of potential sources, most of them unreliable and unrelated to your purposes. Indeed, even those links that do appear helpful might no longer be working, or might take you to a Web site where a promising article or report is no longer available.

In contrast, clicking "search" in a database to which a library subscribes sets off a search of the indexes and archives of sources recommended by experienced researchers and experts in a wide variety of fields. The focus is primarily on print sources, but some databases have begun to index materials from radio and TV broadcasts, particularly public radio and television. Even if a transcript isn't available in the database, the abstract's information about a date and program may enable you to find the audio or video via the network's Web site.

Some specialized databases are available only on CD-ROM in the library itself, but the extensive general interest databases are stored on computers that may be miles away from the library, computers that while conducting your search might also be conducting a search for your best friend from home, who is attending school in another state. When you use these databases from campus, they may seem as free of cost as a Web search engine; however, be assured that libraries do pay subscription fees to the database companies. That is why access is often limited or restricted off campus.

PRINT PERIODICALS AS A STARTING POINT

Librarians usually recommend that student researchers begin a research project by using a periodicals database to look for relevant magazine and journal articles. These materials are easy to access, efficient to use, and more current than books, which take a long time to write and manufacture.

Periodicals databases are indexed according to traditional bibliographic categories (author, article title, publication title, etc.) as well as specialized search terms connected to subject matter. When you enter search terms, the computer checks these indexed categories as well as article abstracts, a process that results in a list of bibliographic citations with the titles and brief abstracts of relevant articles. These lists are usually much smaller and more manageable than those produced by Web searches. As you will see in the next section, rhetorical readers can pick up important evaluative cues from this material.

A bonus of database searches is that most of the citations on a results list will include all the article's official subject terms, which often offer valuable clues about a more efficient way to conduct your research. For example, if you have been using the term "capital punishment" or "secondary school," you might discover that "death penalty" or "high school" would yield more extensive or focused results in that database. However, manipulating subject terms and doing advanced searches can be a complex and frustrating business. If you aren't getting the results you expect, ask a librarian for help.

General Interest and Specialized Periodicals

Your ability to understand your sources will be important to the success of your project, so you need to find material written at a suitable level of expertise. You can count on being able to read general interest publications comfortably, but if they seem oversimplified (perhaps even sensationalized) or don't provide the depth of information you are looking for, try a newsstand periodical that provides in-depth discussion for the general public on certain topics, such as *Sports Illustrated*, *American Health*, *Money*, or *Psychology Today*. These can be good places for a student researcher to find extended but readily understood material. Be forewarned, however: The more specialized the publication, the greater the likelihood that you will find it difficult to understand, either because the material is too technical or because the author assumes readers are more familiar with the subject than you are. If your question has been addressed only at these high levels of scholarship, you will probably need to revise it.

Scholarly Journals

In the academic world, the most highly regarded periodicals are peer-reviewed journals, also known as *refereed journals*. Articles published in them have been approved by several experts as meeting high scholarly standards and contributing to new knowledge. These high levels of credibility make these journals excellent sources for college papers. The drawback is that material written for experts and scholars may be difficult for readers outside the field to understand. However, the abstracts and literature reviews that are standard in this genre can often provide helpful background. Furthermore, even if you cannot understand all the details in material from scientific journals such as the *New England Journal of Medicine* or *JAMA*, reading the abstract, background, and conclusions sections of a study may provide you with better insights than you will find in a newspaper report of that same study.

Evaluating Potential Sources

In this section we offer specific questions to guide your evaluation of texts you are considering as sources for a research project. These questions show how to apply your rhetorical reading skills to infer the original context and purpose of potential sources. Your understanding of a source's context and purpose will give you a basis for answering the following questions:

- How will this source help me answer my research question?
- How can I use this source in my own writing?

QUESTIONS TO ASK ABOUT RELEVANCE

You can determine many basic relevance issues from the bibliographic information you will find in library catalogs and databases. (For Web sources, however, we recommend that you examine the actual source, not just the link supplied by the search engine.)

To evaluate a potential source's relevance to your project, you need to ask three basic questions about its purpose and method.

1. *What ideas and information does this text offer?* For answers about a print publication, examine the title, subtitle, and abstract in the bibliographic citation. Also note carefully the title of the magazine or journal the article appeared in, or, if the publication is a book, note the publisher. What you already know or can discern about the intended audience of the periodical or the book publisher will indicate the article's approach.
2. *Can I trust the source of information?* Consider what you know or can gather about the author's and the publisher's or Web sponsor's credentials and reputation. For Web sources, if there's no evidence of a reputable site sponsor, don't use the source.* (Material from an individual's home page isn't usually acceptable for academic papers, no matter how impressive it may appear.)
3. *Will I be able to understand what the source says—was it written for someone at my level of expertise?* Draw inferences about the intended readers from the title, publisher's reputation, and abstract, then spot read as needed. If the article is full of technical material, concentrate on making sense of the abstract, the literature review, and the conclusions sections.

QUESTIONS TO ASK ABOUT CURRENCY AND SCOPE

Take your evaluation further by using bibliographic information about date of publication and length to determine how usable the material is for your purposes. Abstracts, if supplied, will frequently help you catch a publication's tone and scope, but in many instances you may have to find paper copy that you can skim to see if you want to read the source in detail. Use the following questions as a guide:

1. *How current is the source?* You will usually want the most recent information available, but if you are researching a historical phenomenon, "current" doesn't necessarily mean "recent."
2. *How extensive is the source? How much detail is present? What kind of evidence is used?* A twenty-page article contrasting American and Japanese management styles might be just what you need, or it might be far too detailed for your purposes. A cheery three-paragraph piece in *Glamour* or *GQ* about the value of regular dental checkups might enable you to make a

---

*"Site sponsor" refers to the organization sponsoring the Web page, not to advertisers who may be listed on it.

point about dental education in popular magazines, but it probably won't tell you much about how well people take care of their teeth or the quality of available dental care.

QUESTIONS TO ASK ABOUT
AUTHORS AND EXPERTS

Your background knowledge about subject matter and sources will often help you answer questions about the trustworthiness of an author or expert. When you need more information, look for quick answers within the bibliographical data about the source, then try other available search tools as explained below. Once you have selected certain materials to read in depth, use those texts to consider again the following questions about credibility:

1. *What are the author's credentials and qualifications regarding the subject?* If you recognize the name, it will tell you a lot. But if you don't, see what you can tell about this person's professional expertise. An abstract or a note at the end of a full text article may supply biographical information. Is the writer an expert in the field? A journalist who writes about the subject frequently? A quick search by author (perhaps via a click on the name) will show you what else this person has written recently. You might discover, for example, that the author of a piece on rap music regularly writes about the business side of the entertainment industry. This discovery may signal that the article is not likely to help you if you plan to write about rap's roots in the African American folk tradition, but if you are interested in how rap has been marketed or how it fits into the larger entertainment market, looking for additional articles by this author may lead to just what you need.

2. *What are the credentials and qualifications of experts who are cited?* In journalistic pieces, the writer's expertise is probably less important than that of the sources interviewed. Gathering information about the people quoted usually requires skimming to see what background information is supplied. Looking for material written by those experts can lead to more indepth sources.

3. *What can you tell about the writer's or expert's political views or affiliations that might affect their credibility?* You are more likely to uncover this information in the text than in the citation. (Much of the time you have to use your rhetorical reading skills to infer the writer's ideology—see Chapter 4.) If the purpose of your paper dictates that you find out more about a writer's ideological biases, a quick search in *Books in Print* or in a biography database, or on the Web will probably tell you what you need to know. You might learn, for example, that a particular writer recently received an award from the American Civil Liberties Union or that a medical expert interviewed about the dangers of plastic surgery is a well-known celebrity doctor. It will be up to you to determine the extent to which this

information adds or detracts from the person's credibility in relation to your research project's purposes.

QUESTIONS TO ASK ABOUT PUBLISHERS AND SPONSORS

Crucial information for evaluating a source can become apparent when you examine the purposes and motives of its publisher. Whether you are considering a paper or online source, it is important to consider how and why the material has become available in the first place. These questions about audience, review process, and reputation will help you round out the process of evaluating your sources.

1. *What is the periodical's target audience? Is this a well-known general interest magazine or is it a little-known journal for a specialized audience? Is it known for providing good information about the subject that interests you?* If you are researching antidepressants, for example, you will find that articles in popular magazines are often upbeat about their value. You'll probably find more reliable information about the potential side effects of drugs in medically oriented journals.

2. *How extensive a review process did the article have to undergo before the text was published? Is it from a scholarly journal?* Most Internet materials have not undergone any editorial screening. But not everything on the Web is posted by individuals. As increasing numbers of print periodicals, particularly newspapers, post material on the Web, you will be able to rely on their editorial processes. Nevertheless, it's important to remember that most general circulation publications are driven by marketplace concerns. Their editors choose articles that will help sell copies (or draw eyeballs) because circulation increases advertising revenue. Be alert for overstatement.

3. *Is the publisher or site sponsor known to have a viewpoint that might influence its coverage of material relevant to your question?* Pay attention to liberal and conservative political biases, for example, not because you can avoid bias but because you may want to be sure to consult sources with different leanings. A wide variety of nonprofit, public service, and governmental entities have extensive and useful Web sites. You must determine how the organization's mission may influence its Web presentations. If you use material from an organization known for supporting certain causes or positions, scrutinize it carefully and be sure to let your own readers know any relevant but nonobvious information about the source's reputation.

MORE EXCERPTS FROM JENNY'S RESEARCH LOG

To illustrate how a student might apply these evaluation strategies to her own research project, we conclude this chapter with more excerpts from Jenny's research log.

Evaluating Sources

My Searches

"Romance novels" and "Romance + reading" led me to lots of articles in <u>Publishers Weekly</u> about publishing trends (more emphasis on romance novels from a multicultural point of view, for example) and specific authors. But I don't want to write about the commercial side of this.

Most Relevant Article So Far

TIME, 3/20/2000, "Passion on the Pages" – Paul Gray and Andrea Sachs. (EBSCOhost). Abstract suggests it's much more factual and analytical than the catchy title, but that's TIME. Definitely trustworthy and written for the general reader. It includes reports from a survey. I e-mailed full text to myself.

<u>Currency and Scope</u>? Yes, well-known magazine, fairly recent (more recent than LM, so it's an update!).

<u>Author and experts quoted</u>? Yes. Stats from the Romance Writers Association (self-interested?) and interview of a famous author, Nora Roberts (!). Paul Gray, author of article, writes book reviews for almost every issue of TIME. This is solid.

* * *

Still to Do

- I want to check out the Web page I saw mentioned in an <u>Entertainment Weekly</u> article: theromancereader.com.
- Find book reviews. Where? Do newspapers review romance novels? Seems like a good place to get an everyday view. Check.
- I saw a <u>Library Journal</u> article that reviewed TWO reference books about romance novels. Didn't print it out because I'm not sure how relevant it is. Depends. How could these reference books add to my points about cultural value?
- Most of all, I need to find something related to teaching and education!! Nothing's working on the databases. These books are so popular with

teenagers, people MUST have written about whether to use them in schools. <u>Ask a librarian where I should look.</u>

Summary

This chapter has described how rhetorical reading skills will help you succeed in two of your key tasks as a researcher: formulating questions and evaluating resources. Because college teachers expect students to demonstrate their own thinking about a given research question, successful academic papers are those in which the student's claims and commentary are more prominent than their research sources.

To assist your preresearch and research processes, we discussed the following:

- Question analysis (QA) prompts to use before you begin your active search for sources
- The differences between searching for sources through library databases and using Web search engines
- The differences in publication and editing processes for different kinds of print sources

We then recommended that you evaluate potential sources by applying questions about the following:

- The relevance of a text's purpose and method
- A text's currency and scope
- The background and reputation of authors and experts
- The credibility and likely biases of publishers and Web page sponsors

To illustrate these processes, we provided excerpts from Jenny's research log.

C H A P T E R   7

Making Knowledge: Incorporating Reading into Writing

The mind in action selects and orders, matches and balances, sorting and generating as it shapes meanings and controls their interdependencies.

—Ann E. Berthoff

I n this chapter we address one of the biggest challenges in college writing: incorporating other texts into your own without letting them take over. The techniques we present here will help you foreground your sense of purpose and thus to author strong, rhetorically effective texts. As we have stressed in the preceding chapters, composing a text is an opportunity to add your voice to the ongoing conversation about a particular topic. Your readers, whether your peers or your professors, want to read what *you* have to say, not a rehash of what others have said. Our warning against "passive writing" in Chapter 5 urged you to take an active role in analyzing how the goals and methods of your source materials fit with your purpose for writing. In Chapter 6, we provided guidelines and evaluation questions for selecting source materials directly relevant to the questions that shape your research inquiries. We now turn to specific techniques for using these materials to extend and develop *your* points and for making the distinctions between your ideas (and words) and your sources' ideas (and words) absolutely clear to your readers.

First, we offer guidelines for three methods of incorporating source material into your own writing: summary, paraphrase, and quotation. Your careful use of these techniques will help you avoid the "patch-writing" we described in Chapter 5 and steer clear of any hint of academic dishonesty or plagiarism. Next we explain how to use attributive tags and in-text citations to connect your sources to your own argument. We also show you the rhetorical value of attributive tags for enhancing your own credibility and guiding your reader's response to your sources. In the second half of the chapter, we provide guidelines for in-text parenthetical references in the formats of both the Modern Language Association (MLA) and the American Psychological Association (APA). (Explanations and guidelines for creating bibliographic lists of sources in both formats are provided in the appendix, Building a Citation with MLA and APA Formats, along with numerous model citations.) At the end of the chapter, Jenny's "extending the conversation" paper, "Romance Fiction: Brain Candy or Culturally Nutritious?", which uses MLA format, illustrates many of the principles we discuss.

Summary, Paraphrase, and Direct Quotation

The effective use of sources in your papers will enable you to position your ideas in relation to those of others and will establish your credibility as an informed writer. Success in this aspect of your writing will be measured by your ability to incorporate the words and ideas of others judiciously (keeping readers' attention on *your* points), smoothly (using clear, grammatically correct sentences), and correctly (representing the points and language of your sources without distortion). In the next few pages, we will discuss in detail three techniques for accomplishing these goals: summary, paraphrase, and direct quotation. We summarize our advice in Table 7.1 (p. 141). Because each technique serves a useful and distinct purpose, you should become adept at all three so that you can choose the one that best suits your purpose. The way that you use sources in your texts should be a careful rhetorical choice.

USING SUMMARY

Summary is probably the most common way of incorporating a source in your own writing. As we described in Chapter 3, when you summarize all or part of another writer's text, you present in your own words a condensed version of that writer's points. It is best to introduce a summary of others' work with an attributive tag alerting the reader to the fact that what follows comes from an outside source, and you must provide an accurate reference that pinpoints where others can find that source.

Summarizing is an especially effective rhetorical strategy in the following situations:

- When the source directly supports your thesis, or alternatively, when the source offers a position you wish to argue against or analyze
- When the source offers important background information for your ideas
- When you need to provide readers with an overview of a source's whole argument before analyzing particular ideas from it
- When you want to condense and clarify information from a source

The length of your summary will depend on its location and function in your paper. Your goals for your paper will dictate how much of a source you need to summarize. Usually it's better to summarize only material that is directly relevant to *your* purpose. (See pp. 58–61 for more details about summaries.)

Let's examine two different uses of summaries in Jenny's two papers about Larissa MacFarquhar's article, "Who Cares If Johnny Can't Read?" The first comes from the opening paragraph of Jenny's rhetorical analysis paper at the end of Chapter 4, "Caring If and What Johnny Reads." Notice how the summary gives readers a context for the analysis that will follow. Jenny's one-sentence summary nutshells MacFarquhar's whole argument.

SUMMARY EXAMPLE 1

As the attention-getting title of her essay suggests, MacFarquhar questions some common assumptions regarding reading, specifically that Americans read less than they used to and that reading books is better and more intellectually stimulating than watching television or surfing the Internet.

Our second example is a longer summary from paragraph 6 of Jenny's paper at the end of this chapter, "Romance Fiction: Brain Candy or Culturally Nutritious?" Jenny uses this summary to set up a series of paragraphs that will discuss in detail an article by Carol Ricker-Wilson, a high school teacher who uses romance novels in her classes. Ricker-Wilson is one of several experts Jenny uses to support her claim that romance fiction has cultural value.

SUMMARY EXAMPLE 2

Although not a romance fiction reader herself, Carol Ricker-Wilson, a high school English teacher, offers an interesting perspective on the potential educational value of romance novels in "Busting Textual Bodices: Gender, Reading, and the Popular Romance." Writing in the English Journal for teachers who think of romances as "escapist trash" (58), Ricker-Wilson argues that this widespread belief blinds teachers from seeing romance fiction's personal value to their students and its possibilities for classroom use.

The summary's opening sentence introduces Ricker-Wilson's credentials, which are of key interest here because she is an English teacher, someone whom readers would probably expect to condemn romance fiction. Ricker-Wilson's authority adds authority to Jenny's paper. The summary's second sentence articulates Ricker-Wilson's core point, which Jenny goes on to develop through additional summary as well as paraphrase and a few brief quotations.

We offer two cautions about writing summaries. First, you should summarize only the points that are essential to your purpose. Even though summaries may vary in length, summaries that are too long or that cover too many points will distract readers from your purpose. Second, make sure that your summary fairly and accurately represents the original text's meaning. Be on guard against distorting the original to make it fit your argument. Ask yourself whether the original author would consider your summary to be fair and accurate.

USING PARAPHRASE

Paraphrase involves a more detailed presentation of the ideas from a source. Because paraphrases follow the original wording closely, you must include the page number, if one is available, when you cite the source. Unlike summaries, in which you condense the original text's ideas, paraphrases restate in your words all of the original passage's points. Often, they are as long as or even longer than the original, so it is best to paraphrase only short passages.

Paraphrasing is a particularly valuable rhetorical strategy in the following situations:

- When you want to emphasize especially significant ideas by retaining all of the points or details from the original
- When you want to clarify ideas that are complex or language that is dense, technical, or hard to understand

Because paraphrase involves closely re-presenting the original text, you must take care not to give the impression that these are your ideas. Putting someone else's ideas into your own words does not make these ideas your own. To paraphrase effectively and ethically, you must translate the writer's wording entirely into your own words and acknowledge the source with an attributive tag and a citation.

To illustrate the process and rhetorical effects of paraphrasing, we invite you to consider the parallels and variations between a passage from the Ricker-Wilson article on romance fiction and a paraphrase of it from Jenny's paper about romance fiction.

GUIDELINES FOR EFFECTIVE PARAPHRASE

☐ Avoid mirroring the sentence structure or organization of the original.
☐ Simplify complex ideas by pulling them apart and explaining each smaller component of the larger idea.
☐ Use synonyms for key words in the original and replace unfamiliar or technical vocabulary with more familiar terms.
☐ As a check, try paraphrasing the passage twice, the second time paraphrasing your own paraphrase; then compare your second paraphrase with the original to make sure that you have sufficiently recast it into your own language.

RICKER-WILSON'S ORIGINAL PASSAGE

But while a number of researchers such as Radway and Christian-Smith have maintained that romance reading operates primarily as an unfortunate but justifiable effort to escape from the adversities of real heterosexual relations, it may also offer an escape from what its readers construe to be even less favorable depictions of women in other genres. Fundamentally, I would argue, romance readers *really like to read,* they like to read about women, and they don't want to read about their unmitigated despoliation and dispatch. But once readers venture out of the formulaic romance genre, fiction is a wild card and identification with female protagonists an emotional risk.

JENNY'S PARAPHRASE

Ricker-Wilson acknowledges that some researchers claim that romance fiction provides women readers with escape from their difficult relationships with the men in their lives. She counters this negative view by proposing that romance fiction permits readers to escape something even worse: the negative images of women in other literature. She argues that readers who enjoy romance novels do so because they enjoy reading about women but do not like to read about women who are victimized or killed off, as they often are in other forms of fiction (58).

Jenny's paragraph accomplishes the two important goals of paraphrase. It elaborates and thereby emphasizes two significant and surprising ideas from Ricker-Wilson: that reading romance fiction to escape might actually be a positive thing and that reading other types of fiction might actually be a bad thing for young women. Furthermore, her paraphrase recasts the scholarly language of the *English Journal* article into more everyday terms.

Paraphrasing difficult ideas or dense passages is a good way to help your readers understand the material as well as to demonstrate your own understanding of it. However, recasting scholarly or technical language can be difficult, so we offer some cautionary advice. First, take care to avoid the problem of inadequate paraphrase. If your paraphrase is too close to the original wording, you may open yourself to a charge of plagiarism. Second, to avoid the potential problem of inaccurate presentation, be sure you fully understand any passage you are paraphrasing. One valuable technique is to imagine how you would convey the gist of the source's point conversationally. If you can't move beyond the words of the original, it's likely that you need to obtain a better understanding of the ideas before you use them in your paper. Although students sometimes try to get around this difficulty by quoting entire passages, this tactic can actually make matters worse. Long quotations can suggest that you find the original points so daunting that you can't put them into your own words. As with summary, be concise: Paraphrase from the original only what you need to develop your points. A long paraphrase can draw so much attention to itself that it distracts the reader. Keep readers' focus on your ideas about how the source material fits your points.

USING DIRECT QUOTATION

Direct quotation inserts the words of someone else into your own text. Whenever you use another writer's exact wording, you must mark the beginning and end of the passage with quotation marks and provide as precise a reference to the original source as possible. Used selectively and sparingly, quotations strengthen your credibility by showing that you have consulted appropriate authorities on a particular subject. However, quoting too frequently or using unnecessarily long quotations in your text can actually undermine your credibility. Overreliance on direct quotations weakens your authority and suggests that you have no ideas of your own to contribute to the conversation.

Direct quotations are most effective in enhancing your credibility in the following situations:

- When the language of the source is vivid, distinctive, or memorable
- When the quotation directly supports a key point in your paper
- When the person quoted is such a well-known authority on the matter that even a few well-chosen words carry considerable weight

To demonstrate the importance of these guidelines, we present two versions of a passage from Jenny's paper on romance fiction. When she first composed the paper, Jenny included in the fourth paragraph the following long quotation from MacFarquhar to illustrate derogatory views of romance fiction.

INEFFECTIVE LONG QUOTATION FROM JENNY'S FIRST DRAFT
She says that romance writers are "producing mass-market entertainment that appeals to its consumers for much the same reason as McDonald's and Burger King appeal to theirs: It's easy, it makes you feel good, and it's the same every time. The point of a romance novel is not to dazzle its reader with originality, but to stimulate predictable emotions by means of familiar cultural symbols."

MacFarquhar's vivid comparison to McDonald's and Burger King led Jenny to include this quote in her first draft. But later, when she read over the whole paper to consider revisions, she realized that the quotation was too long for what she wanted to accomplish at that point in her text (the end of paragraph 4). She had already introduced her own claim about the positive aspects of romance fiction and was using the MacFarquhar quote to indicate typical criticisms of romance fiction that the paper would counter. But the long quotation unduly shifted the reader's focus to negative opinions about romance novels. Furthermore, the colorful language from MacFarquhar detracted from Jenny's own important phrase at the end of the paragraph: "brain candy." She decided to pare down her use of MacFarquhar by using paraphrase with a few direct quotations, a decision that shifts the focus to her own argument.

JENNY'S REVISED USE OF QUOTATION

She describes romance fiction as "mass-market entertainment" that appeals to people because "it's easy, it makes you feel good, and it's the same every time." Its purpose, she says, is not to stimulate thinking and the imagination, "but to stimulate predictable emotions by means of familiar cultural symbols."

The quotations that Jenny has woven into her own prose are now serving her purposes instead of competing with them. By using more of her own language, Jenny is able to keep the focus on her own argument. In addition, Jenny's revised version achieves greater coherence because her words "stimulate thinking and imagination" echo concepts she develops earlier in the essay as criteria for judging something's cultural worth. By replacing MacFarquhar's vivid phrase "not to dazzle its readers with originality" with her own less vivid phrase "not to stimulate thinking and imagination," Jenny links this paragraph back to the criteria.

The guidelines on page 140 will help you quote accurately and effectively. We must again add notes of caution. First, not only is absolute accuracy in quotations important ethically, but any inaccuracies will undermine your credibility. Furthermore, be sure that you are not quoting someone out of context. Doing so is a surprisingly common mistake because complex texts or unfamiliar subject matter can make it difficult to recognize changes in tone or references to opposing views. For example, although Larissa MacFarquhar's text isn't technical, its shifts in tone can be tricky. It would misrepresent her to quote her sarcastic statement— "Now, we don't care about reading anymore"—as if it were her opinion when it is actually one of the attitudes she seeks to discredit. Be sure that the way you use a quotation does not misconstrue or misinterpret its original meaning.

Our advice on using summary, paraphrase, and quotation is summarized in Table 7.1.

● **FOR WRITING AND DISCUSSION**

One way to develop skill at incorporating the ideas of others into your own papers is to see how other writers do it. To try this out, track the use of direct quotations in Jenny's paper at the end of this chapter.

ON YOUR OWN

Note all the places where she uses direct quotations, and describe how each quotation is used. Find places, for example, where she uses sources to support or illustrate one of her points, to represent an opinion she opposes, to increase her credibility, or to capture vivid or distinctive language from a source. Some of her direct quotations may serve more than one function.

GUIDELINES FOR USING DIRECT QUOTATIONS EFFECTIVELY

☐ Prefer short quotations. Use long quotations only rarely because they will distract from the focus of your own discussion.

☐ Whenever possible, instead of quoting whole sentences, work quotations of key phrases into your own sentences.

☐ Make sure you are absolutely accurate in the wording of direct quotations.

☐ Punctuate your quotations exactly as in the original.

☐ If you must use a longer quotation, instead of using quotation marks set the material off from the text using block indentation. In MLA format, quotations longer than four typed lines start on a new line, are indented a full inch, and are double-spaced. In APA format, quotations longer than forty words start on a new line, are indented a half inch, and are double-spaced.

☐ Make sure your use of quotations fairly and accurately represents the original source.

☐ Make sure you fully understand the ideas that you quote directly. While the words in a quotation may sound impressive, if you cannot explain them and relate them to your own ideas, incorporating the quotation will detract from your credibility instead of enhancing it.

☐ As part of your proofreading routine, compare all quoted material to the original passage and make any needed adjustments, no matter how small.

WITH YOUR CLASSMATES

Compare your lists and descriptions. Are there differences or disagreements about how a particular direct quotation is being used? How effectively does she use quotations? Are there any quotations that might have been eliminated or shortened? Are there any places where you think her paper might have been strengthened by the use of a direct quotation where there isn't one?   ●

Avoiding Plagiarism

Whether you are summarizing, paraphrasing, or quoting, you must give credit to others' words and ideas by using a recognized system for referring readers to your sources, such as the MLA and APA systems explained later in this chapter and in the appendix. These citation systems, widely used in undergraduate classes, use short in-text citations that refer to a full list of sources at the end of the paper.

TABLE 7.1 • DO'S AND DON'TS WITH SUMMARY, PARAPHRASE, AND QUOTATIONS		
When You Summarize	Do • Make your summary as concise as possible • Represent your source's meaning accurately and fairly	Don't • Distract readers by including points not directly relevant to your purpose
When You Paraphrase	Do • Paraphrase only what you need to develop your points • Be sure you understand the language you are paraphrasing • Recast sentences to create a genuine paraphrase	Don't • Merely change a few words • Distort the original's meaning or intention
When You Quote	Do • Keep the actual quotation as short as possible • Fit the quotation naturally into your own sentence structure • Verify the absolute accuracy of the quotation	Don't • Use quotes as a shortcut around difficult ideas • Distract readers with long quotes

With All Three Techniques

• Link your text to your sources with clear attributive tags and appropriate citations.

• Represent the source fairly and accurately.

You must acknowledge borrowed ideas and information, and all directly quoted language must be marked as such with quotation marks or appropriately indented formatting. Even if your quote is only a short phrase from the original source, quotation marks are essential. Omission of either the quotation marks or the reference information has the effect of creating a text that presents someone else's words or ideas as if they were your own. In that case, you are committing *plagiarism,* a serious form of academic misconduct in which a writer takes material from someone else's work and fraudulently presents it as if it were the writer's own ideas and wording.

The three most common forms of plagiarism are the following:

• Failure to use quotation marks to indicate borrowed language
• Failure to acknowledge borrowed ideas and information

- Failure to change the language of the source text sufficiently in a paraphrase

Student writers sometimes have problems managing the details of quotations because they neglect to take careful notes that clearly mark all directly quoted material. During their revision processes, inexperienced writers sometimes lose track of which sentences and phrases are directly quoted. To avoid such problems and symptoms of potential plagiarism, make sure you take scrupulous care to mark all directly quoted language and its source in your notes. *Write down all relevant bibliographic information even before you begin reading and taking notes.* In drafting papers, some writers use color highlighting or put directly quoted language in a different font so that, as they move passages around during revision, they can keep track of which words are directly quoted. Other writers keep full original quotations at the end of their paper file or in a separate electronic file so that they can check for accuracy and proper citation as part of their final preparations before submission.

You must also acknowledge borrowed ideas and information. That is, all ideas and information that are not your own require citation through attributive tags, internal citation, and the list of sources at the end of the paper. The only exception is common knowledge. Common knowledge, as the phrase suggests, refers to information and knowledge that is widely known. (For example: George Washington was the first president or thunderstorms are more likely in hot weather.) You can verify that certain information is common knowledge by consulting general information sources such as encyclopedias. If you are in doubt about whether something is common knowledge, or if you are concerned that your readers might credit an idea to you that is not yours, cite your source.

Perhaps the most difficult aspect of incorporating sources in a way that avoids plagiarism is sufficiently rewording the language of a source when you paraphrase. (This is why we recommend paraphrasing source material twice.) As we noted in the section on paraphrase, using the same sentence pattern as the original source and changing only a few words does not create an acceptable paraphrase, even if the writer includes a reference to the source. In the following examples, compare the acceptable and unacceptable paraphrases with the original passage from Paul Gray and Andrea Sachs's "Passion on the Pages," one of the sources on romance fiction that Jenny used for her paper:

ORIGINAL

Other genres—mystery, thriller, horror, sci-fi—attract no cultural stigma, but those categories also appeal heavily to male readers. Romances do not, and therein, some of the genre's champions argue, lies the problem.

PLAGIARISM

According to Gray and Sachs, other types of books—horror, mystery, sci-fi—experience no cultural stigma, but these types of books are those that appeal mainly to male readers. Romances, by contrast, do not, and that, some of its champions argue, is the problem (76).

ACCEPTABLE PARAPHRASE

> According to Gray and Sachs, popular books that attract mostly male readers, such as science fiction and thriller novels, do not suffer the same public condemnation as romance novels. Some fans of romance fiction believe that this is no coincidence and that condemnation of it is due to the fact most of its readers are female (76).

By following the guidelines we present for quoting and paraphrasing, you can incorporate the ideas of others while avoiding plagiarism. We close this section by passing along a final bit of advice: when incorporating materials from outside sources, write with your eyes on your own text, not on your source.* Your unfolding text should come from your mind, not someone else's text.

Using Attributive Tags

All three of the techniques we have described for incorporating source material—summary, paraphrase, and quotation—work best with *attributive tags* such as "Ariel Jones says" or "According to Ariel Jones."† These short tag phrases connect or attribute material to its source. In the process of acknowledging the source, the tags can also enhance the rhetorical effect of your text by giving readers valuable information about the credibility of that source, shaping your readers' response to it, and demonstrating that you, not your sources, are in charge. Here's how they do all this.

1. Attributive tags help readers distinguish your sentences and ideas from those in your sources (whether summarized, paraphrased, or quoted). In fact, a lack of attributive tags is often symptomatic of the passive patch-writing we have been warning against. As illustration, consider the difference between two versions of a sentence from Jenny's paper.

CONFUSION CAUSED BY LACK OF ATTRIBUTIVE TAG

> Romance readers insist on formulaic plots of "childlike restrictions and simplicity," and as a result, these books lack "moral ambiguity" (Gray and Sachs 76).

SENTENCE REVISED WITH ATTRIBUTIVE TAG

> The *Time* article mentioned earlier claims that romance readers insist on formulaic plots of "childlike restrictions and simplicity," and says that as a result, these books lack "moral ambiguity" (Gray and Sachs 76).

---

*This advice comes from *The Craft of Research* by Wayne Booth, Gregory Colomb, and Joseph Williams, who say "If your eyes are on your source at the same moment your fingers are flying across the keyboard, you risk doing something that weeks, months, even years later could result in your public humiliation" (Chicago: U Chicago P, 1995), 170.

†We are grateful to freelance writer Robert McGuire, formerly a writing instructor at Marquette University, for his valuable insights and advice about attributive tags.

As the first sentence begins, a reader has every reason to think that it states Jenny's ideas. Matters become confusing when the quotation marks signal that another voice has entered the text, but we don't know its source and the authors' names in the citation are not particularly informative. Readers would have to go to the works cited list to get the contextualizing information that the second sentence provides. In contrast, the attributive tag in the revised sentence not only makes clear the source of the idea, but specifically refers back to earlier discussion of material from the same source.

2. Attributive tags enhance your credibility by showing readers that you are careful with source materials and remain in charge of the paper. You are the one lining up and tying together source materials to fit your purposes for writing. Notice that the tags in these two sentences excerpted from the second paragraph of Jenny's "Brain Candy" paper allow her to link together two sources in a way that helps her build toward her own defense of romance fiction.

> MacFarquhar's essay offers extensive evidence that Americans are reading more than ever, especially "popular fiction" like romance novels. A July 2000 Time magazine article verifies this claim and reports that over 50% of all paperbacks sold in the United States each year are romance novels (Gray and Sachs 76).

3. Attributive tags enhance your text's credibility by indicating the credentials or reputation of an expert you are using as a source. For example, you might say "high school teacher Sam Delaney," "Molly Smith, an avid fan of romance literature," or "Josephine DeLoria, a controversial defense lawyer." Sometimes, credentials will convey more information than a name will: "the Justice Department's main espionage prosecutor for over twenty years."

4. Attributive tags provide a quick method of showing readers the published context of your source material. This context will help you show how the text you are writing fits within a published conversation. Here are some examples: "In her review of Victoria M. Johnson's book, Martha Smith argues . . . ," "Kim Ochimuru, in an article detailing the results of the Harvard study, contends . . . ," or "A letter to the editor objecting to the paper's editorial stance outlines the following complaint."

5. Attributive tags give you the opportunity to shape reader's responses to the material you are presenting. Your choice of verb to describe the source's influence is important because it will imply your attitude toward the source. Some verbs suggest that you agree with the source and others suggest doubt about what the source says. For example, the first two of the following examples convey the writer's positive attitude toward the source material being introduced; the second two convey a skeptical attitude, leading the reader to expect that the writer will counter the source's point:

> A July 2000 *Time* magazine article verifies this claim.
> Research by Carskadon and her colleagues documents the scope of the problem.

Predictable plots, so the argument goes, offer escape.

Some literary critics claim that the books depend too much on magic.

Attributive tags work best near the beginning of a sentence, but can be placed after other introductory phrases at any natural break. Here are some examples of tags placed at different points in sentences:

Published in 1997 in the online journal *Slate,* MacFarquhar's essay offers . . .

At the end of her essay, MacFarquhar challenges readers . . .

Its purpose, she says, is not to stimulate thinking and the imagination, but . . .

Your first attributive tag about a source is likely to be longer than subsequent ones, as illustrated by these contrasting examples from Jenny's paper:

Although not a romance fiction reader herself, Carol Ricker-Wilson, a high school English teacher, offers . . .

According to Ricker-Wilson . . .

Ricker-Wilson argues . . .

In some instances, an author's name may not be as interesting or important to your readers as the place where an article appeared. For example, Jenny's reference to *Time* at the start of the following sentence tells readers much more than the authors' names would have; the parenthetical citation with the authors' names provides the necessary reference information.

PERIODICAL TITLE USED AS ATTRIBUTIVE TAG

A July 2000 <u>Time</u> magazine article verifies this claim and reports that over 50% of all paperbacks sold in the United States each year are romance novels (Gray and Sachs 76).

As the various preceding examples illustrate, attributive tags can offer a variety of information in accordance with a writer's purpose and sense of the intended audience's background knowledge. The possibilities range from facts that appear in citations (e.g., author's name, work's title, publisher, or date) to supplementary details about the author (e.g., credentials or purpose) or about the work (e.g., its context or reputation since publication). Of course, if you used all this information in one tag, the sentence would have hardly any room left for your own ideas. You don't want to overwhelm your readers with details that don't immediately convey significance. Readers can always find complete titles and publication information on your works cited or references list. If you decide readers need a lot of background, you may want to provide it in a separate sentence, as Jenny does at the beginning of her extended discussion of the Ricker-Wilson article: "Although not a romance fiction reader herself, Carol Ricker-Wilson, a high school English teacher, offers an interesting perspective on

---

GUIDELINES FOR USING ATTRIBUTIVE TAGS EFFECTIVELY

☐ Make the tag part of your own sentence.

☐ The first time you bring in a particular source, put the tag before the quotation or summary so that readers will have the background they need when they reach the borrowed source material.

☐ Vary the format and vocabulary of your tags. You want to avoid a long string of phrases that repeat "according to" or "he says."

☐ Provide just enough background to help readers understand the significance of the material you are bringing in, not everything there is to say about the source.

☐ Base your decisions about attributive tags on what you are confident readers will recognize and what will help them recognize the relevance of the source you are using. For example, *Time* is a well-known magazine and the *Journal of Urban History* has a self-explanatory title, so using those titles in a tag would probably provide more context than an author's name would. However, stating that an article appeared in a journal with an ambiguous title—for example, we are aware of at least three periodicals named *Dialogue*—would probably be pointless without further explanation. Rather than use space explaining the audience and purpose of the journal, it would be preferable to supply a brief context-setting phrase about the author's background or about how the material you are using fits the larger published conversation.

---

the potential educational value of romance novels in 'Busting Textual Bodices: Gender, Reading and the Popular Romance.'"

Using Parenthetical Citations

Clear, accurate *citations* of outside sources are an essential element of academic writing. Designed to help readers locate source materials, citations present a formalized statement of a work's author, title, publication date, publisher, and exact location—that is, page numbers for anything shorter than a book and/or an Internet address. As we explained in the section on avoiding plagiarism, citations are required for statistics, quotations, paraphrases, and summaries of other writers' work and ideas—any information that is not common knowledge. Citations give credit where credit is due, and help you show your readers how and where you are positioning your ideas within a published conversation. Furthermore, like attributive tags, citations add to your authority and reveal the quality of the sources you used. When handled well, they also enhance a text's readability.

In the remainder of this chapter, we explain how to create and use parenthetical citations in both MLA and APA formats—what to include and where to place the in-text citations in your sentence. In the Building a Citation appendix you will find guidelines for creating MLA and APA bibliographic lists as well as models for complete bibliographic citations for a variety of sources.

UNDERSTANDING ACADEMIC CITATION CONVENTIONS

All academic disciplines require that you cite sources, but different disciplines use different formats, known as *citation conventions*. Each set of conventions specifies a particular format for presenting information that refers readers to a source. In this book, we discuss the two citation systems most commonly required in undergraduate courses: the Modern Language Association (MLA) format, used widely in the humanities, and the American Psychological Association (APA) format, used widely in the social sciences.* Both systems rely on brief *in-text* or *parenthetical citations* in the body of the paper that are keyed to a list of complete citations—alphabetized by authors' last names—at the paper's end. The short in-text references, placed within parentheses inside any sentence that contains material derived from outside sources, provide readers with enough information to locate the full citation on the list. Full citations help readers see what kinds of materials the writer used as a basis for the current text, what information was used from a particular source, and exactly where the original material can be found.

In-text citations are placed in parentheses to minimize the intrusion of bibliographic information on the reading experience. When a writer has handled the citations well, readers hardly notice them as they read but can return to them and use them to find additional information efficiently. Here's an example from Jenny's paper.

MLA IN-TEXT CITATION

> . . . 50% of all paperbacks sold in the United States each year are romance novels (Gray and Sachs 76).

The authors' names inside the parentheses tell readers where to find the full citation of the work on the alphabetized works cited list at the end of the paper.

CORRESPONDING FULL CITATION ON MLA WORKS CITED LIST

> Gray, Paul, and Andrea Sachs. "Passion on the Pages." Time 20 Mar. 2000: 76-78. Academic Search Elite. EBSCO. Memorial Lib., Marquette Univ. 31 July 2000 <http://www.epnet.com/>.

The page number in the parenthetical in-text citation will help the reader pinpoint the cited material.

---

* Our discussion here and in the appendix is based on Joseph Gibaldi, *MLA Handbook for Writers of Research Papers*, 6th ed. (New York: MLA, 2003) and the *Publication Manual of the American Psychological Association*, 5th ed. (Washington, DC: APA, 2001).

The MLA and APA systems use slightly different formats and punctuation for both in-text citations and the full lists of works those citations refer to. These lists are referred to as "Works Cited" in MLA format and as "References" in APA format. Both systems require that every source on a Works Cited or References list be referred to within the paper (by either a parenthetical citation or an attributive tag) and that full information about every source referred to is available in the list at the end of the paper. Before we go any farther, we want to assure you that the details of citation conventions are not something to memorize. Scholars regularly consult models and guidelines such as those in this chapter and the appendix. You should do the same.

Because accurate use of a discipline's citation format necessitates attention to many formatting details, students sometimes overlook the rhetorical value of carefully prepared citations. First of all, clear, accurate, consistently formatted citations not only acknowledge sources appropriately but present you as knowledgeable and responsible. Furthermore, the content of citations communicates important information about the context and purpose of sources and, thus, about the reliability and authority of the source materials. When you read scholarly articles in specialized courses for your major, you will discover that citations are also an invaluable source of information about where you can find additional resources for research projects.

In some courses, particularly history, instead of in-text citations you may be asked instead to use footnotes that follow the format laid out in the *Chicago Manual of Style* (also called Turabian format, after the author whose handbooks popularized it). Furthermore, professors in political science or sociology might ask you to follow specialized conventions for their discipline. Professors in natural science and technical classes, where it is common to refer repeatedly to many sources, may ask you to use a citation-sequence method for in-text references such as that laid out in the Council of Science (formerly Biology) Editors' *CBE Manual* or a numbering system based on the overall alphabetical order of the sources in a list at the end of the paper. These and other formats are described in many composition handbooks; specialized guides are readily available on line or at library reference desks.* Whenever you aren't sure what is expected regarding citations, check with your instructor.

MLA IN-TEXT CITATIONS

Basic MLA In-Text Citation Format

The basic skeleton of an MLA in-text citation is simple: author's surname plus, if you are quoting or paraphrasing, the page number:

(Name 00)

---

*Online writing centers usually have helpful information that is easy to access. Try the Web sites for the centers at Purdue <http://owl.english.purdue.edu/handouts/research/index.html/> or the University of Wisconsin <http://www.wisc.edu/writetest/Handbook/Documentation.html>.

If your discussion refers to an entire work, not part of it, the *MLA Handbook* suggests that instead of inserting a parenthetical citation, it is better simply to mention the author's name in the sentence, as you would in an attributive tag.

In the examples that follow, note the details of format and punctuation for MLA style in-text citations, which are typically placed at the end of a sentence. The first example indicates that the quotation comes from page 76 of material by authors whose surnames are Gray and Sachs.

end of quote   authors   page number

. . . these books lack "moral ambiguity" (Gray and Sachs 76).

space   space   period

If no author is listed on a source, a shortened form of the work's title is used. The next example indicates that the writer is paraphrasing something on page 15 of a work without a listed author, the title of which begins with "Romance."

title punctuation   page number

. . . increased sales volume over the past decade ("Romance" 15).

space   space   period

Variations on the Basic MLA In-text Citation

The content of in-text citations depends partly on your rhetorical purpose and partly on the information you have about the source. Because these factors will vary, not every MLA in-text citation includes an author's name and a page number. We turn now to MLA guidelines regarding these variations. All of the guidelines stem from this paramount rule: Provide readers with the name or title word(s) that they will find at the left margin of the alphabetized Works Cited list.

When Citation Information Appears in an Attributive Tag. Earlier in the chapter, we pointed out that the inclusion of some bibliographic information in an attributive tag can have valuable rhetorical impact. When an attributive tag does provide bibliographic information, that information does not need to be repeated in a parenthetical citation. As long as there is no chance of confusion, only the page number for a quotation or paraphrase needs to appear in the parenthetical cite. Let's compare the rhetorical effect of two different decisions about combining a tag and a citation. In the first example, the spotlight is on the authors as the source of an idea or phrase.

According to Gray and Sachs, these books lack "moral ambiguity" (76).

In contrast, when the authors' names appear only in the parenthetical citation, the ideas in the sentence receive greater focus.

Some critics find that romance novels lack "moral ambiguity" (Gray and Sachs 76).

The disadvantage of this approach is its lack of clarity. Are Gray and Sachs the critics who complain about moral ambiguity, or do they simply report that some critics feel this way? Furthermore, the citation seems to imply that the work by Gray and Sachs was mentioned earlier. If it wasn't, a reader may feel confused.

When You Must Quote Indirectly. If you want to use something that one source attributes to another source, your best course of action is to find the original version and cite it directly. Only then can you be assured that the quotation is accurate and that you understand its context. If you can't get to the original, combine an attributive tag referring to the original source with a citation for your indirect source that includes the abbreviation "qtd. in"—for "quoted in." For example:

> Robert Hughes says that reading is a collaboration "in which your imagination goes halfway to meet the author's" (qtd. in MacFarquhar 66).*

Use "qtd. in" only when your source quotes from published material. When an author is simply quoting someone else's spoken words, from an interview, for example, no special note is needed—simply follow the guidelines for citing authors or titles.

When an Article Has Only One Page or Page Numbers Are Unavailable. MLA format permits omission of page numbers from an in-text citation, even for a quotation, for three types of materials: (1) a print article complete on one page, (2) a print article retrieved from a periodicals database in a format where it is not possible to pinpoint page numbers, and (3) an article published on a Web site without page or paragraph numbers. In these cases, the in-text citation needs to include only the author's name, even for a quotation. (The full citation on the Works Cited list should include page numbers, however.) The following example sentences quote from a newspaper column by Kathleen Parker that was complete on one page.

MLA IN-TEXT CITATIONS FOR AN ARTICLE COMPLETE ON ONE PAGE

> The shooting death of six-year-old Kayla Rolland outraged many people, including a columnist who said it pushed "the limits of rational thought" (Parker).

> Kathleen Parker responded that the shooting death of six-year-old Kayla Rolland pushed "the limits of rational thought."

When Paragraph Numbers Are Available. Some online publications provide paragraph numbers that both you and your readers can use to pinpoint a refer-

---

*To show how to use a page number in these citations, we've used the page number for the reprint in Chapter 3 of MacFarquhar's 1997 *Slate* article, "Who Cares If Johnny Can't Read?" You can find models for full citations of reprinted articles in the appendix.

ence when page numbers are not available. For MLA format, you should provide a paragraph number only if it appears in the original; don't count paragraphs yourself because different browsers may present the material differently. When you do cite paragraphs by number, use the abbreviation "par." after the author's name and use a comma to separate the two words:

(Stephens, par. 17)

When a Work Has More Than One Author. For two or three authors, include all their names; for four or more authors, you may use the first author's name plus "et al.," which abbreviates the Latin for "and others." The term should not be underlined; "al" is followed by a period. Some examples:

(Fisher and Rinehart 438)

(Fisher, Rinehart, and Manber 12)

(Manber et al. 84)

When a Paper Has More Than One Source by One Author. To avoid potential confusion on a works cited list that has two or more items by the same author, add a *short title* to the citation after the author's name, placing a comma between name and title and using the appropriate title punctuation—quotation marks or underlining. To create a short title, use the first word or the first few words of the full title, enough words for readers to find the right citation readily in the alphabetized works cited list.

MLA IN-TEXT CITATIONS WITH SHORT TITLES

(Friedman, "Eastern")

(Friedman, "Self-Destruction")

CORRESPONDING FULL MLA CITATIONS ON WORKS CITED LIST

Friedman, Thomas L. "Eastern Middle School." New York Times 2 Oct. 2001, late ed.: A25.

---. "Self-Destruction Flourishing." Milwaukee Journal Sentinel 17 June 2003: 15A.

When Two Authors Have the Same Surname. Use first and last name in any attributive tag, or add the author's first initial to the parenthetical citation:

Kathryn Schabel writes . . . (17).

(K. Schabel 17)

Mattias Schabel reports . . . (267).

(M. Schabel 267)

When a Source Doesn't List an Author or Editor. Many Web pages and short articles do not list authors. In these cases, the works cited entry will begin with the title of the article or Web page, so for the in-text citation, use a short title that matches it. For example, for an article without a listed author entitled "Can Antioxidants Save Your Life?" you would use the first two words for a short title:

> ("Can Antioxidants" 5)

(Merely using "can" would seem cryptic.) For some documents, such as a Web site or an annual report, an organization or agency—a *corporate author*—should be listed:

> (Greater Milwaukee Foundation)
> (Centers for Disease Control)

If you are citing an entire document rather than a specific part of it, it will often be better to name the organization in the text itself:

> In its annual report, the Greater Milwaukee Foundation lists . . .

Although some databases label such articles "anonymous," you should not use that word in your citations unless it actually appears in the original publication. In the event that you are working with two works with no listed author and the same title—for example, an encyclopedia article and Web site about jellyfish—MLA recommends that you include a distinguishing element from the full citations that will help readers locate the right source on the works cited list:

> ("Jellyfish," Britannica)
> ("Jellyfish," Ask Jeeves)

Placement of MLA In-Text Citations

For smooth reading, in-text citations work best at the end of the sentence in which you use material from the source. However, a citation can be placed at any natural pause in the sentence and should be placed as close as possible to the material it refers to. All quoted material should be cited immediately at the end of the phrase or sentence in which the quotation appears. Here is a hypothetical example of two citations in one sentence:

> . . . such romances are said to lack "moral ambiguity" (Gray and Sachs 76) or to feed unrealistic fantasies (Hopewell 15).

In disciplines that use MLA style, multiple references in one parenthetical citation are not common, but when they are needed, separate them with semicolons. While the previous example highlighted a direct quotation and a paraphrase, the following example with combined citations foregrounds a generalization based on ideas in those works:

> In the 1990s, several commentators noted that the plots of romance novels turn on unrealistically simple moral questions (Gray and Sachs; Hopewell).

MLA does not specify a particular sequence for references inside parentheses, but using alphabetical order would be a convenience to your readers.

When a summary of a source covers several sentences in a row, your citation may come at the end of the summary, but an attributive tag at its beginning should make it clear that you are about to draw someone else's work into your text and thus alert readers to expect the citation. In the following example of a multisentence summary, notice Jenny's placement of page number citations for the quotations. The attributive tags referring to Ricker-Wilson make it unnecessary to repeat her name in parenthesis.

Writing in the English Journal for teachers who think of romance fiction as "escapist trash" (58), Ricker-Wilson argues that this widespread belief blinds teachers from seeing romance fiction's personal value to their students and its possibilities for classroom use. By allowing a group of young women in her lower-track English class to read the novels of Danielle Steele for extra credit, she learned about the many benefits romance fiction offered her students. Among these were camaraderie and escape in a positive sense. According to Ricker-Wilson, these students became an "authentic community" of readers, regularly exchanging books and eagerly sharing their ideas about them (62).

APA IN-TEXT CITATIONS

Basic APA In-Text Citation Format

Developed for disciplines where scholars publish frequently and the currency of research is very important, APA format emphasizes dates of publication by requiring dates in parenthetical citations. Specific page or paragraph numbers are used only for direct quotations.

The basic APA internal citation provides the author's surname (or the work's title if no author is given) and the publication date, separated by a comma:

> (Name, year)

If a quotation is used, its page number is added after the abbreviation "p." or "pp." In APA style, this page information must be included even for articles that are complete on one page:

> (Parker, 2000, p. 10A)

To familiarize you with APA style, we draw attention to punctuation details in the following examples. The first is from the research article about adolescents' need for sleep by Wolfson and Carskadon (1998) that was discussed in Chapter 2 (pp. 25–28).* This reference tells readers where they can find major research that supports the sentence's assertion.

> Persistent sleep problems have also been associated with learning difficulties throughout the school years (Quine, 1992).
>
>   ↑   ↑   ↑
>
>   space   comma   period follows parenthesis

The second example is from a hypothetical student paper that quotes from the Wolfson and Carskadon article; it cites the pagination of the original publication. Notice that this format saves space inside the parentheses by using an ampersand between authors' names. However, in regular text, use "and" between authors' names as you normally would.

> Researchers suggest that "adolescent moodiness" is partly "a repercussion of insufficient sleep" (Wolfson & Carskadon, 1998, p. 885).
>
>   ↑↑   ↑   ↑ ↑↑   ↑
>
> closing space ampersand   commas │ period after parenthesis
> quotation mark   abbreviation

When you read articles that use APA style, you will see that authors often use long strings of citations as a shorthand way of establishing a foundation for the research they are reporting. Consider, for example, how much information is packed into the following sentence. Note that the four citations in the list are separated by semicolons.

> Over the past 2 decades, researchers, teachers, parents, and adolescents themselves, have consistently reported that they are not getting enough sleep (Carskadon, 1990a; Carskadon, Harvey, Duke, Anders, & Dement, 1980; Price, Coates, Thoresen, & Grinstead, 1978; Strauch & Meier, 1988).

The combination of the authors' names and the dates of publication provides the key to finding each work's full citation on the alphabetized list at the end of a paper or article, called "References" in APA style.

In the sections that follow, we explain some important variations in APA format for parenthetical citations. The following four guidelines will give you a solid foundation for creating APA parenthetical citations:

---

    *Many of our examples of sentences with APA citations are taken from or refer to this article. An APA references list entry for the article would look like this:

> Wolfson, A. R. and Carskadon, M.A. (1998). Sleep schedules and daytime functioning in adolescents. *Child Development 69,* 875–887.

An MLA style works cited citation for it can be found on page 35.

- Provide readers with the information they need to find a full citation on the references list. The word(s) in parentheses should match the word(s) at the left margin of the list.
- Always provide a date or the notation "n.d." for "no date."
- Use a comma between author and date.
- Page numbers, required for direct quotations, are marked with the abbreviation "p." or "pp."

Variations on the Basic APA In-Text Citation

APA format, like MLA format, provides for the content of in-text citations to vary according to the information available and the writer's rhetorical intent. The guidelines in this section show how to avoid repeating information already in attributive tags and how to distinguish among similar references when confusion is possible.

When Citation Information Appears in an Attributive Tag. If the author's name is already present in the sentence, the parenthetical cite includes only the date of publication. For example:

> A 6-year longitudinal summer sleep laboratory study by Carskadon and colleagues (1980) . . .

Conversely, if your sentence highlights the date, only the name would be needed in the parentheses.

> In 1980, the results of an important longitudinal study were published (Carskadon et al.).

Sentences highlighting a date are likely to include an author's name as well, making a parenthetical citation unnecessary unless a page number is needed for a quotation, as in these examples.

> In 1980, Carksadon and her colleagues published their important longitudinal study.

> In their 1998 study, Wolfson and Carskadon suggest that "adolescent moodiness" is partly "a repercussion of insufficient sleep" (p. 885).

When You Must Quote Indirectly. Finding the original source is always preferable because you may make incorrect assumptions about the context of a quotation. When you must indirectly cite a quotation from a published work, use an attributive tag to refer to the original publication and in the parenthetical citation insert APA's phrase "as cited in."

> Robert Hughes says that reading is a collaboration "in which your imagination goes halfway to meet the author's" (as cited in MacFarquhar, 2005, p. 66).

This citation of MacFarquhar's article refers to the reprint in Chapter 3 of this book. Note that APA format calls for using the date of the reprinted work.

When Page Numbers Are Unavailable. APA requires page numbers for articles complete on one page, but it does recognize that complete page numbers are sometimes not available in online databases or Web pages. In some instances, you may be able to use paragraph numbers to document quotations (see below). When a page number is unavailable, use just the author's name and the date in the citation, unless they are already provided in an attributive tag. If the source originally appeared in print, take careful notes so that you can provide beginning and ending page numbers—known as *inclusive pagination*—on the references list citation, which should follow APA format for material retrieved from a database or Web site.

When Paragraph Numbers Are Available. Because of the variations in Internet browsers and professors' expectations, we advise you to ask your instructor if citations by paragraph number are expected when page numbers are unavailable. APA suggests that if the original doesn't have page or paragraph numbers you can use headings to pinpoint the relevant section, and then count paragraphs from the heading to the location of the quoted material. To cite a paragraph instead of a page, put a comma after the date, insert either the ¶ symbol or the abbreviation "para.", and add the number. In the following reference to the online version of the MacFarquhar article, a paragraph number pinpoints the paraphrase:

> According to survey data, books on personal hygiene were popular at least as long ago as the 1930s (MacFarquhar, 1997, para. 7).

The next example illustrates how to provide headings plus a paragraph number. Note the punctuation and that APA format capitalizes only the first word of headings.

> Wolfson and Carskadon suggest that "adolescent moodiness" is partly "a repercussion of insufficient sleep" (1998, Discussion: Additional consequences section, ¶ 3).

When a Work Has More Than One Author. Multiple authorship is more common in the social sciences than in the humanities. To avoid confusing your reader you must designate the authorship of coauthored works carefully. Here are the APA guidelines for using "et al." (for "and others") in in-text references with multiple authors. For reference list entries, the guidelines are slightly different; see the appendix.

FOR WORK BY TWO AUTHORS

Use both names in all in-text references.

FOR WORK WITH THREE TO FIVE AUTHORS

On the first reference use each name; on subsequent references, use the first author's name, then "et al." You can use "et al." in attributive tags as well as in parenthetical citations.

FOR WORK WITH SIX OR MORE AUTHORS

Use the first author plus "et al." for all references.

In any instance where the "et al." form could refer to two or more articles on your list with the same publication date, give as many names as needed to identify each before inserting "et al." For example, the following citations refer to two articles published in 1997 by Carskadon (lead author) and Acebo (second author). In the subsequent references, note that "al" is followed by a period, then a comma before the date.

FIRST IN-TEXT REFERENCES

(Carskadon, Acebo, Richardson, Tate, & Seifer, 1997)

(Carskadon, Acebo, Wolfson, Tzischinsky, & Darley, 1997)

SUBSEQUENT IN-TEXT REFERENCES

(Carskadon, Acebo, Richardson, et al., 1997)

(Carskadon, Acebo, Wolfson, et al., 1997)

When a Paper Has More Than One Source by an Author. On most APA references lists, the year of publication serves to distinguish among several works by the same author or group of authors. However, if a list includes more than one work published in a given year with the same authorship, lowercase letters inserted immediately after the date serve to prevent confusion. These letters should be inserted according to the alphabetical order of the works' titles in the references list.

APA IN-TEXT CITATIONS WITH DATE AND LETTER

(Kramer, 2000a)

(Kramer, 2000b)

CORRESPONDING FULL APA CITATIONS ON REFERENCES LIST

Kramer, M. (2000a). Dreaming has content and meaning not just form. *Behavioral and Brain Sciences, 23*, 959.

Kramer, M. (2000b). The variety of dream experience: Expanding our ways of working with dreams. *Journal of the American Academy of Psychoanalysis, 28*, 727–729.

When Two Authors Have the Same Surname.   For the sake of clarity, use the author's first initial in either the text or a parenthetical citation, even if the years of publication are different:

> E. Sutton's study (2001)…
>
> (E. Sutton, 2001)
>
> According to M. Sutton (1990) . . .
>
> (M. Sutton, 1990)

When a Source Doesn't List an Author or Editor.   For short articles and Web pages that do not list an author, use the first few words of the title to create a short title for the parenthetical reference. APA style capitalizes only the first word of titles and subtitles and does not use title punctuation (quotation marks) for articles:

> (Can antioxidants, 1998)

Some works, particularly Web sites and print publications such as program brochures, annual reports, or publications of a government agency should be cited as having a group or corporate author:

> (Greater Milwaukee Foundation, 2002)
>
> (Centers for Disease Control, 2003)

If readers will understand an abbreviation sufficiently to find full information on the references list, group authors can be abbreviated. Indicate the abbreviation parenthetically when you first refer to the entity in a reference or attributive tag.

FIRST REFERENCE
> (Centers for Disease Control [CDC], 2003)

SUBSEQUENT REFERENCES
> (CDC, 2003)

If abbreviations can be misleading or confusing, such as "NSF" for both the National Science Foundation and the National Sleep Foundation, continue to spell out the group name in all references. If you want to refer to an entire Web site in general, not to cite a specific document within it, APA guidelines say that putting the URL in the text is sufficient reference, as in the following sentence:

> Much of this sleep research has been boiled down to advice for average consumers and is available at the Web site of the National Sleep Foundation (http://www.sleepfoundation.org/).

When a Source Doesn't Provide a Date Because dates are so important in APA format, when a work has none available, the in-text citation should include "n.d." (for "no date") where the date would normally be placed:

(McCormick, n.d.)

Dates are frequently not available on Web sites, where author names and page numbers are also frequently unavailable. In these cases, formulate the full reference, then for the parenthetical reference use the first few words as a title and insert "n.d." where the date would go. Consider the following example, which refers to a self-test for which no author or date is given on the National Sleep Foundation Web site:

(How's your sleep? n.d.)

We might have used the Web site sponsor, the National Sleep Foundation, as author but the reference communicates more both to a reader and to someone looking for the quiz if the title is used. We used the quiz's complete title because shortened versions, "How's" or "How's your," would be puzzling. The citation on the references page would begin with the title and list the Sleep Foundation, along with the URL and a date of retrieval. (See the appendix for models.)

Placement of APA In-Text Citations

Papers and scholarly articles that follow the APA citation style typically use parenthetical references not only to acknowledge the source of summarized, paraphrased, or quoted material, but to refer to and build on entire studies. Because clarity is crucial, APA references to published work should not be deferred to the end of a sentence or a natural sentence break; instead, they must be provided as soon as the work is mentioned. Thus, parenthetical citations of dates usually follow immediately after an author or group of authors is named in a sentence. Cites may even be placed between a subject and verb, as in the following examples from the introduction to Wolfson and Carskadon (1998).

> Price et al. (1978), for example, found . . .

> Although sleeping less than when younger, over 54% of high school students in a Swiss study (Strauch & Meier, 1988) endorsed a *wish for more sleep* (emphasis in original).

> Another consistent report (Bearpark & Michie, 1987; Petta, Carskadon, & Dement, 1984; Strauch & Meier, 1988) is that . . .

Similarly, all quoted material should be cited immediately. As a result, page references are often separated from the author-date reference. To illustrate, we have rewritten in APA style two excerpts from the earlier example in which Jenny uses short quotations from the Ricker-Wilson *English Journal* article.

> Ricker-Wilson (1999), writing for teachers who think of romance fiction as "escapist trash" (p. 58), argues that . . .

According to Ricker-Wilson (1999), these five women students became an "authentic community" (p. 62) of readers, regularly exchanging books and eagerly sharing ideas about them.

Finally, when you combine references within the same parentheses, use semicolons to separate items by different authors. APA specifies that the author-date items should appear in the same order as the works are listed on the references list; that is, arrange them first in alphabetical order; then put dates of works by the same author in chronological order, separated by commas. Arrange dates for works published by one author in the same year according to the alphabetical order of the lowercase letters appended to them. Here is a hypothetical example based on items in the Wolfson and Carskadon (1998) references list:

(Carskadon, 1982, 1990a, 1990b; Carskadon et al., 1986; Carskadon, Orav, & Dement, 1983; Carskadon et al., 1989.)

Summary

In this chapter we described the differences among summary, paraphrase, and direct quotation, and explained that skillful incorporation of source materials into your own texts enhances your credibility and clarifies how your ideas fit into the larger published conversation about a topic. Throughout the discussion we emphasized the importance of subordinating source materials to your own purposes, ideas, and organization. We stressed the importance of careful note-taking as a means of avoiding even inadvertent plagiarism. The guidelines we provided show how to

- Incorporate brief summaries, paraphrases, and direct quotations into your work
- Avoid plagiarism by using genuine paraphrases, taking careful notes, and attending to the details of bibliographic information
- Use attributive tags to help shape the response you desire from readers
- Provide clear and correct in-text citations using both MLA and APA formatting

In the sample student paper that follows, you will find numerous examples of these techniques. The appendix to this book offers models of full MLA and APA citations for many types of materials you will be likely to use in your own papers.

Incorporating Reading into Writing: An Example in MLA Format

Here is Jenny's researched evaluation argument, written in response to the assignment at the beginning of Chapter 6 (p. 119). It uses MLA format for citing sources.

Romance Fiction: Brain Candy or Culturally Nutritious?

In junior high school, I was a big fan of Sweet Valley
High novels. I read every one I could get my hands on, and
my friends and I passed them around and talked about the
characters as though they were a part of our group of
friends. Even then, I could see that there was a formula:
heroine pines for popular boy who doesn't know she's
alive; things look hopeless for a long time; then something
happens and he notices her; and in the end they walk off
into the sunset. Actually, knowing that there would be a
happy ending was part of the fun. The interesting thing
was how it would work out. My parents, who are both
teachers, considered these books a waste of time, but I
loved them anyway.

I haven't read novels like this since junior high, but
reading Larissa MacFarquhar's "Who Cares Why Johnny
Can't Read?" reminded me of this early fondness for
romance fiction and the widespread idea that these books
lack cultural value. MacFarquhar's essay offers extensive
evidence that Americans are reading more than ever,
especially "popular fiction" like romance novels. A July
2000 Time magazine article verifies this claim and reports
that over 50% of all paperbacks sold in the United States
each year are romance novels (Gray and Sachs 76). At the
end of her essay, MacFarquhar challenges readers to
consider whether it is reading in and of itself that has
cultural value or whether it is what people read (or watch
on television) that contributes to "the fertility of our
culture." Since romance fiction is so popular, it seems to
me that we ought to ask this question of romance fiction.
Does it have cultural value and contribute to "the fertility
of our culture"? Is it only brain candy or does it have
some cultural nutrition?

But how do we determine what contributes to cultural
growth or nutrition? Although it is unclear how
MacFarquhar herself might define and judge cultural
value, she refers disapprovingly to the "reputation for

Margin annotations:

1. Opens with a personal anecdote

Introduces tension

2. Explicitly connects to assignment

Detailed tag provides context

First MLA citation gives page number for statistic

No page or paragraph numbers online; author named in tag, so in MLA style, no citation for quotation

Clear statement of evaluation issue

3. New paragraph raises issue of criteria

educational and even moral worthiness" that books have acquired. According to MacFarquhar, book advocates claim that books activate the imagination and encourage original thinking by being "quirky and individualistic and real." Despite MacFarquhar's sarcasm about these claims for books, it seems to me that educational and moral worth as well as stimulation of the imagination and intellect are all legitimate bases for judging cultural value. However, research and the memory of my early reading experiences have convinced me that these criteria, though valid, are too limited. Other factors such as emotional sustenance and community building also contribute to our cultural welfare. In this essay, I review briefly the arguments of those who believe romance fiction is without cultural value, then offer arguments for why romance fiction does have cultural value, even in terms of traditional criteria, and certainly in terms of other, equally important, criteria.

4   The key reason many people believe that romance fiction has no cultural value is its lack of originality. Predictable plots, so the argument goes, offer escape but not intellectual stimulation. The Time article mentioned earlier claims that romance readers insist on formulaic plots of "childlike restrictions and simplicity," and says that as a result, these books lack "moral ambiguity" (Gray and Sachs 76). Although MacFarquhar makes no direct judgment about the cultural value of romance fiction, her description of this genre echoes the criticism of Gray and Sachs. She describes romance fiction as "mass-market entertainment" that appeals to people because "it's easy, it makes you feel good, and it's the same every time." Its purpose, she says, is not to stimulate thinking and the imagination, but "to stimulate predictable emotions by means of familiar cultural symbols." As my friends would put it, MacFarquhar describes romance fiction as brain candy.

Margin annotations:

Counters MacFarquhar; offers her own criteria

Maps how rest of essay will proceed; forecasts her delayed thesis

Clear statements acknowledge opposing views

Elaborates on views opposing hers

Compares MacFarquhar and *Time* critics

Weaves short quotations into her own prose

Ends paragraph with echo of "brain candy" from paragraph 2

However, many intelligent fans of romance fiction   5
would disagree. They, in fact, describe romance fiction as
having some of the characteristics that people traditionally
associate with cultural value. Katherine Hennessey Wikoff,
an English professor at Milwaukee School of Engineering
and a self-described "life-long romance reader," for
example, says that "Years of romance fiction amply
reinforced my own character growth." In her review of
Victoria M. Johnson's book, <u>All I Need to Know in Life I
Learned from Romance Novels</u>, Wikoff says that she "cut
her romance novel teeth" at age twelve on <u>Gone with the
Wind</u>, from which she learned both positive and negative
lessons: to be resourceful like Scarlett but not to be so
proud like Scarlett, who lost Rhett because she wouldn't
risk telling him she loved him for fear of rejection. Wikoff
goes on to list the life lessons she, like Johnson, claims to
have learned from romance fiction. A few examples are
these: "Communication is the key to a healthy
relationship"; "Attitude makes all the difference"; and
"Love changes everything." In Wikoff's opinion, and
apparently Victoria Johnson's, reading romance fiction can
be morally uplifting and contribute to character growth,
surely important cultural values.

Although not a romance fiction reader herself, Carol   6
Ricker-Wilson, a high school English teacher, offers an
interesting perspective on the potential educational value
of romance novels in "Busting Textual Bodices: Gender,
Reading, and the Popular Romance." Writing in the <u>English
Journal</u> for teachers who think of romances as "escapist
trash," Ricker-Wilson argues that this widespread belief
blinds teachers from seeing romance fiction's personal
value to their students and its possibilities for classroom
use. By allowing a group of young women in her lower-
track English class to read the novels of Danielle Steel for
extra credit, she learned about the many benefits romance
fiction offered her students. Among these were camaraderie

Rebuttal begins

Attributive tag gives credentials of expert

Attributive tag sets context for quotations and paraphrases

Review was complete on one page—in MLA format, no page references needed in an in-text citation

Moves to second expert supporting her view—entire sentence as attributive tag—title adds flavor

Summary sets up discussion in paragraphs 7–9

and escape in a positive sense. According to Ricker-Wilson, these students became an "authentic community" of readers, regularly exchanging books and eagerly sharing their ideas about them (62).

7   Ricker-Wilson acknowledges that some researchers claim that romance fiction provides women readers with escape from their difficult relationships with the men in their lives. She counters this negative view by proposing that romance fiction permits readers to escape something even worse: the negative images of women in other literature. She argues that readers who enjoy romance novels do so because they enjoy reading about women but do not like to read about women who are victimized or killed off, as they often are in other forms of fiction (58).

8   Finally, Ricker-Wilson argues that romance novels have educational benefits if they are treated seriously. Her one requirement for reading these books was that students write about them in response to her romance questionnaire, which asked about the depiction of women, romantic relationships, and other aspects of the novels (58). What Ricker-Wilson discovered was that her students were quite capable of criticizing these books and seeing the mixed messages they give to women. Despite Ricker-Wilson's reservations about some of the "troubling" messages sent by these books, she concludes that "popular romance offers one of the richest imaginable repositories for exploring conflicting understandings of gender and sexuality" (63).

9   Ricker-Wilson's point about the potential of shared reading experiences for building community is something that the publishers of romance novels seem to understand. A November 1999 Publishers Weekly article describes the trend of targeting new romance books to "niche markets," particularly African Americans, Latinos, and readers looking for a spiritual dimension in their romance reading

Annotations in left margin:

Cites page for quotation

Paraphrase recasts R-W's points into everyday language

Page citation for paraphrase

Summary continues

Page citation pinpoints information

Closes Ricker-Wilson discussion with quotation and page reference

Jenny's response to Ricker-Wilson begins, supported by another source

(Rosen). Another aspect of community is evident at The Romance Reader (TRR) Web site, where many fans of romance novels post reviews and comments. In an article for the TRR Forum, Linda Mowery tells of the pleasure of rereading favorite books and the personal benefits offered by these novels. She calls the romance books that she rereads "comfort reads" and "emotional safety nets." She writes, "Rereading favorite books is being with old friends, friends who understand us and accept us." Tina Engler, one of the TRR reviewers who posted comments in response, adds, "To me, rereading a favorite book is like crawling under the covers with a cup of hot cocoa on a rainy day. . . it's relaxing, invigorating, and acts as an emotional security blanket in that I already know everything that's going to happen."

No page number available for quotation from article accessed online

No parenthetical citations for Mowery or Engler because authors' names in tags and no page or paragraph numbers on Web site

Comments such as these remind me of all the good times my friends and I had talking about Sweet Valley High novels. These books gave us a way to talk indirectly about our own insecurities about being popular and liking boys who often didn't notice us. If romance novels can create bonds among people, honor their ethnic or spiritual identity, and help them cope with difficult times by escaping into a book from time to time, aren't these important cultural values? Like comfort food, romance novels may not provide the same nutrition that the literary equivalents of granola and tofu do, but apparently they provide a kind of nutrition that many people in our culture need.

10

Wraps up argument by returning to personal experience

Presents delayed thesis in full

Works Cited

Engler, Tina. The Romance Reader Forum. 11 July 2000. 8
    Aug. 2000 <http://www.theromancereader.com/
    forum21.html>.

Gray, Paul, and Andrea Sachs. "Passion on the Pages." Time
    20 Mar. 2000: 76-78. Academic Search Elite. EBSCO.
    Memorial Lib., Marquette Univ. 31 July 2000
    <http://www.epnet.com/>.

Works cited list would start on new page in actual paper

Uses double spacing and hanging indents throughout

Provides inclusive pagination for print publication from database

MacFarquhar, Larissa. "Who Cares If Johnny Can't Read?" Slate 16 Apr. 1997. 23 May 2000 <http//slate.msn.com/ Concept/97-04-16/Concept.asp>.

No punctuation between date of access and URL

Mowery, Linda. "The Second Time Around: The Magic of Rereading." The Romance Reader Forum. 11 July 2000. 8 Aug. 2000 <http://www.theromancereader.com/ forum21.html>.

URLs can break across lines at slash, only at slashes

Ricker-Wilson, Carol. "Busting Textual Bodices: Gender, Reading, and the Popular Romance." English Journal 88.3 (1999): 57-64.

Rosen, Judith. "Love Is All Around You." Publishers Weekly 8 Nov. 1999: 37-43. ProQuest. Memorial Lib., Marquette U. 31 July 2000 <http://proquest.umi.com/>.

Inclusive pagination for print publication from database

Wikoff, Katherine Hennessey. "Romance Novels More than Heaving Bosoms." Rev. of All I Need to Know in Life I Learned from Romance Novels by Victoria M. Johnson. Milwaukee Journal Sentinel 4 Feb. 1999: E2.

Format for book review citation

Building a Citation with MLA and APA Formats

Providing accurate, conventionally formatted documentation of your sources will enhance your own authority as well as give your readers essential information for follow-up. This appendix provides model citation formats you can use to prepare lists of research sources in either Modern Language Association (MLA) format—entitled "Works Cited"—or American Psychological Association (APA) format—entitled "References." In both citation systems, the list of sources is regarded as an integral part of the paper. Readers work with both types of lists in the same way. They use the information from the brief parenthetical references in the body of the paper to find full citations on the alphabetized list at the end of the paper. (For guidance about creating in-text citations keyed to these lists, see Chapter 7.)

If you cannot find an appropriate citation model in this appendix or need advice about how to include additional details, consult the current edition of the *MLA Handbook for Writers of Research Papers* (we used the sixth edition, 2003) or of the *Publication Manual of the American Psychological Association* (we used the fifth edition, 2001). Both are almost certainly available in your library's reference section. Your campus writing center will also be a valuable source of information, as are the online writing centers at Purdue <http://owl.english.purdue.edu/handouts/research/index.html/> and at the University of Wisconsin <http://www.wisc.edu/writetest/Handbook/Documentation.html>.

The Basics for MLA and APA Citation Lists

The important guidelines in this section will help you format your works cited and references lists accurately and efficiently. The care you take in formatting citations will convey the care with which you have approached your writing project and will thus enhance your credibility. In other words, the quality of your lists reflects the quality of your work.

SETTING UP MLA AND APA LISTS

1. Your list of sources should begin on a separate page at the end of your paper. Center the title "Works Cited" (MLA) or "References" (APA) at the top of the page.

2. Use double spacing throughout.
3. Include in this list only materials that you refer to in the body of your paper.
4. Arrange all citations alphabetically according to the author's last name. If the source lists no author, begin with the title, fitting it into the overall alphabetical order. When alphabetizing, ignore *the*, *a*, and *an* in book and article titles. For sequencing entries for two or more works by the same author, use the guidelines that appear under "Citations for Books" in both the MLA and APA sections that follow.
5. Use the hanging indent format illustrated in the model citations: the first line of each citation starts at the left margin, and subsequent lines are indented a half inch. This format helps readers quickly locate the word(s) provided by in-text citations. If you have trouble setting up the indents, consult your software's help screens.

PROCESS ADVICE ABOUT PREPARING MLA AND APA LISTS

1. To avoid omissions and confusion, add citations to your list while you are composing, as you integrate each source into your paper. An efficient technique for doing this is to keep a separate computer file open so that whenever you use outside material in your paper you can immediately put full information for a citation into the second file. (You can polish the citation format later.) Working this way will help you avoid last-minute scrambles to recover missing bibliographic information.
2. As part of final proofreading, take a few minutes to verify that each of your in-text citations matches a full citation on your works cited or references list. Then check in reverse—use your word processor's search function to move from the list to the in-text citations. The first part of this procedure will reveal any citations missing from your list. The second part will help you notice whether any in-text citations have been accidentally deleted during revision. (Missing in-text citations can prompt questions from your instructor and be embarrassing.) Checking your list against your text will also help you discover any citations listed during early drafting that are no longer relevant. Simply delete them.

Specifics about MLA citation formats follow; the APA section begins on p. 184.

MLA Citation Formats for Books

The basic book citation has three information elements separated by periods.

Author. <u>Title</u>. City, State: Publisher, Date.

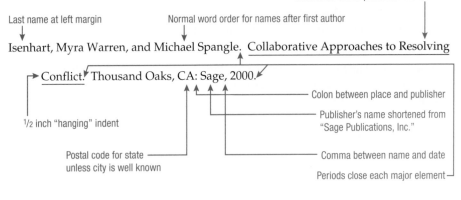

Underlined title is preferred MLA format

Last name at left margin

Normal word order for names after first author

Isenhart, Myra Warren, and Michael Spangle. Collaborative Approaches to Resolving

Conflict. Thousand Oaks, CA: Sage, 2000.

Colon between place and publisher

Publisher's name shortened from "Sage Publications, Inc."

½ inch "hanging" indent

Postal code for state unless city is well known

Comma between name and date

Periods close each major element

MODEL BOOK CITATIONS

Book by One Author

Radway, Janice A. <u>Reading the Romance: Women, Patriarchy, and Popular Literature</u>. Chapel Hill: U of North Carolina P, 1984.

Book with Two or Three Authors

Brooke, Robert, Ruth Mirtz, and Rick Evans. <u>Small Groups in Writing Workshops: Invitations to a Writer's Life</u>. Urbana, IL: NCTE, 1994.

Lutz, Catherine A., and Jane L. Collins. <u>Reading National Geographic</u>. Chicago: U of Chicago P, 1993.

- Note the commas after the first and second authors' names.
- Use regular name order for the second and subsequent authors.
- The names of university presses can be shortened to "U of [school name] P," as in this example, or "[school name] UP."

Using "et al." for More Than Three Authors

In MLA style, when a book or article has more than three authors, you may list all names or you may use "et al." ("and others") after the first name.

Mabey, Nick, Stephen Hall, Clare Smith, and Sujata Gupta. <u>Argument in the Greenhouse: The International Economics of Controlling Global Warming</u>. London: Routledge, 1997.

OR

Mabey, Nick, et al. <u>Argument in the Greenhouse: The International Economics of Controlling Global Warming</u>. London: Routledge, 1997.

Two or More Works by the Same Author

Alphabetize first by the author's name, then by the works' titles. On the second and any subsequent entries, instead of the author's name, type three hyphens, a period, and then the title.

Quindlen, Anna. <u>How Reading Changed My Life</u>. New York: Ballantine, 1998.
---. "It's the Cult of Personality." <u>Newsweek</u>. 14 Aug. 2000: 68.
---. <u>One True Thing</u>. New York: Random, 1994.

Book with Corporate Author

In this sense "corporate" means authored by any group where individual members are not identified.

Hayward Gallery. <u>Rhapsodies in Black: Art of the Harlem Renaissance</u>. Berkeley: U of
    California P, 1997.

Book with No Author or Editor Listed on Title Page

<u>Strong Hearts: Native American Visions and Voices</u>. New York: Aperture, 1995.

Translated Book

Aristotle. <u>On Rhetoric: A Theory of Civic Discourse</u>. Trans. George A. Kennedy. New
    York: Oxford UP, 1991.

If your discussion primarily concerns the translation, begin the citation with the translator's name, followed by "trans." Include the author after the title, preceded by the word "by."

Kennedy, George A., trans. <u>On Rhetoric: A Theory of Civic Discourse</u>. By Aristotle.
    New York: Oxford UP, 1991.

Second or Later Edition of a Book

If a title page doesn't include an edition number, the book is probably a first edition, which is not noted in a citation. If the book's title page does have an edition number, you need to include it in the citation because content and page numbers have probably changed since the first edition. Place edition information as a separate element between the title and publication information.

White, Edward M. <u>Teaching and Assessing Writing</u>. 2nd ed. San Francisco: Jossey-Bass,
    1994.

Book from a Series

If the title page or the page preceding it indicates that the book is part of a series, place the series name as a separate element after the title without underlining or quotation marks, then add the series number, then the publication information.

Folsom, Marcia McClintock, ed. Approaches to Teaching Austen's Pride and Prejudice. Approaches to Teaching World Lit. 45. New York: MLA, 1993.

Special Considerations When Titles Include Titles

To indicate that a book title includes the title of another book, omit the underlining on the included title.

Sten, Christopher. Sounding the Whale: Moby-Dick as Epic Novel. Kent, OH: Kent State UP, 1996.

To indicate that a book title includes a short story or essay title, add quotation marks around the shorter title and retain underlining for the entire book title.

Dock, Julie Bates, ed. Charlotte Perkins Gilman's "The Yellow Wall-Paper" and the History of Its Publication and Reception: A Critical Edition and Documentary Casebook. University Park, PA: Penn State UP, 1998.

Edited Collection

Citations for edited collections follow the book models, with the label "ed." or "eds." inserted after the last editor's name.

Ward, Harold, ed. Acting Locally: Concepts and Models for Service-Learning in Environmental Studies. Washington, DC: American Association for Higher Education, 1999.
Severino, Carol, Juan C. Guerra, and Johnnella E. Butler, eds. Writing in Multicultural Settings. New York: MLA, 1997.

Selection from an Edited Collection

Present inclusive (i.e., first and last) page numbers for the selection as a separate item after the date.

Christian-Smith, Linda K. "Voices of Resistance: Young Women Readers of Romantic Fiction." Beyond Silenced Voices: Class, Race, and Gender in U.S. Schools. Ed. Lois Weis and Michelle Fine. New York: State U of New York P, 1993. 169-89.
"The Dream of the Rood." Longman Anthology of British Literature. Ed. David Damrosch, et al. Vol. 1A. New York: Longman, 1999. 120-24.
Welch, James. "Christmas Comes to Moccasin Flat." A Geography of Poets. Ed. Edward Field. New York: Bantam, 1979. 43.

If the selection is from a book that collects work by one author, use the same format, including an editor only if relevant.

Hribal, C. J. "Consent." The Clouds in Memphis. Amherst, MA: U of Massachusetts P, 2000. 55-67.
Williams, William Carlos. "The Red Wheelbarrow." Selected Poems. New York: New Directions, 1968. 30.

Work Reprinted in an Anthology

When information about the original publication date and venue are important but your page references are from a reprinted version, use the following format to provide publication information for both versions.

Beck, Evelyn Torton. "From 'Kike' to 'JAP': How Misogyny, Anti-Semitism, and Racism Construct the 'Jewish American Princess.'" Sojourner Sept. 1988: 18-26. Rpt. in Race, Class, and Gender. Ed. Margaret L. Andersen and Patricia Hill Collins. 2nd ed. Belmont, CA: Wadsworth, 1995. 87-95.

Selection from a Multivolume Work

Volume information comes between any edition note and the publication information.

"The Dream of the Rood." Longman Anthology of British Literature. Ed. David Damrosch, et al. Vol. 1A. New York: Longman, 1999. 120-24.

Melville, Herman. "Bartleby the Scrivener." Norton Anthology of American Literature. Ed. Nina Baym et al. 5th ed. Vol. 1. New York: Norton, 1999. 2330-55.

List only the material or volumes you use. If you were discussing the entire two-volume collection referred to in the previous example, the citation would begin with the editor.

Baym, Nina, et al., eds. Norton Anthology of American Literature. 5th ed. 2 vols. New York: Norton, 1999.

Introduction, Preface, Foreword, or Afterword of a Book

Hirsch, Edward. Introduction. Transforming Vision: Writers on Art. By Art Institute of Chicago. Boston: Little, 1994. 9-11.

Selection from a Reference Book

Cite material from reference books as you would work in a collection, but omit the editor's name. If the article is signed, begin with the author's name. If contents in the reference book are arranged alphabetically, you may omit volume and page from the works cited list citation, but you should include them in the parenthetical citation in your text. If the reference work is well known and appears in frequent editions, full publication information is not needed. If you are drawing information from an online or electronic source, you will find information about formatting details later in this appendix.

MATERIAL FROM FAMILIAR SOURCE ARRANGED ALPHABETICALLY

"Rembrandt." The New Encyclopedia Britannica. 1998.

MATERIAL FROM LESS FAMILIAR SOURCE ARRANGED ALPHABETICALLY

Blasing, Mutlu Konuk. "Poetry: Since 1960." Benet's Reader's Encyclopedia of American Literature. New York: Harper, 1991.

"Hegira." Merriam-Webster's Dictionary of Allusions. Springfield, MA: Merriam-
    Webster, 1999.

MATERIAL FROM LESS FAMILIAR SOURCE WITH MULTIPLE SECTIONS

"Kentucky Living." Magazines for Libraries. New Providence, NJ: Bowker, 2000. 382.

SPECIFIC DICTIONARY DEFINITION AMONG SEVERAL

"Story." Def. 9. Random House Dictionary of the English Language. 2nd ed. 1987.

Cross References

When you cite several works from the same collection, avoid repetition and
save space by using one main entry to which citations for specific works within
it can refer. Note the absence of punctuation between the editor's name and the
page numbers in this sample list of works from one collection.

Atwan, Robert. Foreword. Gould viii-xii.
Gould, Stephen J., ed. The Best American Essays 2002. Boston: Houghton, 1999.
---. "Introduction: To Open a Millenium." Gould xiii-xvii.
Mayblum, Adam. "The Price We Pay." Gould 213-18.

MLA Citation Formats for Articles
in Periodicals

This section presents model citations for articles from print periodicals that you
access either from a paper issue or through a database subscription service such
as ProQuest or Academic Search Elite. The next section will present models for
citing periodical articles that you access through a free, public Web site.

   The increasing number of full text articles available through libraries' subscription databases gives students the advantage of quick, convenient access to
materials they need. However, when it is time to format citations for those materials, determining the best way to show readers how the materials were retrieved can often be a challenge. The models and notes supplied in this section
should help you meet this challenge.

INFORMATION TO INCLUDE WHEN
CITING PERIODICALS

Citations for periodical articles that originated in paper form should begin with
the print information, then provide any details about electronic retrieval. To illustrate, we provide an annotated MLA style citation that provides information
as follows:

Information Elements Needed for MLA Citations of Print Periodicals

Author. "Article Title." Periodical Title volume (date): page number(s).

Information Elements Needed for Adding Database Retrieval Details

<u>Database Name</u>. Database Company. Library, Place. Date accessed <URL for database homepage>.

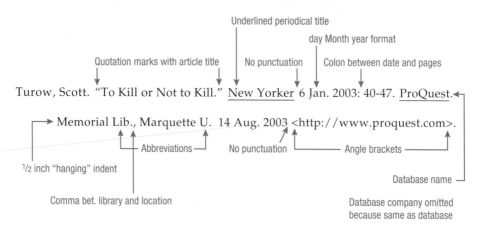

Additional Notes

- Note periods after each major element: author, article title, journal information, database name, location/subscriber for database, and retrieval date plus URL.
- If no author is listed, begin with the title. Do not use the word "anonymous" that appears in some databases unless it appears on the article in the periodical itself.
- MLA format calls for capitalizing all words of a title except *the, a, an,* and short prepositions, even if they are not capitalized in the original or the database.
- MLA format drops an initial *the* from names of periodicals.
- For variations in format for scholarly and general circulation periodicals, see the model citations. The two important distinguishing details to remember are these:
  1. Include volume numbers only for scholarly journals.
  2. Include edition information for newspaper articles when it is available.
- Providing first and last page numbers of an article is preferred unless the article pages are not consecutive.
- If the article's pages are not consecutive, provide the first page number followed by a plus sign.
- If a database service provides only the initial page, put a hyphen after the first page number, then a space, then a period, like this: 40- .
- In general, you may omit information that the electronic database omits.
- You may omit the name of the database company if it is not readily apparent from the search pages or if the name is the same as that of the database, as in the annotated example.

MODEL ARTICLE CITATIONS

Work from Scholarly Journal with Continuous Pagination Through Each Volume

ORIGINAL PAPER VERSION

Krabill, William, et al. "Greenland Ice Sheet: High-Elevation Balance and Peripheral Thinning." <u>Science</u> 289 (2000): 428-30.

ELECTRONIC VERSION RETRIEVED THROUGH LIBRARY DATABASE

Krabill, William, et al. "Greenland Ice Sheet: High-Elevation Balance and Peripheral Thinning." <u>Science</u> 289 (2000): 428-30. <u>Academic Search Elite</u>. EBSCO. Memorial Lib., Marquette U. 15 Sept. 2000 <http://www.epnet.com/>.

Work from Scholarly Journal That Begins with Page One in Each Issue

Pivnick, Janet. "A Piece of Forgotten Song: Recalling Environmental Connections." <u>Holistic Education Review</u> 10.4 (1997): 58-63.

- The numbers between the periodical title and date indicate the volume (10) and issue (4).

Magazine Articles

PUBLISHED WEEKLY (PAPER COPY)

Woodard, Colin. "The Great Melt: Is It Normal, or the Result of Global Warming?" <u>Chronicle of Higher Education</u> 14 July 2000: A20-21.

- The letter "A" is included with the page number because this publication, like many newspapers, has more than one section, each with separate page numbers.

PUBLISHED MONTHLY (FULL TEXT ACCESSED THROUGH LIBRARY DATABASE)

Tyler, Varro E. "Medicinal Teas: What Works, What Doesn't." <u>Prevention</u> Apr. 2000: 127+. <u>ProQuest</u>. Memorial Lib., Marquette U. 10 Sept. 2000 <http://proquest.umi.com/>.

PUBLISHED QUARTERLY (PAPER COPY)

Stephenson, Sam. "Nights of Incandescence." <u>Doubletake</u> Fall 1999: 46-51.

Newspaper Articles

SPECIAL CONSIDERATIONS WHEN CITING NEWSPAPER ARTICLES

- Give the paper's name as it appears in the masthead, but omit introductory *the*.
- If the city is not included in the name, add it in square brackets after the name: e.g., *Times-Picayune* [New Orleans].
- If an edition is listed, include it after the date because different editions of the same issue include different material and pagination.

- If sections of the paper are paginated separately, include identifying letters or labels (e.g., A9 or Sun. Mag. 15).

ARTICLE ACCESSED FROM PAPER COPY OF NEWSPAPER

Claiborne, William. "Iowa Looks Abroad for Workers." Washington Post 16 Sept. 2000, final ed.: A3.

ARTICLE ACCESSED VIA LIBRARY DATABASE

Claiborne, William. "Iowa Looks Abroad for Workers." Washington Post 16 Sept. 2000, final ed.: A3. Lexis-Nexis Academic Universe. Memorial Lib., Marquette U. 13 Oct. 2000 <http://web.lexis-nexis.com/universe>.

Editorial or Opinion Piece

"Soft Money Travesties." Editorial. New York Times 16 Sept. 2000, natl. ed.: A26.

Letter to the Editor

Use the label "letter" after the title, if a title is given. Otherwise, the word "letter" follows the author's name.

Clark, Diana Shaw. "Money and Horses." Letter. New Yorker 18 Sept. 2000: 18.

Review

Include title of the work reviewed (film, book, play, etc.) with the label, "Rev. of," then the author of the reviewed work, as relevant.

Denby, David. "Four Kings." Rev. of The Original Kings of Comedy. New Yorker 4 Sept. 2000: 88-89. [film review]

If the review is untitled, the reviewer's name is followed directly by the "Rev. of" label. Note the comma between the title of the reviewed work and "by."

Grimm, Nancy Maloney. Rev. of Between Talk and Teaching: Reconsidering the Writing Conference, by Laurel Johnson Black. College Composition and Communication 52 (2000): 156-59. [book review]

If the review is untitled and unsigned, begin with "Rev. of" and alphabetize the entry under the work's title. The following citation would be alphabetized under "J."

Rev. of The Jerusalem Syndrome. New Yorker 4 Sept. 2000: 8+. [theater review]

MLA Citation Formats for Internet Sources

As with citations for print sources, citations for material used from Web pages or other areas of the Internet should convey to readers two important matters: the quality of the source (author, sponsor, currency) and information about how to locate the material. For citations of Web sources, the writer's first challenge is finding the relevant information for a citation; the second is using conventional format consistently. MLA style guidelines recommend that citations of electronic materials closely follow the format conventions for print citations. When formats are familiar, readers can take in their content quickly.

With electronic sources, not every detail will be available or relevant for every citation. Keep in mind your goals for providing readers with meaningful information and context, and include what you can. Err on the side of providing too much information rather than too little. In this section the annotated sample citation is followed by additional notes about what to include in MLA Internet citations, then a list of model citations for a variety of material types. One note of caution: if a Web site offers information about how to cite the page, use the information elements provided, but present them in MLA format.

INFORMATION TO INCLUDE WHEN CITING INTERNET SOURCES

The *MLA Handbook* divides Web citations into five basic elements:

Author. "Document Title." Information about print publication. Information about electronic publication. Access information.[1]

Note that each of the five elements is followed by a period. However, within the final element, there is no punctuation between the date of access and the URL. The result links the two, as if to say, "on this date this material was available at this address."

Corporate (i.e., group) author

Underlining for title of the Internet site —

Quotation marks around title of material used

Document length (.pdf format) ¬

Task Force on College Drinking. "A Call to Action: Changing the Culture of Drinking at U.S. Colleges." Apr. 2002. College Drinking: NIAAA Reports. 66 pp.

National Institute on Alcohol Abuse and Alcoholism. 14 Aug. 2003

<http://www.collegedrinkingprevention.gov/Reports/TaskForce/ TaskForce_TOC.aspx>. ← Angle brackets around URL

No punctuation

Date of print publication

Sponsor of Web site

---

[1]Joseph Gibaldi, *MLA Handbook for Writers of Research Papers*, 6th ed. (New York: MLA, 2003) 208.

Additional Notes

AUTHORS

- You will sometimes need to decide whether to put the name of a corporate author at the left margin or after the document and site titles, in the "sponsor" slot. This decision will depend on what details are available and what you want to emphasize in your text, because the word that begins the works cited entry appears in the parenthetical citation. To see different possibilities, contrast the model citations listed under "Material from an Organization Site" and the examples from Trek Bicycle and Harley-Davidson under "Material from a Commercial Site."

- If the work or the entire site has an editor, translator, or compiler not already cited in the "author" slot, include that name (in regular name order) after the title of the work or site, then add an appropriate abbreviation (e.g., "Ed.") if available.

DOCUMENT TITLE

- In most cases, the Web site and document titles will be distinct. The document title comes first; the format is analogous to an article title followed by a book or periodical title. Punctuate titles according to the guidelines for book and article citations.

PRINT PUBLICATION

- If the work has appeared in print but you are retrieving it from a Web site, simply follow the guidelines in the previous sections when you format this element of the citation.

ELECTRONIC PUBLICATION

- The site title is one of the most important identifiers in the citation. It should be underlined. If this title is not absolutely clear on the page itself, use the title that appears at the very top of your browser screen. If the site title is already evident from the name of a corporate author such as Trek Bicycle or American Library Association, you can omit it here. When no title is immediately apparent, break down the URL to find the larger site or consider using a label (e.g., "Home page") if it would be helpful.

- Numbers for the date of electronic publication or last update (if available), volume and issue numbers (if relevant), and the electronic document's total number of pages or paragraphs (if numbered) should be placed after the site title.

- The name of the institution or organization sponsoring the site—if not already listed earlier as corporate author or in the site title—concludes the electronic publication portion of the citation. This detail provides important information about context. In cases where it is difficult to discern a

sponsor, it would be wise to spend a few minutes looking for one by
breaking down the URL.

ACCESS INFORMATION
- Unlike the format for periodicals accessed through a subscription database, citations for public access Web sites must present the specific URL
  for the material used. For accuracy, copy and paste the URL from your
  browser window. Remove any hyperlink that transfers with the address.
- MLA style places URLs in angle brackets. Break URLs across lines only at
  a slash mark.

ALTERNATIVES TO PROVIDING A URL

When the URL of a document you refer to is unique to a particular subscription,
not evident, or unmanageably long, you have several options.

- Provide the URL for the subscription service's home page:

  "Suzan-Lori Parks." Contemporary Authors Online. Biography Resource
      Center. 8 Aug. 2003. 15 Aug. 2003 <http://www.galenet.com>.

- End with the date of access:

  "Suzan-Lori Parks." Contemporary Authors Online. Biography Resource
      Center. 8 Aug. 2003. 15 Aug. 2003.

- Provide the URL for the sponsoring Web site's search page:

  "Manatee Mortality." Save the Manatee Club. 2002. 29 July 2003 <http://
      www.savethemanatee.org/search_post.cfm>.

- Provide the keyword used by a personal subscription service, labeled as
  such:

  "AOL Latino Fact Sheet." AOL Keyword: Latino. America Online. 15 Aug. 2003.
      Keyword: Latino.

- Conclude with the path to follow from an organization's or a personal subscription service's home page:

  Mellon, Margaret, and Jane Rissler. "Environmental Effects of Genetically
      Modified Food Crops: Recent Experiences." Union of Concerned Scientists.
      31 July 2003. 31 July 2003 <http://www.ucsusa.org>. Path: Food;
      Biotechnology; Special Features.

MODEL INTERNET CITATIONS

An Entire Web Site

Nonprofit Portal of Greater Milwaukee. Barbara Duffy. 16 July 2003. Center for
    Initiatives and Research, University of Wisconsin–Milwaukee. 15 Aug. 2003
    <http://epic.cuir.uwm.edu/NONPROFIT/>.
Bill of Rights Defense Committee. 15 Aug. 2003. 15 Aug. 2003 <http://bordc.org/>.

A Course or Department Home Page

McManus, Barbara F. Greek Tragedy. Course syllabus. Sept.-Dec. 1999. Classics, College of New Rochelle. 15 Aug. 2003 <http://www.cnr.edu/home/bmcmanus/ tragedysyl.html>.

Peace Studies. Program home page. Cornell U. 2003. 15 Aug. 2003 <http:// www.einaudi.cornell.edu/PeaceProgram/>.

A Personal Home Page

Tannen, Deborah. Home page. 17 April 2000. 29 July 2003 <http:// www.georgetown.edu/faculty/tannend/index.htm>.

Material from an Online Reference Database

"Kempe, Margery." Encyclopaedia Britannica Online. 13 Oct. 2000 <http:// www.eb.com:180/bol/topic?eu=46106&sctn=1>.

Material from an Online Scholarly Project

"Yoknapatawpha County." William Faulkner on the Web. John B. Padgett. 31 May 2000. University of Mississippi. 13 Oct. 2000 <http://www.mcsr.olemiss.edu/~egjbp/ faulkner/glossaryy.html#Yoknapatawpha>.

E-Book

Bok, Edward William. The Americanization of Edward Bok. New York: Scribner's, 1921. Bartleby.Com. 5 Oct. 2000. 13 Oct. 2000 <http://www.bartleby.com/197/>.

Article from a Scholarly E-Journal

Mazer, Emmanuel, Juan Manuel Ahuactzin, and Pierre Bessière. "The Ariadne's Clew Algorithm." Journal of Artificial Intelligence Research 9 (1998): 295-316. 10 Nov. 1998. 13 Oct. 2000 <http://www.cs.cmu.edu/afs/cs/project/jair/pub/volume9/ mazer98a-html/ariane.html>.

Periodical or Newspaper Article Published Online

Appelbaum, Richard, and Peter Dreier. "The Campus Anti-Sweatshop Movement." American Prospect Online 46, Sept.-Oct. 1999. 7 June 2000 <http:// www.prospect.org/archives/46/46appelbaum.html>.

Scodel, Harvey. "Illiteracy Test." Email to the Editors. Slate 24 Apr. 1997. Microsoft. 23 May 2000 <http://slate.msn.com/Email/97-04-24/Email.asp>.

Stolba, Christine, and Sally Satel. Rev. of Genes, Women, Equality, by Mary Briody Mahowald. New England Journal of Medicine 8 June 2000. Massachusetts Medical Society. 19 Sept. 2000 <http://www.nejm.org/content/2000/0342/0023/1761.asp>.

Streitfeld, David. "Court Says Napster Must Stop." washingtonpost.com 12 Feb. 2001. 12 Feb. 2001 <http://www.washingtonpost.com/wp-dyn/articles/ A59310-2001Feb12.html>.

Article Posted on a Web Site

Cohn, Ed. "The Civil Society Debate." Electronic Policy Network. 13 Oct. 2000
    <http://tap.epn.org/issues/civilsociety.html>.
Puentes, Robert. "Flexible Funding for Transit: Who Uses It?" Center on Urban and
    Metropolitan Policy. 17 May 2000. 11 pp. Brookings Institution. 13 Oct. 2000
    <http://www.brookings.org/es/urban/flexfunding.pdf>.

Material from an Organization Site

"CIPA Updates." American Library Association. 15 Aug. 2003. 15 Aug. 2003
    <http://www.ala.org/>. Path: Our Association; Offices; Washington Office; Issues;
    Civil Liberties; Intellectual Freedom and Privacy; CIPA.
National Sleep Foundation. "How's Your Sleep?" 12 July 2003 <http://
    www.sleepfoundation.org/howsyoursleep.html>.
Thacker, Shane. "Dos and Don'ts of Grant Proposals for Tech Funding." The
    Grantsmanship Center Magazine. Fall 2000. The Grantsmanship Center. 15 Aug. 2003
    <http://www.tgci.com/magazine/00fall/dosdonts.asp>.

Cartoon or Comic Strip

Horsey, David. "Letter from Home." Cartoon. Seattle Post-Intelligencer: David Horsey.
    17 Aug. 2003. 15 Aug. 2003 <http://seattlepi.nwsource.com/horsey/>.

Posting to a Discussion List, Online Forum, or Weblog

Sullivan, Andrew. "Marriage Again." Online posting. "Daily Dish."
    Andrewsullivan.com. 10 July 2003. 15 Aug. 2003 <http://www.andrewsullivan.com/
    index.php?dish_inc=archives/2003_07_06_dish_archive.html>.

- Whenever possible, provide the URL for the posting's archival version
  so that readers can find it readily.

Material from an Online Information Service

"Guillain-Barré Syndrome." OnHealth.Com. OnHealth Network Company. 15 Feb. 2000
    <http://onhealth.webmd.com/conditions/resource/conditions/item,41282.asp>.

Online Transcript from Television or Radio Program

Havel, Vaclav. "Newsmaker Interview." With Margaret Warner. Online NewsHour.
    PBS. 16 May 1997. Transcript. 21 May 1997 <http://www.pbs.org/newshour/bb/
    europe/jan-june97/havel_5-16.html>.

Television or Radio Broadcast Available Online

Sound Portraits Productions. "Witness to an Execution." All Things Considered. 12 Oct.
    2000. NPR. 12 Oct. 2000 <http://www.npr.org/programs/atc/witness/>.

Material from a Commercial Site

"Harley-Davidson History." Harley-Davidson Motor Company. 17 June 2000 <http://
    www.harley-davidson.com/company/history/history.asp>.

Trek Bicycle Corporation. "Mission Statement." Home page. 18 July 2000. 15 Oct. 2000
<http://www.trekbikes.com/abouttrek/index.html>.

MLA Citation Formats for Other Materials and Media

Government Publications

The information and formats required for citing government documents varies
considerably, so it is advisable to consult a specialized handbook such as the
Complete Guide to Citing Government Information Resources. The following citation,
which identifies the government "author" first by country, then by three increasingly smaller bodies, provides a basic model.

United States. Cong. Senate. Committee on Energy and Natural Resources. Global
Climate Change: Hearing. 104th Cong., 2nd sess. Washington, D.C.: GPO, 1997.

Historical documents and federal laws—the United States Code (USC)—do not
need to be listed in the works cited list because they can be cited adequately with
an in-text parenthetical citation, for example: "(US Const., art. 3, sec. 1)" or "(17
USC 554, 2000)."

If you want to cite the text of a federal bill or law directly, you can retrieve
it from *Thomas*, the Library of Congress's data bank of legislative information.
Use the citation model that follows below. The first date is the date of enactment
(usually different from the day it was approved by Congress). The last is the date
of retrieval; if a date of posting were available, it would be placed between the
site title and sponsor (as in other citations for Web material).

Children's Internet Protection Act. Pub. L. 106-554. 21 Dec. 2000. Thomas: Legislative
Information on the Internet. Lib. of Congress, Washington, DC. 18 Jan. 2001
<http://thomas.loc.gov/cgi-bin/cpquery/R?cp106:FLD010:@1(hr1033):URL>.

If you are working on something that requires numerous legal citations, refer to
the current edition of *The Blue Book: A Uniform System of Citation*, the standard editorial reference for attorneys. Always check with your professor about the citation systems preferred for a given course.

Biblical Citations

Whenever you plan to discuss any sacred texts in a paper, be sure to ask your
instructor what kind of citation information you need to provide and what format to use.

Material from the Judeo-Christian Bible as well as from sacred writings in
other traditions is typically cited in the text by an abbreviation for the name of
the book, then chapter and verse numbers. Page numbers are not used because
the citation already permits the reader to find the passage in any version of the
Bible. Include the edition of the Bible in your first reference. For example, (New
Oxford Annotated Bible, Ps. 19:7) refers to this full citation:

The New Oxford Annotated Bible. New Revised Standard Version. Ed. Bruce M.
    Metzger and Roland E. Murphy. New York: Oxford, 1991.

In MLA format, a particular published edition of the Bible is underlined, but the
version is not. In some classes, especially in religious studies or theology courses,
you may be expected to note only the version, thus eliminating the need for a citation on your works cited list. You would then use in-text citations such as
these: (New Revised Standard Version Bible, Ps. 19:7) or (New English Bible, Col.
3:12-17). On later references, the version may be omitted or abbreviated, in these
cases to "NRSV" and "NEB."

Lecture, Speech, or Conference Paper

Jamieson, Kathleen Hall. "Deliberation, Democratic Politics, and Journalism." James A.
    Moffett '29 Lecture in Ethics. Princeton University. 17 Feb. 2000.

Material in Varying Media from an Information Service

Follow guidelines for the original media (print publication, lecture, or paper presentation, etc.), adding the information service identification code at the end. The
example is for a document available through ERIC (Educational Resources Information Center) in both paper and microfiche as well as online full text.

CITATION FOR PRINT OR MICROFICHE

Barrow, Lloyd H. "Preservice Methods Students' Response to a Performance Portfolio
    Assignment." Paper presented at the Annual Meeting of the American Educational
    Research Association. New Orleans. April 24-28, 2000. ED 442 826.

CITATION FOR ONLINE TEXT

Follow the model for periodicals accessed through a database. First provide information for paper copy, then add the database information:

Barrow, Lloyd H. "Preservice Methods Students' Response to a Performance Portfolio
    Assignment." Paper presented at the Annual Meeting of the American Educational
    Research Association. New Orleans. April 24-28, 2000. ED 442 826. ERIC Document
    Reproduction Service. Ovid. Memorial Lib., Marquette U. 10 Sept. 2000
    <http://gateway2.ovid.com/>.

CD-ROM

Follow guidelines for print publications, but specify the publication medium, any
vendor (e.g., SilverPlatter, Microsoft, etc.), and dates for both print and electronic
publication/update, as available.

"Haiti." Concise Columbia Encyclopedia. 1995. CD-ROM. Microsoft Bookshelf, 1995.

Video Recording

Unless your discussion focuses on the contributions of a particular person (performer, director, narrator, etc.), begin with the title, underlined, and include the
director, distributor, and year of release. Add other pertinent material between
title and distributor.

<u>Australia's Twilight of the Dreamtime</u>. Writ/Photog. Stanley Breeden. National
   Geographic Society and WQED, Pittsburgh, 1988.

Sound Recording

Your decision about whom to cite first—the performer, composer, or conductor—
depends on the point you are making. The following citation, for example, emphasizes the performers and notes the composer.

Ma, Yo-Yo, and Bobby McFerrin. "Grace." By Bobby McFerrin. <u>Hush</u>. Sony, 1992.

   If you cite liner notes or a libretto, provide that genre label before the title.
If the original recording date is important, provide it after the title; then indicate
any medium other than a CD followed by the manufacturer and production
date.

Coltrane, John. Liner notes. <u>A Love Supreme</u>. Rec. 9 Dec. 1964. LP. Impulse, 1964.

TV or Radio Program

"Take This Sabbath Day." <u>The West Wing</u>. Writ. Aaron Sorkin. Dir. Thomas Schlamme.
   NBC. WTMJ, Milwaukee. 9 Feb. 2000.

APA Citation Formats for Books

The most prominent features of APA format are that initials are used for author's
first names and that the date of publication is placed in parentheses immediately
after the author's name. Indeed, scholars accustomed to using APA citations typically refer to works by author-date shorthand, such as "Wolfson and Carskadon
1991" or "Tannen 1997." (For further discussion about this, see the discussion of
APA parenthetical references in Chapter 7.)
   If you do not find a model citation that fits the type of material you need to
cite either in this appendix or in the APA *Publication Manual*, follow APA's advice to look over the available models, choose one that most closely matches
your source, and use that format. (We have followed this advice in the sample
citations for entire Web sites and for an online transcript.) Finally, as the manual says, "when in doubt, provide more information rather than less."[2]

INFORMATION TO INCLUDE WHEN CITING BOOKS

The annotated citation for an entire book presents four information elements in
this format:

Author. (Date). *Title*. City, State: Publisher.

---

[2]*Publication Manual of the American Psychological Association*, 5th ed. (Washington, D.C.:
APA, 2001), 232.

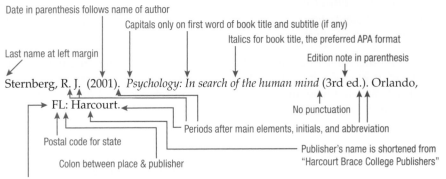

Date in parenthesis follows name of author

Capitals only on first word of book title and subtitle (if any)

Italics for book title, the preferred APA format

Last name at left margin

Edition note in parenthesis

Sternberg, R. J. (2001). *Psychology: In search of the human mind* (3rd ed.). Orlando,

FL: Harcourt.

No punctuation

Periods after main elements, initials, and abbreviation

Postal code for state

Publisher's name is shortened from "Harcourt Brace College Publishers"

Colon between place & publisher

½ inch "hanging" indent

MODEL BOOK CITATIONS

Book by One Author

Firstenberg, P. B. (1996). *The 21st century nonprofit: Remaking the organization in the post-government era.* New York: Foundation Center.

Book with Two or More Authors or Editors

Banta, T. W., Lund, J. P., Black, K. E., & Oblander, F. W. (1996). *Assessment in practice: Putting principles to work on college campuses.* San Francisco: Jossey-Bass.

- APA reference entries list all authors by surname plus initials, listing surname first for all. See Chapter 7 for guidance about using "et al." in APA parenthetical citations.
- Ampersand (&) is used instead of "and."

Two or More Works by the Same Author

Alphabetize the references first by author's name, using the full name for each entry, then arrange them by year of publication, earliest first. One-author entries precede and are sequenced separately from multiple-author entries. Multiple-author entries are alphabetized first by the first author's surname, then by the surname of the second author, third author, and so on. When authorship is identical, put earlier articles first. (See Chapter 7 for details about internal citations with multiple authors.)

Carskadon, M. A. (Ed.). (1993). *Encyclopedia of sleep and dreaming.* New York: MacMillan.
Carskadon, M. A. (Ed.). (2002). *Adolescent sleep patterns: Biological, social, and psychological influences.* New York: Cambridge University Press.
Carskadon, M. A., & Mancuso, J. (1988). Sleep habits in high school adolescents: Boarding versus day students. *Sleep Research, 17,* 74.
Carskadon, M. A., & Taylor, J. F. (1997). Public policy and sleep disorders. In M. R. Pressman & W. C. Orr (Eds.), *Understanding sleep: The evaluation and treatment of sleep disorders* (pp. 111–122). Washington, DC: American Psychological Association.

Book or Brochure with Corporate Author
National Sleep Foundation. (2002). *ABC's of ZZZ's: When you can't sleep.* [Brochure].
Washington, DC: Author.

- When the corporate author and publisher are the same, the word "Author" is placed where the publisher's name usually appears.
- The bracketed label informs readers about what type of document is being cited.

Book with No Author or Editor Listed on Title Page
Publication manual of the American Psychological Association (5th ed.). (2001). Washington,
DC: American Psychological Association.

Translated Book
Freud, A. (1935). *Psycho-analysis for teachers and parents: Introductory lectures* (B. Low,
Trans.). New York: Emerson.

- If it is available, include the original publication date in parenthesis at the end of the citation with the following phrase: "(Original work published [insert year])"—omit final punctuation.
- APA uses conventional name order for editors, translators, and so on, when their names are placed after the main title that is cited in the entry.

Subsequent and Revised Editions of a Book
White, E. M. (1994). *Teaching and assessing writing* (2nd ed.). San Francisco: Jossey-Bass.

- The edition note is treated as part of the title but not italicized, and the period ending the title element comes after the closing parenthesis.

Technical and Research Reports
Task Force on College Drinking. (2002). *A call to action: Changing the culture of drinking at
U.S. colleges.* (National Institutes of Health Pub. No. 02-5010). Washington, DC:
National Institute on Alcohol Abuse and Alcoholism.

- This citation refers to the paper publication of the report.

Edited Collection
Buley-Meissner, M. L., Thompson, M. M., & Tan, E. B. (Eds.). (2000). *The academy and the
possibility of belief.* Cresskill, NJ: Hampton.

- Parentheses are used around "Ed." or "Eds." after the name(s).
- The period after "(Eds.)" signals that the editor designation is part of the author element.

Selection from an Edited Collection

Carskadon, M. A. (2002). Risks of driving while sleepy in adolescents and young adults. In M. A. Carskadon (Ed.), *Adolescent sleep patterns: Biological, social, and psychological influences* (pp. 148–158). New York: Cambridge University Press.

- APA style capitalizes only the first word of chapter and article titles and any subtitle.
- The phrase about the larger collection (editor, title, pages) begins with "In" and is treated as a single element.
- Note conventional name order for editor.
- APA uses the abbreviations "p." and "pp." to locate works within a book and does not shorten the second number in inclusive pagination.

Work Reprinted in an Anthology

Use the date of the reprint after the author's name; provide information about the original publication, if available, in parenthesis at the end of the reference without end punctuation.

Villanueva, V., Jr. (1996). *Inglés* in the colleges. In M. Wiley, B. Gleason, L. W. Phelps, *Composition in four keys: Inquiring into the field* (pp. 503-519). Mountain View, CA: Mayfield. (Reprinted from *Bootstraps*, pp. 65–90, by V. Villanueva, Jr., 1993, Urbana, IL: National Council of Teachers of English)

- An in-text, parenthetical reference to this reprint would read: (Villanueva, 1993/1996).

Selection from a Multivolume Work

Melville, H. (1987). Bartleby, the scrivener. In H. Hayford, H. Parker, & G. T. Tanselle (Vol. Eds.), *Piazza tales and other prose pieces: Vol. 9. The writings of Herman Melville* (pp. 13–45). Evanston & Chicago: Northwestern University Press and Newberry Library.

Introduction, Preface, Foreword, or Afterword of a Book

Lacroix, C. (1993). Preface. In J. Peacock, *20th-century fashion: The complete sourcebook* (pp. 6–7). New York: Thames & Hudson.

Selection from a Reference Book

Chambers of rhetoric. (2001). *The new Penguin dictionary of the theater* (p. 113). London: Penguin.

Pincus, A.L., & Ruiz, M.A. (2001). Five-factor model of personality. *The Corsini encyclopedia of psychology and behavioral sciences* (3rd ed., Vol. 2, pp. 582–585). New York: Wiley.

- When the reference article or entry has no byline, begin with the title.

APA Citation Formats for Articles in Periodicals

In this section of the appendix you will find model APA style citations for print periodical articles that are accessed either directly from a paper issue or through a database subscription service such as ProQuest or Academic Search Elite. Models for formatting periodicals materials accessed through free, public Web sites are presented in the next section.

INFORMATION TO INCLUDE WHEN CITING PERIODICALS

Acknowledging the widespread use of subscription databases as a tool for retrieving research materials, the latest edition of the *APA Publication Manual* (2001) announced a simplified method for referencing these materials that involves just two parts: (1) information about print publication, and (2) a retrieval statement that indicates the name of the database and the date of access. Here is the format:

Author. (Date). Article title. *Periodical Title, vol #,* page number(s). Retrieved Month Date,
    Year, from Database Name.

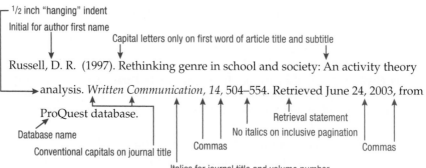

Additional Notes

- APA style does not abbreviate the names of months.
- Periods close each major element: author, date, article title, periodical information (*name, volume,* pages), retrieval statement.
- If no author is listed, begin with the title. Do not use the word "anonymous" that appears in some databases unless it appears on the article in the periodical itself.
- When an article's pages are not consecutive, APA format requires numbers for all pages on which it appears.
- APA format does not drop *the* from names of periodicals.
- For variations in format for scholarly and general circulation periodicals, see the model citations. Two distinguishing details are worth noting:

1. Add publication month and day for weeklies and dailies.
2. Use "p." and "pp." when there is no volume number.

MODEL ARTICLE CITATIONS

Work from Scholarly Journal with Continuous Pagination Through Each Volume

Revonsuo, A. (2000). The reinterpretation of dreams: An evolutionary hypothesis of the function of dreaming. *Behavioral and Brain Sciences, 23,* 877–901.

Work from Scholarly Journal that Begins with Page One in Each Issue

Kessler, R. (1997). Social and emotional learning: An emerging field builds a foundation for peace. *Holistic Education Review, 10*(2), 4–15.

- Note that the italics stop with the volume number; the parenthetical issue number is not italicized even though it follows without a space.

Magazine and Newsletter Articles

PUBLISHED WEEKLY (PAPER COPY)

Hertzberg, H. (2003, June 9). Building nations. *The New Yorker,* pp. 39–40.

PUBLISHED MONTHLY, ARTICLE NOT ON CONTIGUOUS PAGES (PAPER COPY)

Tremain, K. (2003, September–October). Pink slips in the parks: The Bush administration privatizes our public treasures. *Sierra, 88*(5), 26–33, 52.

MONTHLY NEWSLETTER WITH VOLUME AND ISSUE NUMBERS

Spinal stenosis. (2001, June). *Mayo Clinic Health Letter, 19*(6), 1–3.

PUBLISHED MONTHLY (FULL TEXT ACCESSED THROUGH LIBRARY DATABASE)

Lamb, J. (2003, July). How to write a marketing plan, part 1: Product. *Stitches,* p. 8. Retrieved August 24, 2003, from LexisNexis database.

PUBLISHED QUARTERLY, INDIVIDUAL ISSUES NUMBERED (PAPER COPY)

Alter, S. K. (2003, Spring). Business planning for social enterprises. *The Grantsmanship Center Magazine, 46,* 21–22.

Newspaper Articles

ARTICLE ACCESSED FROM PAPER COPY

Coyne, A. (2002, November 3). How to visit your mother in prison. *Milwaukee Journal Sentinel,* p. 1L.

ARTICLE ACCESSED VIA LIBRARY DATABASE

Boxer, S. (2003, May 25). Prospecting for gold among the photo blogs. *The New York Times,* p. 2.1. Retrieved August 24, 2003, from ProQuest New York Times database.

Work Without a Listed Author
Seeing the light. (2003, Summer). *Cathedral Age*, pp. 16–17.

Editorial or Opinion Piece
An empty energy bill [Editorial]. (2003, May 12). *The New York Times*, p. A24.
Ehrenberg, R. G. (2003, August 15). Who pays for the growing cost of science? [Opinion article]. *The Chronicle of Higher Education*, p. B24.

> • Identify nonroutine materials with a label in brackets immediately after the work's title, before the period. When there is no title, brackets signal that the words are a label, not a title, as in the Letter to the Editor example below).

Letter to the Editor
Kushner, H. (2003, February 3). [Letter to the editor]. *The New Yorker*, p. 7.

Review
Lahr, J. (2003, February 17 & 24). Rhythm and blues: "Ma Rainey" and August Wilson's mighty music [Review of the play *Ma Rainey's black bottom*]. *The New Yorker*, pp. 190–191.
MacFarquhar, L. (2003, February 3). Bark: Do dogs have history? [Review of the book *The pawprints of history*]. *The New Yorker*, pp. 88–92.
Wilkey, C. (2003). [Review of the book *Community action and organizational change: Image, narrative, identity*]. *College Composition and Communication, 54,* 664–666.

APA Citation Formats for Internet Sources

Use the model citations in this section for materials that you access electronically through the free, public part of the Internet. The APA manual lays out two primary guidelines for citing Internet sources: (1) "Direct readers as closely as possible to the information being cited—whenever possible, reference specific documents rather than home or menu pages"; (2) "Provide addresses that work" (2001, p. 269). APA style does not offer alternatives to providing a URL and does not put a period at the end of a URL. One note of caution: if a Web site offers information about how to cite the page, use the information elements provided, but convert them to APA format.

INFORMATION TO INCLUDE
WHEN CITING INTERNET SOURCES

APA format for Internet materials uses a retrieval phrase that includes the date of retrieval and the URL for the source. These phrases read almost like a sentence but do not have end punctuation. Here is the basic model:

Author. (Date). *Title of the work.* Retrieved Month day, year, from http://www.fillin.URL

Month day, year, format for retrieval

Authors — Year first for date of posting   Italics for title of material cited

Mellon, M., & Rissler, J. (2003, July 31). *Environmental effects of genetically modified*

food crops: Recent experiences. Retrieved July 31, 2003, from

Union of Concerned Scientists Web site: http://www.ucsusa.org/

food_and_environment/biotechnology/page.cfm?pageID=1219

APA style treats "Web site" as two words   No period after URL means
                                                       none at end of reference

Retrieval phrase names site sponsor, followed by a colon before URL

Break a URL across lines *only* at a slash

Additional Notes

- When relevant, the name of the Web site sponsor should be inserted in the retrieval statement, as in the annotated example.
- Distinguish between article and periodical titles by using italics only on the periodical title.
- Use parentheses to provide relevant information about the role played by individuals listed (e.g., writer, producer) and brackets to provide descriptive labels for media (e.g., broadcast, CD, online posting).

MODEL INTERNET CITATIONS

An Entire Web Site

APA does not provide a reference model for entire Web sites, but following the *Publication Manual*'s advice to use a model most like the source, we worked from the format for documents from Web sites. In the place of the publication date we used the most recent update, and for natural phrasing, we used "accessed . . . at" in the retrieval phrase.

Bill of Rights Defense Committee [Web site]. (2003, August 29). Accessed September 1, 2003, at http://bordc.org/

Site Within a University Program or Department Site

This example is also extrapolated from the models for material available from Web sites.

Nonprofit Portal of Greater Milwaukee. (2003, July 16). Accessed August 15, 2003, from University of Wisconsin–Milwaukee, Center for Initiatives and Research Web site: http://epic.cuir.uwm.edu/NONPROFIT/

- Use a colon before the URL when the retrieval statement includes descriptive information after "from."

Material from an Online Reference Database
Calligraphy. (2003). In L. Macy (Ed.), *The Grove dictionary of art online*. Retrieved September 3, 2003, from http://www.groveart.com

Material from an Online Scholarly Project
Johnson, B. R. & Larson, D. B. (2003). *The InnerChange Freedom Initiative: A preliminary evaluation of a faith-based prison program*. Retrieved September 4, 2003, from University of Pennsylvania, Center for Research on Religion and Urban Civil Society Web site: http://www.sas.upenn.edu/crrucs/8_research.html

E-Book
Carpenito, L. J. (1999). *Nursing care plans and documentation*. Retrieved September 4, 2003, from Books@Ovid.com Web site: http://pco.ovid.com/lrppco/index.html

Article from a Scholarly E-Journal
ARTICLE BASED ON A PRINT SOURCE

Henze, G. P. (2001). Building energy management as continuous quality control process [Electronic version]. *Journal of Architectural Engineering, 7,* 97–106.

ARTICLE FROM AN INTERNET-ONLY JOURNAL

Kirsch, I., Moore, T. J., Scoboria, A., & Nicholls, S. S. (2002, July 15). The emperor's new drugs: An analysis of antidepressant medication data submitted to the U.S. Food and Drug Administration. *Prevention & Treatment, 4,* Article 23. Retrieved September 4, 2003, from http://journals.apa.org/prevention/volume5/pre0050023a.html

Periodical or Newspaper Article Published Online
Orenstein, C. (2003, September 5). What Carrie could learn from Mary. *The New York Times*. Retrieved September 5, 2003, from http://www.nytimes.com/2003/09/05/opinion/05OREN.html?th

Article Posted on a Web Site
Greenberg, D. H. & Pasternak, J. (1998, Spring). Age discrimination in the workplace. *The Successful California Accountant*. Retrieved March 5, 2002, from the Discriminationattorney.com Web site: http://www.discriminationattorney.com/article-age.html

- When available, volume, issue, and page numbers should be provided.

Material from an Organization Site
American Library Association. (2003, September 4). CIPA updates. Retrieved September 5, 2003, from http://www.ala.org/Content/NavigationMenu/Our_Association/Offices/ALA_Washington/Issues2/Civil_Liberties,_Intellectual_Freedom,_Privacy/CIPA1/CIPA.htm

Cartoon or Comic Strip
Trudeau, G. (2003, September 6). Doonesbury [Comic strip]. Retrieved September 6, 2003, from http://www.ucomics.com/doonesbury/

Posting to a Discussion List, Online Forum, or Weblog

Pax, S. (2003, March 25). Where is Raed? [Online posting]. Retrieved September 6, 2003, from http://dear_raed.blogspot.com/2003_03_01_dear_raed_archive.html

- References lists should cite only archived material that readers can retrieve. If you are using personal communication, refer to it only in the text, as in this example: "Scott (personal communication, June 27, 2004) reported . . ."

Material from an Online Information Service

Grayson, C. (2002, January 1). Understanding snoring. Retrieved September 6, 2003, from http://my.webmd.com/content/article/8/1680_54137

Online Transcript from Television or Radio Program

Crystal, L. (Executive Producer). (2000, April 14). Love and knowledge [Transcript of television interview with Margaret Edson]. *Online NewsHour.* Retrieved January 10, 2003, from http://www.pbs.org/newshour/bb/entertainment/jan-june99/edson_4-14.html

- This example adds a bracketed label and a retrieval statement to the APA model for a television broadcast.

Television or Radio Broadcast Available Online

Arnold, E. (Reporter). (2002, April 9). ANWR [Broadcast segment]. *All Things Considered.* Washington, D.C.: National Public Radio. Retrieved August 7, 2003, from http://discover.npr.org/features/feature.jhtml?wfId=1141379

Data File

Department of Health and Human Services. Substance Abuse and Mental Health Services Administration. Office of Applied Studies. (2000). *National Household Survey on Drug Abuse, 2000* (Study #3262) [Data file]. Available from Substance Abuse and Mental Health Data Archive, http://www.icpsr.umich.edu/SAMHDA/

APA Citation Formats for Other Materials and Media

Government Publications

Columbia Accident Investigation Board. (2003). Final report. Washington, DC: U.S. Government Printing Office.

The APA *Publication Manual* has a lengthy appendix regarding citation of legal materials—consult it or the current edition of *The Blue Book: A Uniform System of Citation* if you need to reference court cases, statutes, or legislative proceedings.

Lecture, Speech, or Conference Paper

Suskind, R. (2003, September 4). [Public lecture]. Marquette University, Milwaukee, WI.

Material in Varying Media from an Information Service

CITATION FOR PRINT OR MICROFICHE

Hopkins, S. (2000). *VET and the voluntary sector: Dealing with ambiguities.* (ERIC Document Reproduction Service No. ED470938)

CITATION FOR ONLINE TEXT

Hopkins, S. (2000). *VET and the voluntary sector: Dealing with ambiguities.* (ERIC Document Reproduction Service No. ED470938). Electronic version retrieved September 7, 2003, from Ovid.

Video Recording

Taylor, D. (Translator/Director). (1991). *Antigone* [Video recording]. BBC & Films for the Humanities. (Available from Films for the Humanities, PO Box 2053, Princeton, NJ 08543-2053)

Sound Recording

Fields, D. & McHugh, J. (n.d.). Exactly like you. [Recorded by T. Bennett & K. D. Lang]. On *A wonderful world* [CD]. New York: Sony. (2002)

TV or Radio Program

Cohen, D. (Writer), & Kirkland, M. (Director). (1995). Lisa the vegetarian [Television series episode]. In B. Oakley & J. Weinstein (Producers) *The Simpsons.* Los Angeles, CA: Fox Broadcasting Company.

Credits

Chapter 2

"The Voice You Hear When You Read Silently" from *New and Selected Poems 1975–1995* by Thomas Lux. Copyright © 1997 by Thomas Lux. Reprinted by permission of Houghton Mifflin Company. All rights reserved.

Chapter 3

Larissa MacFarquhar, "Who Cares If Johnny Can't Read?" *Slate* 16 Apr. 1997. Copyright © Slate/Distributed by United Feature Syndicate, Inc.

"The Need for Environmental Ethics," pp. 101–05 from Anthony Weston, *Toward Better Problems: New Perspectives on Abortion, Animal Rights, the Environment, and Justice.* Reprinted by permission of Temple University Press. Copyright © 1992 by Temple University. All rights reserved.

Chapter 4

From "Christina's World" by Jeremy Helligar and Lori Majewski, *Us Weekly* 3 Feb. 2003. Copyright © 2003 Us Weekly LLC. Used with permission.

Index